AF608155

BLACK LIVES MATTER IN US SCHOOLS

SUNY series, Critical Race Studies in Education

Derrick R. Brooms, editor

BLACK LIVES MATTER IN US SCHOOLS

RACE, EDUCATION, AND RESISTANCE

EDITED BY

BONI WOZOLEK

Cover: D'nae Harrison, *Patterns for New Horizons* (2021), 14" × 20" acrylic on Masonite panel, from the private collection of Boni Wozolek.

Published by State University of New York Press, Albany

Printed in the United States of America

For information, contact State University of New York Press, Albany, NY
www.sunypress.edu

Library of Congress Cataloging-in-Publication Data

Name: Wozolek, Boni, editor.
Title: Black lives matter in US schools : race, education, and resistance / Boni Wozolek.
Description: Albany : State University of New York Press, [2022] | Series: SUNY series, Critical Race Studies in Education | Includes bibliographical references and index.
Identifiers: ISBN 9781438489179 (hardcover : alk. paper) | ISBN 9781438489193 (ebook)
Further information is available at the Library of Congress.

10 9 8 7 6 5 4 3 2 1

Contents

Introduction: From Cooper and Woodson to Schools Today

BLM and American Schools

Boni Wozolek

Black. Lives. Matter.

In the spring of 2013, a high school student, Rochelle,[1] was recalling her reaction to hearing Billie Holiday's "Strange Fruit" for the first time with her grandmother. In my role as a teacher-researcher, I was thinking with students of color about how they negotiated difficult contexts within their overwhelmingly white[2] and conservative high school. In the interview, Rochelle noted she felt Black students were the metaphorical "strange fruit of the school." She explained that her white peers, teachers, and administrators did not "care if [Black students] rot or if they die . . . as long as they are out of the way." I left the interview thinking about all the ways that this young person came to see herself as the "bitter crop" of schools.

As time passed after the study's conclusion, I remained haunted by Rochelle's words, often finding myself reflecting on them over the years. Specifically, I am haunted because I know her story does not exist in isolation. It is part of an assemblage on which past, present, and future iterations of violence de- and reterritorialize (Wozolek, 2021). I have heard her words echoed in narratives from students across contexts who have articulated similar perspectives on the dehumanization they experienced in schooling. Like many scholars and activists, I remain troubled knowing that every day in school, children are treated as if their voices, perspectives, and lives are disposable. Since 2013, I have remained in contact via social media with Rochelle and several other participants who wished to stay in touch. As I observe the next stages in their lives, I remain intimately aware that the anti-Black norms they described during our time together have spilled from classrooms and into communities, impacting them along the way.

For those who work with Black youth in schools or consider the impact of schooling on Black ways of being, knowing, and doing, Rochelle's reflection about being the strange fruit of the school, while enough to make one's blood boil (Du Bois, 1903), is often not surprising. After all, there are long-standing dialogues stemming from scholars across African American intellectual traditions (e.g., Bethune, 1938; Cooper, 1892; Du Bois, 1903; Woodson, 1933) that discus the constant circulation of racism between schools and communities. Or, as Woodson (1933) more pointedly wrote, "There would be no lynching if it did not start in the schoolroom" (p. 3). More recently, contemporary scholars across fields have theorized what Rochelle expressed in the interview as a kind of onto-epistemological death for Black and Brown youth that is too often engendered and maintained in schools (e.g., Jocson et al., 2020; Morris, 2016; Noguera & Leslie, 2014).

The Black Lives Matter movement can be thought of as a societal response to the same anti-Blackness that students like Rochelle—and, more broadly, her family and intersecting communities—continue to experience both in and outside of educational contexts. As I will discuss later, while the overarching BLM movement is intimately connected to police brutality, the purpose of this book is to think critically about how such violence is tangled up in systems of schooling (Nespor, 1997) while considering the curricular implications of what it would mean for Black Lives to *actually* matter in schools.

Again, the idea of honoring Black lives in systems of schooling is certainly not new. Educators like Mary McLeod Bethune, Fanny Jackson Coppin, Susie King Taylor, Carter G. Woodson, W. E. B. Du Bois, Bettina Love, Crystal Laura, Denisha Jones and Jesse Hagopian, Keeanga-Yamahtta Taylor, and countless others have examined the theoretical and practical implications of Black Lives as they intersect with educational contexts. This book is meant to add to those voices with an emphasis on curriculum theory. This text comes at a time when teacher education programs across the United States have prioritized a focus on neoliberal practices over curriculum theory for teacher candidates (Pugach et al., 2020). Yet, as I will discuss later in this chapter, curriculum theory is not only inclusive of instruction and the official knowledge of schooling (Apple, 2014) but it also critically considers all the ways that learning happens. Curriculum theory is therefore imminently complex; braiding theoretical lenses and disciplines to think about educational contexts and systems. Woven into teacher education programs not as a singular "curriculum" but as the polyvocal "curricula," curriculum theory seeks to critically engage with ways of being, knowing, and doing as they spring from (or die out because of) schools (Berry & Stovall, 2013).

The authors pose questions like: What would it mean for *all* teachers to actively combat white supremacy on a daily basis in schools? What would it mean for schools to consider—and to intentionally create spaces for—the multiplicity of "being" within Black communities? What do city spaces offer as sites of curriculum? What is the curriculum that communities offer to us as academics? Steeped in curriculum theory and other critical fields of education, the contributors in this volume consider the many ways we learn from the presences and absences of Black lives across forms of curriculum—formal, enacted, hidden, and null—and the way that such lessons have impacted sociopolitical and cultural norms and values.

In light of the multiple and ongoing forms of violence against Black bodies and communities, this book is dedicated to the memory of those whose lives were cut short, to those whose ways of being, knowing, and doing have been irrevocably changed, and to those whose young lives will continue to be shifted in explicit and implicit ways through white supremacy. First and foremost, the work presented in this volume has been curated to honor Black experiences across systems of schooling, and to attend to the relationship between schools and communities. Additionally, honoring the significance of coalition building, this book recognizes those who live as accomplices (e.g., Love, 2019)—those who engage in equity and access across contexts to promote Black excellence, and to interrupt anti-Blackness that is sociopolitically and culturally normalized in the United States and around the globe.

Scholars such as Audre Lorde (1984), Monique Morris (2016), Beverly Tatum (1997), Carter G. Woodson (1933), and others have explored the "how," "what," and "where" learning takes places as an always already complex assemblage of spaces, places, events, and affects. Rather than a linear line between contexts, the rest of this introduction tacks back and forth between schools, communities, and the content of this book.

Much like the chapters included in this book that move between the curriculum, classrooms, personal experiences, and broader sociocultural narratives, this introduction honors the many ways the curricula speak, leak (Helfenbein, 2010) and spill (Gumbs, 2016) across contexts. I will begin by describing my positionality as it is related to how this book has taken shape over time.

Coming into Being

All books have their own origins stories. The first iteration of this book was a newsletter that was published by the Curriculum Studies Division (Division B) of the American Educational Research Association (AERA). At that time, I was a graduate student who served as the division's newsletter editor. I was asked by Vice President Ming Fang He to craft a response to the Charleston Church shootings that occurred on June 17, 2015, taking the lives of nine African American congregants at the hands of a white supremacist. While I was honored to undertake such an important task at an early stage in my career, I felt uneasy. As a first-generation, queer, biracial woman with Indian roots, I certainly understand the devastating impact of colonization. I identify as a queer Brown person who grew up in an overwhelmingly white and straight town in the Midwest. I am therefore no stranger to the everyday racisms and antiqueer bias that were likely behind the reasons my white neighbors chained me to a tree and left there for hours at a young age (Wozolek, 2021).

I also recognize that while my personal experiences with racism might be similar in kind to those of my Black peers, they are ultimately different in critical ways that should not be conflated or overlooked. With this in mind, and in the spirit of coalition politics, both the original newsletter and this volume foreground the voices and perspectives of those who have experienced the vitriol of anti-Black violence personally; be it sociopolitically, culturally, physically, emotionally, institutionally, or across the many other ways that such violence pervades our society. It also includes the perspectives of scholars like me who work as accomplices to the Black Lives Matter movement, particularly as it resonates with and against systems of schooling.

Since the inception of this book, there have been multiple attacks on people of color carried out by white extremists and at the hands of police who proport to "serve and protect" all United States citizens. One of the difficulties in editing a volume like this is that the sociopolitical and historical context of the United States means that there is always "one more" event that could, and should, be included as examples of why Black Lives should be honored, recognized, and respected everywhere—from the curricula in schools to every single community across the nation. The *Washington Post*, for example, reports over 5,000 fatal police shootings by on-duty police officers across the United States since 2015, when the first iteration of this text was released. In the past year alone, there have been 950 fatal police shootings (*Washington Post*, 2021). Within these troubling numbers, Black Americans are killed by police at more than twice the rate of white Americans (Hemenway et al., 2019). Amid the COVID-19 pandemic, the United States witnessed the murder of George Floyd and a backlash from conservatives on the inclusion of Critical Race Theory (CRT) in classrooms. Needless to say, an attention to how, what, and when schools teach about Black lives is important. This is not only true when considering the significant contributions that Black people have made around the globe that resonates through every discipline taught in school but, as Critical Race theorists have explored, it is critical when exploring how racism is sociohistorically enmeshed with the very fabric of the United States. A critical attention to both Black excellence and the tenets of CRT as it related to historical and contemporary lessons taught in schools continues to be of utmost importance in interrupting various forms of violence—from police brutality, to mass shootings, to the silencing of Black voices, histories, and perspectives—that continue to be normalized across spaces in the United States.

In the original version of this introduction, I had included several examples of police violence and mass shootings where communities of color were targeted. However, given the collective trauma experienced by witnessing the 9 minutes and 29 seconds of George Floyd's murder, and as forms of media continuously air other atrocities that are in a similar vein to Floyd's murder, I reconsidered these examples. While I refer to these events, rather than describe them in great detail, I have left citations available in the references for readers to explore on their own. Borrowing from Rochelle, I recognize that some of the work included in this book can be triggering enough without recounting the many ways that too often Black people become the strange fruit of, in, and through schools and communities. To better contextualize this work, this chapter will now turn to the national and global significance of the Black Lives Matter movement.

#BlackLivesMatter across Contexts

In the African American intellectual traditions, the image of fire has often been used to symbolize aggression carried out by white supremacists against people of color (e.g., Baldwin, 1963; Truth, 1850), and as a general metaphor for the state of the nation within these violent interactions (e.g., Cooper, 1892; Douglass, 1855; Garvey, 1922; Woodson, 1933). In our contemporary context, cities burning from uprisings in places like Ferguson, Baltimore, Philadelphia, and Minneapolis, mirror the literal and metaphorical fires explored by educational ancestors. As Baldwin (1963) argued, these fires burn as a symbol of the necessary life-and-community-saving changes that must happen to ensure equity and access, but more pressing in an era when white supremacy is again on the rise, the necessity of basic human rights for all citizens. While these scenes might evoke a sense of much needed urgency and attention, it is important to remember that the desire to rise against violence is not new in the United States. For example, the genocide of Indigenous people and cultures laid the groundwork for the normalization of trafficking and enslaving people, for eugenics, and for the unabated murders of Black and Brown people (Dunbar-Ortiz & Gilio-Whitaker, 2016). In short, the United States is a country founded on the bedrock of oppression and violence against Black and Indigenous people, and People of Color.

Given the historical and contemporary iterations of violence that are central to white supremacy, it is not surprising that Black Lives Matter (BLM) is simply the most recent example of sociopolitical movements aimed at dismantling oppressive structures across the country. BLM was started in 2013 by Alicia Garza, Patrisse Cullors, and Opal Tometi. This movement was sparked as a direct response to the acquittal of George Zimmerman, who murdered Trayvon Martin, a 17-year-old African American high school student on February 26, 2012. Martin was unarmed and simply visiting relatives in Zimmerman's gated community. Zimmerman's acquittal understandably raised tensions across the country and the hashtag #BlackLivesMatter quickly trended on social media. BLM continued to develop when in 2014 Michael Brown, another unarmed Black man, was murdered by the Ferguson police. Brown's death became another watershed moment in the movement, with Black Lives Matter chapters popping up across the country (Jones & Hagopian, 2020; Taylor, 2016). Since these early roots took hold, the movement has become internationally recognized as an "ideological and political intervention in a world where Black lives are systemically and intentionally targeted for demise" (Black Lives Matter, 2020, n.p.).

Although Black death continued to be normalized, with cases of police brutality continuing well after BLM chapters became established, the murder of George Floyd was yet another defining moment in the movement. The public lynching of Mr. Floyd sparked protests across the nation in the summer of 2020, with activists calling for legal and policing reforms that would impact several sociopolitical systems, including education. A few months prior to Floyd's death, Nikole Hannah-Jones's "1619 Project" was published by the *New York Times*. This project aimed to "reframe the country's history by placing the consequences of slavery and the contribution of Black Americans at the very center of the United States' national narrative" (Hannah-Jones, 2019, n.p.). Although Hannah-Jones and the *New York Times* faced backlash from this project (with Hannah-Jones eventually being denied tenure from the University of North Carolina and finding an academic home at Howard University), the project itself generated curricular questions in schools by asking when Black voices emerge, and in what light, through the curriculum. The murder of George Floyd, along with the publication of "The 1619 Project," became important catalysts for the exploration of Black narratives (or the lack thereof) in schools.

In September 2020, amid BLM protests after Floyd's murder, the Trump administration launched an assault directly on Critical Race Theory. Specifically, in a series of tweets and through an executive order, Trump banned federal contractors from conducting racial sensitivity training, emphasizing that such work indoctrinates "government employees with divisive and harmful sex-and race-based ideologies." Trump tweeted that CRT and antiracist training was "divisive, un-American propaganda." Missing the fact that any nation's history with racism is significant in contemporary norms, and the fact that citizens of the United States are not living in a postracial utopia, the Trump administration saw the banning of CRT as a way to "defend the virtue of America's heroes, and the nobility of the American character." The impact of the Trump administration's ban on CRT has significantly impacted schools, with districts across the country banning any dialogue that might relate to Critical Race Theory from the curriculum. One might argue that the current moment in the BLM movement is a fight for a formal curriculum that includes an accurate representation of the nation's history with racism.

Finally, it is significant to note that Black liberation movements in the United States have been central in creating space for Black people and communities against oppressive ideologies and violence. It is also important to recognize that such movements have historically been disproportionate in that they overwhelmingly carved out space mostly for straight, cisgender men—leaving women and queer people either absent from or in the background of the movement (Garza, 2014; Taylor, 2016). BLM activists have attended to this disparity, working to create more inclusive spaces and to honor Black experiences across ways of being, knowing, and doing, both in and outside of the cis-hetero patriarchy. Alicia Garza, one of the cofounders, openly identifies as queer and, along with her cofounders, has argued for the necessary inclusion of voices across the Black experience. As Ray Charles (1993) once sang, "None of us are free if one of us is chained."

The Black Lives Matter movement has been significant in resisting and refusing deadly oppressions while affirming the significance of Black communities across historical and contemporary events in the United States (Hannah-Jones, 2019; Ransbury, 2018). While Black Lives Matter as a movement is relatively new, its ideologies have been central to the work of antiracist and abolitionist educators who actively resist exclusionary systems of schooling (Morris, 2016; Nespor, 1997). For example, the journal *Theory, Research, and Action in Urban Education* (TRAUE), put together a special issue on #BlackLivesMatter committed to sparking a dialogue across educational experiences for students, educators, scholars, administrators, and community organizers (Menjivar, Vogel, Laksimi-Morrow, & Robinson, 2017). In addition, there are several scholars who have argued that schools and systems of schooling are essential in the resistance and refusal of sociopolitically normalized racism (e.g., Au, Brown, & Calderón, 2016; Gordon, 1993; Howard, 2019; Huckaby, 2019; Love, 2019; Pinar, 1991). Following this call to action by scholars, this chapter will now attend specifically to schools and curricula before thinking about the contributions of each chapter.

The Curriculum: The Being and Doing of Black Lives in School

The forms of curriculum can be envisioned as a gordian knot—an impossibly entwined set of knowledges, ontologies, and actions that happen in, through, and between educational spaces and places. While scholars might momentarily attend to one form of curriculum by falsely bracketing it from the others, the sticky, messy nature of schooling almost demands that it be quickly folded back into the rest of the curricular assemblage. Yet, there is a danger in falsely bracketing any form of curriculum without recognizing its impossibly entwined nature with other forms of curriculum. That is, by assuming that the formal curriculum is "the" curriculum, it easily allows educational stakeholders to be self-congratulatory about what is taught (see, for example, the idea that the nation's virtue must be defended by silencing a CRT curricular lens), while releasing educators from the responsibility engaging students with difficult histories with race, genders, disabilities, and the like that are central to current sociocultural ideologies. An attention to only the formal curriculum allows people to overlook oppression through the practice of silencing while ignoring the many places that learning happens in schools in ways that only reinforces oppressive norms and values. This book, much like the forms of curriculum, remains and entangled mess, asking the reader to imagine curricular possibilities, challenges, and oppressions within the assemblage that is curriculum theory, rather than as siloed ideas about how, what, when, and where we learn. The purpose of this section is twofold: the explicate the forms of curriculum while underscoring one of the themes of this book: everything is always already a form of curriculum. In short, this book asks: Where does learning *not* happen?

Curriculum scholars have asked similar questions across traditions, specifically thinking about what counts as knowledge and whose knowledge is of most worth (Grant et al., 2015; Malewski, 2009; Pinar, 2004; Spencer, 1860; Watkins, 2001). This book attends to these traditions by weaving chapters that follow a narrative style (see Ngozi Williams, Roland Mitchell, David Stovall, and Denise Taliaferro Baszile) with other forms of inquiry (see Kirsten Edwards, Yolanda Sealey-Ruiz, Marcelle Haddix, Cluny Lavache, Walter Gershon, Sherick Hughes, and Reagan Mitchell). The purpose of braiding these chapters is twofold: To honor the polyvocal ways of engaging with the topic of Black Lives Matter and education, while recognizing that each chapter is in and of itself a form of curriculum. Although each chapter resides under the broad umbrella of Black Lives Matter and education, they all hold curriculum as a common touchstone.

An attention to curriculum studies is important because systemic oppressions in schools are enacted and maintained across curricular forms. Entangled with broader norms and values, the curricula of schooling can be understood an assemblage that functions as a set of "sociopolitical processes that discipline humanity into full humans, not-quite-humans, and nonhumans" (Weheliye, 2014, p. 4). In short, curricular entanglements in schools facilitate dehumanization, eventually teaching students, educators, and administrators across identities that Black lives, voices, and perspectives are inferior (Woodson, 1933). The racialized nature of the curricula is insidious in that it permeates every layer of scale in schools. For example, every semester, I ask students that take my educational foundations class to think of every scientist that they can in 20 seconds who has the perceived identity of a white man. The room is generally filled with names like Isaac Newton, Albert Einstein, Charles Darwin, or Stephen Hawking as students shout names confidently and quickly. Then, I reset the timer. I ask them to shout out the names of every white woman scientist that they can. There is far more silence but, generally, at least one student usually yells out, "Marie Curie!" I repeat this activity by asking students to respectively name Black men, Black women, and, finally, any queer scientists that they can think of without using the internet. By the last round, there is complete silence and uneasy tension. Every student who is enrolled the courses I teach managed to get through high school, pass the ACT or SAT, and have been admitted to the institution. Yet, regardless of race, ability, genders, sexual orientations, home language, and other such factors, the result has been the same—enthusiastic, fast replies for the first round and silence, if not embarrassment, for the last three rounds.

What one learns in school, what Michael Apple (2014) called the "official knowledge" of schooling, can be understood as the lessons that are intended through schools (Page, 1991). Often, when I work with teacher candidates, this is what they are referring to when they mention "the" curriculum in terms of state standards, textbooks, and the district curriculum. This can also be thought of as the names that students easily recall during the activity discussed above. The null curriculum (Eisner, 1985) is what is unintentionally not taught. These are the scientists that students could not easily name as these are the scientists who are often absent from the formal curriculum. The contributions of scientists like Alice Ball, Mae Jemison, George Washington Carver, Benjamin Banneker, Sara Josephine Baker, Richard Summerbell, and others, remain largely absent from the formal curriculum but rather present within the null curriculum. As scholar like Berry (2010) and Watkins (2001) argued, the null curriculum is often haunted by those pushed out of the formal curriculum as a way of engendering and maintaining hegemonic norms and values. The formal and null curriculum deeply impact both the hidden (Giroux & Penna, 1983) and enacted curricula (Page, 1991; Schwab, 1969). The hidden curriculum can be thought of as the broader cultural norms and values that are often hidden to those participating in a cultural context. Students, teachers, and administrators tend to unconsciously attach value to the voices represented in the formal curriculum and, similarly, degrade those that are relegated to the null curriculum. Trump's perspective on the "virtue of American heroes" is but one example of how the formal curriculum posits mostly white, straight men as the "heroes" of American history. This narrative impacts the core values, beliefs, and attitudes of any person who participated in systems of schooling and, over time, such beliefs become taught through the hidden curriculum.

As people interact, the attitudes and values across the hidden curriculum become apparent through what is known as the enacted curriculum. Page (1991) argues that learning is ubiquitous. Students do not just interact with each other and adults in the building. Any person entering a school interacts with the physical building. Think, for example, what can be learned from the placement of classrooms for students with disabilities that are often hidden in the school, or what students with disabilities learn about their role in the building from the placement of their classroom (Jones & Hensley, 2012). Similarly, students, teachers, and administrators alike learn from interacting with the voices that are present (or absent) from textbooks, how the school-to-prison pipeline functions not just outside but as a part of school culture (Kim et al., 2010; Love, 2019; Meiners, 2016), and through the school-to-coffin pipeline that is a normalized way of pushing queer youth out of school and into the hospital or grave (Wozolek, Wootton, & Demlow, 2017). It is no small wonder that through the various forms of curriculum many citizens—from police officers to white extremists, and teachers to administrators—are comfortable "exploiting . . . or exterminating a class that everybody is taught to regard as inferior" (Woodson, 1933, p. 3).

While schools and systems of schooling regularly dehumanize Black youth and communities, it is significant to note that the curriculum of racism (Bethune, 1983; Cooper, 1892; Love, 2019; Morris, 2016) has not gone unabated. Scholars across fields of education have a long-standing history of arguing the broader implications of racialized practices in schools that express sociocultural norms and values (Cooper, 1892; Du Bois, 1903; Watkins, 2001; Winfield, 2007; Woodson, 1933). As a result, arguments for equity and access in schools have made several significant inroads that have resulted in the proliferation of questions about representation, voice, and power in schooling. For example, scholars have unpacked the relationship between broader cultural movements, ideas, and ideals as they are entwined with schooling (e.g., Apple, 1971; Skutnabb-Kangas; 2000; Taliaferro Baszile, Edwards, & Guillory, 2016), analyzing, for example, how eugenics or cultural genocide has shaped the curricula. Scholars have also discussed how schools can interrupt raced and racist cultural norms (e.g., Au, Brown, & Calderón, 2016; Bracho & Hayes, 2020; He & Ross, 2012). While such inroads to discussing race and schooling are not mutually exclusive, it should be noted that regardless of positionality or questions of scale, these dialogues have significantly contributed broader conversations regarding marginalization and violence against people of color in schools and across the country. As people of color in schools, and the communities with which they are knotted (Nespor, 1997), continue to experience violence that has been taught and normalized across spaces, it becomes abundantly clear that academic dialogues and ideas are not just theoretical. They are enacted in daily, targeted violence against bodies of color across the United States.

Given that the indelible images of contemporary lynchings are entangled with what scholars like Du Bois (1926) referred to as a "choking away" of onto-epistemologies through white educational ideologies, it becomes clear that schooling provides a form of ontological death that is mirrored in the physical murders of Black people across community contexts. In short, because schooling normalizes the dehumanization of all bodies outside of the white cis-hetero patriarchy, racist police officers and white extremists have sanctioned inflicting physical pain on Black people and in Black communities. This brings to the fore the following questions: What does it mean for a child to be metaphorically lynched or choked through the schoolroom, as scholars like Du Bois (1926) and Woodson (1933) have described? As such, how does the everyday choking away (Du Bois, 1926) of a child's way of being and knowing contribute to larger sociocultural violence against people of color? What roles do and should scholars play in the interruption of this marginalization, both in theory and practice? These are difficult questions that the contributors to this book wrestle with as they explore the intersection of schooling and less local aggressions.

The rest of this introduction focuses on unpacking contributions to this volume. Although strong scholarship has been dedicated to the Black Lives Matter movement (Taylor, 2016), this book is devoted to continuing such dialogues through the lens of schooling, curriculum, and the multiple ways in which educational contexts effect and affect students of color. Examining the intersections between schooling and Black Lives Matter is significant because while the normalization of aggression against people of color is always already in broad circulation between schools and their communities (Brockenbrough, 2016; Dumas & Nelson, 2017; Woodson, 1933), interrupting this violence should also be central to the everyday experiences of schooling.

Honoring Black Lives across the Pages and Beyond

The recent murders of George Floyd, Breonna Taylor, and Ahmaud Arbery—alongside the ubiquitous harassment of Black folks enjoying a barbecue, a Black child selling water in her neighborhood, Black people enjoying time watching birds in the park, and other stories that might not have made national news—resonate within the echo chamber of racism that is prevalent across the United States. The chapters in this book speak directly to these tensions, showing a necessity for the ideas shared across the chapters presented in this work. While I engage in bracketing some of the forms of curriculum represented in each chapter, it is important to note that every form of curriculum is always at work in and across contexts.

The first chapter of this book highlights the work of Sherick A. Hughes. Aligned with Bethune's (1938) dialogue on how one might clarify sociopolitical and cultural contexts with the facts, and building on Pinar's (1991) conversation on curriculum as a racialized text, Hughes's chapter can be understood as an interruption of the hidden curriculum that proliferates false narratives and news around Black lives, the BLM movement, and the Black experience in the United States. Almost a forward to the other chapters, Hughes's work is first in this volume because it is intended to stand as a corrective curriculum to what is often read as the official knowledge that propagates in communities and leaks into schools. In short, Hughes's chapter is a way of setting the record straight before the other chapters build various forms of curriculum. Hughes investigates the facts behind #BlackLivesMatter to interpret the myths constructed by white nationalists that are in opposition to the BLM movement. In this chapter, Hughes weaves literatures that are related to the Black Lives Matter movement to think about intraracial crime, policing, and affirmative action. Hughes's work is significant in that he not only lays out the opposition's ideas about BLM but he deeply and critically engages with the implications of the myths, the realities, and their relationship with sociopolitical norms, values, and movements. By challenging schools and colleges of education to revisit how racial epistemologies can be hidden within the curriculum, Hughes argues that in resolving this challenge, Black Lives Matter in schools can no longer be easily dismissed or distorted, something that schools and universities desperately need if white supremacy is to be interrupted, resisted, and refused.

Following Hughes's work, the next chapter focuses on the experiences of Ngozi Williams. It is important to note that Williams began writing the first iterations of this chapter in high school. Her voice is significant to this text because Black youth are, in many ways, the backbone of not only the BLM movement but, one could argue, perhaps one of the most significant reasons to create a safer sociopolitical and cultural context. Williams boldly asks, "If not for Black youth, then for whom do we do this work?" The book therefore follows Hughes's corrective curriculum with Williams's salient call to action as a reminder that despite the BLM movement, Black youth around the nation still struggle with various forms of oppression that they learn through iterations of the enacted curriculum. Using narrative inquiry, Williams highlights the challenges of learning through the enacted and hidden curricula. As the daughter of immigrant parents in an overwhelmingly white context, her chapter explores the imbrications of race and queerness that many young people experience. Attending to many salient issues that Black queer youth face, Williams discusses topics such as physical health, beauty standards, and social exclusion. Williams's work brings to the fore the lived experience and voice of Black queer youth as it is entangled with sociocultural violence in her local and less local contexts.

Roland Mitchell's chapter compliments Williams's work in that their respective narratives are both related to racist affects and events that are normalized within the enacted and hidden curricula. While Williams's work focuses on racism experienced by Black youth, Mitchell expresses events entangled with racism as a Black adult. Mitchell uses the deluge of and after Katrina, and the murder of Alton Sterling, as a backdrop to his dialogue about what it means to be a Black academic and a dean. Through his narrative he shows how his personal mantra—Know who you are, control what you can, and stay focused—has shifted as a result of these events, as they are knotted with his academic experiences. By exploring how the "river of white supremacy has shaped the institutional coastline" and the many ways that "levees of resistance in communities of color" have refused to accept further floods of racism, Mitchell explicates how we might all function as systems of refusal for raced and racist norms in the academy.

Following Mitchell's dialogue, Kirsten Edwards's work can be understood as an exploration of the null and enacted curricula. Edwards unpacks how traditional theoretical frameworks and methodologies not only limit Afrocentric inquiry but often fail to disrupt anti-Blackness in and across academic spaces. Edwards's work is significant in that it questions how Black spaces are made in and across Critical Race Theory, intersectionality, and collegiate marronage. The implications of reconceptualizing institutional spaces that Edwards discusses offer programmatic and systemic possibilities that reject inquiry rooted in anti-Blackness to "draw on the strength of critical, dexterous, Black curiosity." Edwards's work puts into action what she calls for throughout the chapter—the pursuit of unapologetically recognizing and using Black intellectual thought and traditions to create a space against white patriarchal values that are business-as-usual in higher education.

Continuing Edwards's dialogue on dismantling systemic oppression in educational spaces and places, Yolanda Sealey-Ruiz, Marcelle Haddix, and Cluny Lavache discuss the absence of Black voices in literacy education. Their contribution explores the formal and null curricula, considering what it might mean to foreground Black Lives Matter in literacy by asking: What would it look like? How would it be enacted? Who creates it, teaches it, and how is it taught? Their work mirrors those of educators who contributed to early editions of the *Journal of Negro Education*, where contributors similarly thought through a curriculum that not only foregrounds but is constructed with Black lives, experiences, and ideas first, rather than as an afterthought. This means that teacher candidates, as the authors argue, "have the ability to see greatness in the Black students they may one day service, and not only understand and theorize that Black lives matter, but believe . . . and demonstrate that through their actions, deeds, and instructional practices."

Mirroring Sealey-Ruiz, Haddix, and Lavache's call for teacher candidates who are concerned with equity and access, Walter S. Gershon's chapter attends to the necessary work of being an accomplice as an educator concerned with antiracist policies and practices. A strong example of how the forms of curriculum are entangled, Gershon explicates what he calls a "curriculum of lying, choking, and dying," that pervades systems of schooling across the United States. The argument for what a curriculum of onto-epistemological death might mean for Black youth, while hauntingly evocative, is well aligned with other scholars within the African American intellectual traditions that have explicated the link between physical and metaphorical violence to what is learned through schooling (e.g., Cooper, 1892; Du Bois, 1926; Woodson, 1933). Gershon's work is significant in that it carefully traces the roots of a racialized curriculum in the United States—from Franklin Bobbitt to Simon-Binet IQ tests. Gershon's chapter also critically considers how curricular roots have given life to the tree where students' onto-epistemologies are metaphorically—yet intentionally—killed by and through the classroom and corridors as students of color become the strange fruit (Meeropol/Holiday, 1939) of today's schools. Similar to Schwab's (1969) curriculum in-action or Love's (2019) dialogue of a curriculum that moves as much as it is moving, Gershon argues that "curricular understandings indicate actions as they convey content and normalize violence" against Black people and communities.

Following Gershon's historical and contemporary account of a curriculum fraught with violence, David Omotoso Stovall considers how the Black Lives Matter movement is often reduced to images of reactionary protests, rather than an ideal of consistent, and constant, work that demands justice, equity, and access. Echoing the narrative styles of Williams and Mitchell, Stovall gives a personal account of living in Chicago. Drawing lines between gentrification, the execution of Laquan McDonald, Obama-era politics, and a "curriculum of fugitivity," this work is important because it unmasks the hypersegregation that impacts communities and schools that displace and dispossess people and communities. While Stovall attends to Chicago, it is critical to remember that his points are applicable across contexts and layers of scale. As Stovall argues, because of this lived reality in and across the United States, it is time to recognize that "the claim to Black life is a claim to the humanity of all."

Connecting Stovall's complicated conversation on Black voices and feminisms in and across city spaces, Reagan P. Mitchell engages in an enacted curriculum through a letter to Pauli Murray. Mitchell's work can also be understood as an engagement with the null curriculum as Murray's legacy is often absent from K–12 and many university spaces. Through his letter, Mitchell thinks about southern queerhood as it lives within, and sometimes against, the call for equity and access in Black communities. Mitchell argues that Afro-surrealism is significant as a means to "permeate, envelope, and destroy the template" of the Enlightenment that has sustained "linear trajectories [for] queer, feminist, gender fluid/

nonconforming, dis/abled, impoverished senses of time as deficient." Mitchell's work is important in that it uses a Black feminist praxis to articulate the line between voices like Zora Neale Hurston, Angela Davis, Patricia Hill-Collins, and Pauli Murray that is disruptive to normalized ideas and ideals within the cis-hetero patriarchy.

Finally, this book concludes with the deeply personal and strong scholarly voice of Denise Taliaferro Baszile. In her chapter, Taliaferro Baszile thinks critically about how memory is formed and informed by oppression and, toward that end, how such memory might be interrupted through the praxis of protest. Theorizing "democracy in the break," Taliaferro Baszile argues that engaging the breaking and breaking open of democratic practices is central to moving beyond current sociopolitical and cultural norms and values. Taliaferro Baszile offers readers a moment to pause, heal, and (re)consider what lies beyond everyday oppressions that are business-as-usual across American cultures.

Conclusion

In her book, *In the Wake: On Blackness and Being*, Christina Sharpe (2016) argues that the ocean still swells with the violence from slave ships traversing its waters. Looking at the time it takes for a substance to enter and then leave the ocean, a process that is known as "residence time," Sharpe found that sodium has a residence time of 260 million years. The "human body," Sharpe writes, "is salty [and] what happens to energy produced in the waters? It continues cycling like atoms in residence time . . . Black people exist in the residence time of the wake, a time in which 'everything is now. It is all now' " (p. 40). In this case, I'm speaking literally, not metaphorically. Salt is shared and recursive. The violence is literally in the salt, in the water, in our bodies. But it is also metaphorically true. This is where it gets complicated. The trauma of America's history with racism is always at once metaphorical and material.

This begs the question: What violence exists in the soil, churned constantly as the next wave of whiteness impacts, and too often kills, the bodies and ways of being of Black and Brown people and communities? Racism, and its toxic remnants are therefore in our oceans, on our lands, and in the air. In schools, this manifests as a curriculum of violence (Wozolek, 2019, 2021), where racism is akin to lead in water. It is not a question of the lead being in the water but, rather, how much of the water one has to drink and whether or not you have the privilege of a filter. In the case of this book, racism is the lead that impacts Black people across sexual orientations, gender identities, ability, home languages, and the like—is always in the water. Drinking water is a necessity to live. However, the ability to purchase, or being given, a filter to protect you from the carcinogens of racism is a question of privilege. How one uses the filter, as an ally or accomplice for those who do not have filters, is a matter of agency.

Black Lives Matter in US Schools is a significant text in that it thinks about how schools—from kindergarten through to the academy—are responsible for the violence that normalizes the murders of Black people across the United States. Additionally, it is significant because it considers not only how one might filter out racism, but the authors actively attempt to construct educational spaces that are inherently and intentionally antiracist. If, to recall the words of Woodson, we are to overcome the contemporary lynchings that are all-too-familiar headlines, we must begin with curricula that are more than inclusive, respectful, and responsible to and for Black lives. We must enact, engender, and maintain curricular spaces that are antiracist at their core. Returning to Rochelle's dialogue at the beginning of this chapter, this book asks what it might mean for children to never feel like strange fruit in school, at home, or in their communities again. We must therefore be more than well-intentioned but, rather, explicitly intentional about how Black Lives Matter in our communities in general and, especially, in the place where they should be foregrounded as a mechanism for abolishing sociopolitically normalized racism—at school.

Notes

1. A pseudonym given to the student to protect her anonymity.

2. Throughout this book, the authors follow Crenshaw's (1991) capitalization of *Black*, because it refers to a cultural group and therefore requires capitalization. Alternatively, *white* does not refer to a specific cultural group and therefore is not capitalized.

References

Apple, M. W. (1971). The hidden curriculum and the nature of conflict. *Interchange*, *2*(4), 27–40.

Apple, M. W. (2014). *Official knowledge: Democratic education in a conservative age*. New York: Routledge.

Au, W., Brown, A. L., & Calderón, D. (2016). *Reclaiming the multicultural roots of US curriculum: Communities of color and official knowledge in education.* New York: Teachers College Press.

Baldwin, J. (1962). *The fire next time.* New York: The Dial Press.

Berry, T. R., & Stovall, D. O. (2013). Trayvon Martin and the curriculum of tragedy: Critical race lessons for education. *Race Ethnicity and Education, 16*(4), 587–602.

Berry, T. R. (2010). Honoring our founders, respecting our contemporaries: In the words of a critical race feminist curriculum theorist. In E. Malewski (Ed.), *Curriculum Studies Handbook: The Next Moment* (pp. 138–141). New York: Routledge.

Bethune, M. M. (1938). Clarifying our vision with the facts. *Journal of Negro History, 7*(2), 10–15.

Black Lives Matter. (2020). Herstory. Retrieved from https://blacklivesmatter.com/herstory/

Bracho, C. A., & Hayes, C. (2020). Gay voices without intersectionality is white supremacy: narratives of gay and lesbian teachers of color on teaching and learning. *International Journal of Qualitative Studies in Education, 54*(1), 1–10.

Brockenbrough, E. (2016). Becoming queerly responsive: Culturally responsive pedagogy for Black and Latino urban queer youth. *Urban Education, 51*(2), 170–196.

Charles, R. (1993). None of us are free. *My world.* Warner Brothers.

Cooper, A. J. (1892). *A voice from the south (by a Black woman from the south).* Xenia, OH: Aldine Printing House.

Crenshaw, K. (1991). Mapping the margins: Intersectionality, identity politics, and violence against women of color. *Stanford Law Review, 43*(6), 1241–1299.

Douglass, F. (1855). What is the slave to the Fourth of July? Extract from an oration at Rochester, NY, July 5, 1852.

Du Bois, W. E. B. (1903). *The souls of Black folk.* Chicago, IL: McClurgand.

Du Bois, W. E. B. (1926). Criteria of Negro art. *The Crisis, 32*, 290–297.

Dumas, M. J., & Nelson, J. D. (2016). (Re)Imagining Black boyhood: Toward a critical framework for educational research. *Harvard Educational Review, 86*(1), 27–47.

Dunbar-Ortiz, R., & Gilio-Whitaker, D. (2016). *"All the real Indians died off": And 20 other myths about Native Americans.* Boston, MA: Beacon Press.

Eisner, E. (1985). *The educational imagination: On the design and evaluation of school programs* (2nd ed.). New York: Macmillan.

Fatal force. (January, 2021). *Washington Post.* Retrieved from https://www.washingtonpost.com/graphics/investigations/police-shootings-database/

Garvey, M. (1922). Address to the second UNIA convention. Talk given in Harlem, NY.

Garza, A. (2014). A herstory of the #BlackLivesMatter movement. In J. Hobson (Ed.), *Are all the women still white?: Rethinking race, expanding feminisms* (pp. 23–28). Albany, NY: State University of New York Press.

Giroux, H., & A. Penna (1983) *The hidden curriculum and moral education.* Berkeley, CA: McCutchan.

Gordon, B. M. (1993). African-American cultural knowledge and liberatory education: Dilemmas, problems, and potentials in a postmodern American society. *Urban Education, 27*(4), 448–470.

Grant, C. A., Brown, K. D., & Brown, A. L. (2015). *Black intellectual thought in education: The missing traditions of Anna Julia Cooper, Carter G. Woodson, and Alain Leroy Locke.* New York: Routledge.

Gumbs, A. P. (2016). *Spill: Scenes of Black feminist fugitivity.* Durham, NC: Duke University Press.

Hannah-Jones, N. (2019). The 1619 Project. Retrieved from https://www.nytimes.com/ interactive/2019/08/14/magazine/1619-america-slavery.html

Helfenbein, R. J. (2010). Thinking through scale: Critical geographies and curriculum spaces. In E. Malewski (Ed.), *Curriculum studies handbook: The next moment* (pp. 304–317). New York: Routledge.

Hemenway, D., Azrael, D., Conner, A., & Miller, M. (2019). Variation in rates of fatal police shootings across US states: The role of firearm availability. *Journal of Urban Health, 96*(1), 63–73.

Howard, T. C. (2019). *Why race and culture matter in schools: Closing the achievement gap in America's classrooms.* New York: Teachers College Press.

Huckaby, M. F. (2019). *Researching resistance: Public education after neoliberalism.* Sterling, VA: Stylus Publishing.

Jocson, K. M., Dixon-Román, E., & Jean-Denis, A. J. (2020). Embracing the speculative: Pedagogical and methodological crossroads. *Equity & Excellence in Education, 53*(3), 263–270.

Jones, D., & Hagopian, J. (2020). *Black lives matter at school: An uprising for educational justice.* Chicago, IL: Haymarket Books.

Jones, J. L., & Hensley, L. R. (2012). Taking a closer look at the impact of classroom placement: Students share their perspective from inside special education classrooms. *Educational Research Quarterly, 35*(3), 33.

Kim, C. Y., Losen, D. J., & Hewitt, D. T. (2010). *The school-to-prison pipeline: Structuring legal reform.* New York: NYU Press.

Lorde, A. (1984). *Sister Outsider: Essays and Speeches by Audre Lorde.* Berkeley, CA: Crossing Press.

Love, B. (2019). *We want to do more than survive: Abolitionist teaching and the pursuit of educational freedom.* Boston, MA: Beacon Press.

Malewski, E. (Ed.). (2009). *Curriculum studies handbook: The next moment.* New York: Routledge.

Meeropol, A. (1939). "Strange fruit" [Recorded by B. Holiday]. On [78 rpm]. *Classics in Swing.* New York: Commodore Records.

Menjivar, J. A., Vogel, A., Laksimi-Morrow, S., & Robinson, R. (2017). Special issue on #BlackLivesMatter, *Theory, Research, and Action in Urban Education, 5*(1), 1–3.

Meiners, E. R. (2016). *For the children? Protecting innocence in a carceral state.* Minneapolis: University of Minnesota Press.

Morris, M. W. (2016). *Pushout: The criminalization of Black girls in schools.* New York: The New Press.

Moyer, J. (2016). White high school teacher arrested in Texas after classroom attack on Black student caught on video. *Washington Post.* Retrieved from https://www.washingtonpost.com/news/morning-mix/wp/2016/04/11/white-high-school-teacher-arrested-in-tex-after-classroom-attack-on-black-student-caught-on-video/

Nespor, J. (1997). *Tangled up in school: Politics, space, bodies and signs in the educational process.* Mahwah, NJ: Lawrence Erlbaum.

Noguera, P. A., & Leslie, T. (2014). Risk, Resilience, and Response. In C. A. Grant & E. Zwier (Eds.), *Intersectionality and Urban Education: Identities, Policies, Spaces & Power* (pp. 79–96). Charlotte, NC: Information Age Publishing.

Page, R. (1991). *Lower-track classrooms: A curricular and cultural perspective.* New York: Teachers College Press.

Pinar, W. F. (1991). Understanding Curriculum as a Racial Text. *Scholar and Educator, 15*(2), 9–21.

Pinar, W. F. (2004). *What is curriculum theory?* Mahwah, NJ: Lawrence Erlbaum.

Pugach, M. C., Blanton, L. P., Mickelson, A. M., & Boveda, M. (2020). Curriculum theory: The missing perspective in teacher education for inclusion. *Teacher Education and Special Education, 43*(1), 85–103.

Ransbury, B. (2018). *Making all Black lives matter: Reimagining freedom in the 21st century.* Oakland: University of California Press.

Schwab, J. J. (1969). The practical: A language for curriculum. *The School Review, 78*(1), 1–24.

Sharpe, C. (2016). *In the wake: On Blackness and being.* Durham, NC: Duke University Press.

Skutnabb-Kangas, T. (2000). *Linguistic genocide in education—or worldwide diversity and human rights?* New York: Routledge.

Spencer, H. (1860). What knowledge is of most worth? In H. Spencer, *Education: Intellectual, moral, and physical* (pp. 21–96). New York: D. Appleton & Company.

Taliaferro Baszile, D., Edwards, K. T., & Guillory, N. A. (2016). *Race, gender, and curriculum theorizing: Working in womanish ways.* Lanham, MD: Rowman & Littlefield.

Tatum, B. D. (1997). *"Why are all the Black kids sitting together in the cafeteria?" And other conversations about race.* New York: Basic Books.

Taylor, K. Y. (2016). *From #BlackLivesMatter to Black liberation*. Chicago, IL: Haymarket Books.

Thebault, R. (2019). Video shows police officer tackling an 11-year-old girl he accused of being 'disruptive' at school. *Washington Post*. Retrieved from https://www.washingtonpost.com/education/2019/10/23/video-shows-police-officer-tackling-an-year-old-girl-he-accused-being-disruptive-school/

Truth, S. (1851). Ain't I a woman? Paper presented at the Women's Convention. Akron, OH.

Watkins, W. H. (2001). *The white architects of Black education: Ideology and power in America 1865–1954*. New York: Teachers College Press.

Winfield, A. G. (2007). *Eugenics and education in America: Institutionalized racism and the implication of history, ideology, and memory*. New York: Peter Lang.

Wozolek, B. (Ed.). (2015). Black Lives Matter. *AERA's Division B News, 1*(1).

Wozolek, B. (2019). War of the half-breeds: Communities of color, resistance, and racist education in a high school in the Midwest. In W. S. Gershon (Ed.), *Sensuous curriculum: The politics of the senses in education* (pp. 67–84). Charlotte, NC: Information Age Press.

Wozolek, B. (2021). *Assemblages of violence in education: Everyday trajectories of oppression*. Routledge.

Wozolek, B., Wootton, L., & Demlow, A. (2017). The school-to-coffin pipeline: Queer youth, suicide and resilience of spirit, *Cultural Studies ↔ Critical Methodologies, 17*(5), 392–398.

Zaveri, M. (2020). Body camera footage shows arrest by Orlando police of 6-year-old at school. *New York Times*. Retrieved from https://www.nytimes.com/2020/02/27/us/orlando-6-year-old-arrested.html

Revisiting Claims about #BlackLivesMatter

Toward an Equity Literate Fact-Checking Approach

Sherick A. Hughes

> "I hope these [White Lives Matter] shirts convince ALL white people to look at the TRUE FACTS. Facts like, more whites are killed by police than blacks. Blacks kill more police annually than police kill blacks, and the fact that ANY black that feels whites have it over them HAS to be a racist. That's a whole lot of blacks! I started designing shirts like this one the very instant I heard that horrible statement BLACK LIVES MATTER."
>
> —Bobby, 2018[1]

> "The same educational process, which inspires and stimulates the oppressor with the thought that he is everything and has accomplished everything worthwhile, depresses and crushes at the same time the spark of genius in the Negro by making him feel that his [racial identity] does not amount to much and never will measure up to the standards of other peoples. The Negro thus educated is a hopeless liability."
>
> —Woodson, 1933/1990, p. ix

Introduction

Here is some more bad news. The Southern Poverty Law Center (SPLC) identified white Lives Matter, a neo-Nazi group now growing into a movement[2] with a potential renewable energy source of misleading "TRUE FACTS" (Bobby, 2018). The US has a highly publicized, incessant, and insidious problem—racial identity informs lived experience in complex, conditional, and sometimes hidden ways. Similar to scholar-activist Van Jones, I anticipated backlash, or *whitelash*, following the ascendance of President Barack Obama (Ryan, 2016). As the first US president to self-identify as Black or African American, President Obama triggered for some, and reinforced for others, strong misperceptions of increasing Black advantages and declining white advantages; even moving some authors to argue prematurely for the country as representing a postracial society (SPLC, 2018). Has there been such parity in Black versus white racialized experiences? The answer to this question not only depends on the obvious—how race informs lived experiences—but also on the degree to which one learns to interpret race-related data as a critical self-monitor engaging critical reflexivity, and acting to sustain equitable practices.

As a Black man with the vast majority of my educational life at historically and predominantly white institutions (HPWIs) of public education, I find Woodson's (1933/1990) message in the opening of this chapter to be instructive. Limited critical self-monitoring and critical reflexivity in my research could lead me to join miseducated Blacks who become "exceedingly loyal to America's economic and political system and in most cases [turn] away from protest" and counterevidence (Watkins, 2001, p. 172). *Miseducation of the Negro* instructs me to remain vigilant and engaged in the work of problematizing my racialized "education" to challenge the allure at most HPWIs to embrace and support a hidden or explicit white-centered curriculum (Woodson, 1933/1990). Adding to this allure is the fraction of Blacks who become celebrated Black intellectuals with a frequent media presence—and the relatively few student-athletes that dominate men's basketball and football, the two most highly visible, revenue-generating sports (Hughes, Thompson-Dorsey, & Carrillo, 2016; Hughes, 2007; Tanaka, 2007). The media visibility of these few faculty members and students can skew the prominence of Blacks at HPWIs, which can provide a form of confirmation bias for white observers, like Bobby and potentially for Blacks lives more or less like mine.

Readers may be asking by now, "Is there any *good* news?" The good news is that while HPWIs can be sites for reproducing racial inequity, they also can become sites to develop racial equity. Inspired in part by Mary Macleod Bethune (1938), this chapter was developed to *clarify the vision* of research on #BlackLivesMatter (BLM) by introducing equity literacy as a tool for critiquing claims of "true facts" (Bobby, 2018) from data associated with the movement. It addresses one central question: "What key claims about the BLM movement are supported or refuted by an equity literate fact-checking (ELF) approach to data interpretation?"

The field of curriculum studies has several long-standing dialogues that describe how education curricula remain organized in ways that reify ideas and ideals of white entitlement and greater life worth (e.g., Grant, Brown, & Brown, 2015; Watkins, 2001; Winfield, 2007). This chapter builds on the metaphor of curriculum as racialized text (Pinar, 1993; Berry & Hughes, 2005; Winfield, 2007; Watkins, 2001). Evidence of hidden and explicit racialization may lead one to accept plausible, but misleading evidence about Black versus white lives in the US. The remaining text: (a) presents *equity literacy* as a theoretical framework, (b) offers a brief history of #BlackLivesMatter movement, (c) describes the data assemblage process, (d) applies an equity literate fact-checking approach to interpret data related to key claims about the movement, and (e) offers concluding thoughts, including implications for curriculum as a racialized text at HPWIs.

Theoretical Framework: Equity Literacy

This chapter is for the *chronic egalitarians* who have goals of monitoring their own reactions and behaviors in an effort to root out stereotypes and feelings that counter their espoused values (Johnson, 2007). Although, chronic egalitarians may not always meet their goals or even know where to start, after viewing counterevidence revealing their biased reactions, and allowed to practice debiasing strategies, they are more likely to make equitable judgments than their nonchronic counterparts (Johnson, 2007). Perhaps, the "key to developing *equity literacy*" for chronic egalitarians involves "cultivating four abilities" (Gorski & Swalwell, 2015, pp. 36–37; Gorski, 2013). Those include the ability to:

1. *Recognize* even subtle forms of bias, discrimination, and inequity;
2. *Respond to* bias, discrimination, and inequity in a thoughtful and equitable manner;

3. *Redress* bias, discrimination, and inequity, not only by responding to interpersonal bias, but also by studying the ways in which bigger social change happen;

4. *Cultivate and sustain* bias-free and discrimination-free communities, which requires an understanding that doing so is a basic responsibility for everyone in a civil society. (Gorski & Swalwell, 2015, p. 37)

Educators commonly espouse egalitarian views, which suggests that P–16 schools, colleges, and universities can be home to many chronic egalitarians positioned to engage an equity literacy curriculum. There are four essential questions regarding an equity literacy curriculum: (a) What makes something equitable or inequitable? (b) What (local, regional, global) inequities exist? (c) How have they changed over time, and why? (d) What individual and collective responsibilities do we have to address them? The questions require rigorous attention to evidence and ethics. In addition, the questions fit well with the inquiry approach to curriculum frameworks (Gorski & Swalwell, 2015, p. 37) that can be used to address common claims about BLM. The internet hosts a plethora of conflicting claims regarding the BLM movement, from data available through popular public media sources to data available via government, NGO, and academic experts. Next, this chapter revisits key claims about the BLM movement by applying equity literate fact-checking as an alternative approach to data interpretation.

Brief History of #BlackLivesMatter

Contrary to popular belief, the hashtag that quickly became the signature of a movement started with a Facebook exchange in 2013. The portrait of despair and protest painted the day of the acquittal of George Zimmerman in Sanford, Florida, now includes two Black women in the foreground grieving after the shooting death of his victim, Trayvon Martin, an unarmed, Black teenager. "I continue to be surprised at how little black lives matter," typed author/activist, Alicia Garza. "Black people, I will NEVER give up on us. NEVER," she wrote to friend and fellow activist, Patrisse Khan-Cullors. Equally distraught by the verdict, Patrisse replied powerfully, and yet, parsimoniously, "#BlackLivesMatter" (Khan-Cullors & Bandele,

2018). The hashtag has come to embody the struggle for racial equity and the fight against structural racism, particularly as experienced by Black Americans. While the movement is decentralized, messages crediting the initial leadership of Garza, Khan-Cullors, and Opal Tometi pervade. Opal was the master communicator credited with developing the initial digital components needed to get people comfortable saying the words Black Lives Matter (Khan-Cullors & Bandele, 2018). Even some people closest to the trio initially felt the words would be viewed as separatist, and thereby lead to isolation (Khan-Cullors & Bandele, 2018). They persist and today some credit the group for sparking a resurgence of Black activism (e.g., Lartey, 2018). Many who oppose the Black Lives Matter campaign also blame it for sparking a resurgence of white activism.

By 2016, white supremacists cofounded White Lives Matter. As aforementioned, it represents a designated hate group with Neo-Nazi ideology as per the Southern Poverty Law Center (SPLC). The SPLC website explains that the group is "growing into a movement as more and more white supremacist groups take up its slogans and tactics" (SPLC, 2018, n. p.). Moreover, some scholars of peer-reviewed journal sources describe US racial inequity as reaching an all-time high (Carter, 2018) adding, "White supremacists are targeting college campuses like never before" (Wilcher, 2018, p. 2). The alt-right white nationalists arguably gained the widest national attention during white supremacist rally at the University of Virginia at Charlottesville. Notable for their chants of "White Lives Matter" during the Charlottesville tragedy, the group is comprised predominantly of young, white, college-educated men (Pitofsky, 2018, n.p.). Equity literate fact-checking seems imperative for chronic egalitarians to consider, as the alternative-fact messages of designated hate groups, like white Live Matters grow in opposition to #BlackLivesMatter, and as stewards of public grounds are compelled to uphold the groups' constitutional rights.

The Data: A Process of Assemblage

A diverse array of scholars representing a range of schools of thought from Foucault to Deleuze, have applied the term assemblage to their practice (Schatzki, 2002). The research for this chapter draws from qualitative assemblage techniques for data collection (Denshire & Lee, 2013; Hughes & Pennington, 2017). Assemblage data collection involves a multilayered process. The process relies on literature, items, and accounts assembled in order to respond to the central research question (Hughes & Pennington, 2017, p. 27). Assemblage data collection is comparable "to the assembling of artifacts from an archaeological site . . . made up of different forms and modes of representation" (Denshire & Lee 2014, slide 7). Accordingly, the data assembled here reflects a compilation of literature selected from publicly available federal government, nonpartisan NGO, and other nonpartisan nonprofit databases (e.g., U.S. Census, FBI, DOJ-BJS, SPLC, and ACLU,[3] The *Washington Post*'s Fatal Force data, Killed by Police, Fatal Encounters, Mapping Police Violence, and The Counted). In addition, the data assembled represents reputable peer-reviewed academic research (e.g., Carter, 2018; DeGue, Fowler, & Calkins, 2016; Hughes, Thompson-Dorsey & Carrillo, 2016; Wise, 2013; Cambell, Nix, & Maguire, 2018, p. 398; Tregle, Nix, & Alpert, 2019; Johnson, St. Vil, Gilbert, Goodman, & Johnson, 2019). Moreover, the data assembled here include relevant research found in the reference sections and bibliographies of those texts.

Data Interpretation Violations

From an ELF framework, there are at least four data interpretation violations with my initial attempts to respond to claims about BLM in 2018. Data Interpretation Violation #1 involves a failure to consider the limitations of population proportion data as a common, an acceptable, but insufficient benchmark (Ross, Winterhalder, & McElreath, 2020) for claims about fatal interactions with police (FIPs). In fact, scholars of criminology noted having "yet to identify an appropriate benchmark to put observed racial disparities in officer-involved shootings into context" (Tregle et al., 2019, p. 18). Data Interpretation Violation #2 involves the failure to consider the relevance of reputable databases, like Fatal Force of the *Washington Post*, which may not be enough, alone, to make defensible claims that withstand the utmost scrutiny. Scholars of sociology, criminology, social work, behavioral sciences, and health education apply the research industry standard triangulation of data as necessary to render the most defensible findings on the topic (Tregle et al., 2019; Johnson, et al., 2019). It is imperative to consider that as many as 70 cases may be in Database A that are not in Database B, while some 227 cases may be Database-B that are note in Database-A (Johnson et al., 2019, p. 228). Including incidents appearing in both databases would be an equitable way to resolve this disparity (Johnson et al., 2019, p. 228). Thus, ELF researchers should consider triangulating data sources, as well as citing sources that triangulate data. For example, some databases on police shootings do not include all killings, (i.e., deaths where no shooting was involved), as in the killing of George Floyd. Researchers may also want to know whether the officer who killed the victim was white or Black, which is available in some database and not in others.

Data Interpretation Violation #3 involves the failure to acknowledge the potential of critical approaches to hierarchical linear modeling (HLM), multiple regression, and other inferential statistical analyses (Johnson et al., 2019; Ross, Winterhalder, & McElreath, 2020). Such statistical analyses move beyond the highly criticized population benchmarking (Ross, Winterhalder, & McElreath, 2020; Tregle et al., 2019) to provide a more robust computations of statistical significance (e.g., effect sizes) for making causal claims about what racial identity groups reflect more FIPs. Statistical methods like HLM also afford the built-in disaggregation of data beyond *who was killed* to offer information about *where they were killed, why they were killed,* and *under what contexts and conditions,* with related statistical significance. Data Interpretation Violation #4 involves the failure to consider data regarding police killings of unarmed victims as a central concern (MPV, 2019, n.p.). Victims of FIPs who were unarmed sparked the BLM movement, as well as current international protests following the murder of George Floyd.

Equity Literate Fact-Checking (ELF) Claims about BLM

Given the brief history of the movement, it is perhaps no surprise to readers that the math data used most often to oppose #BlackLivesMatter, is crime statistics. An equity literate fact-checking approach involves a deeper, more comprehensive investigation of those statistics and reveals key math logic that tends to be misunderstood, ignored, and/or suppressed. Accordingly, the ELF process includes the interpretation of (a) data on FIPs and (b) court sentencing data with the racial identity of the victims. The opening text of the chapter necessitates an application of the ELF process to two revisited claims: (1) "more whites are killed by police than blacks," and (2) "Blacks kill more police annually than police kill blacks" (Bobby, 2018). After checking Bobby's claims to his "TRUE FACTS," I revisit and fact check another common counterclaim to the BLM movement that emerged from the literature: "All Lives Matter" (Gallagher et al., 2018, p. 2). The three claims about BLM are revisited with the ELF approach by:

(a) explaining the initial data interpretation, and (b) naming and accounting for relevant data interpretation violation(s).

Claim #1: More Whites Are Killed by Police than Blacks

Bobby claims, "More whites are killed by police than blacks. Blacks kill more police annually than police kill blacks." An ELF approach requires me to consider first check my own bias as a Black man who does not support the White Lives Matter movement. It requires a consideration that Bobby's claim may be correct, before then moving to checking the sources of data he uses to support this claim. Since, Bobby offers no sources, the next step requires a search for sources without clear bias toward a political campaign or racialized group. As a trained researcher, my default is to begin with a Google search for data from research by scholars in journals that adhere to a blind, peer-review process to ensure quality. As noted previously, my training in equity literacy, also led me to search for federal government, nonpartisan NGO, and other nonpartisan nonprofit databases, and the references and bibliographies of those sources. I began with the *Washington Post* database, which continues to be cited by scholars as one of the most up-to-date and comprehensive databases on the topic of police shootings[4] (Tregle, Nix, & Alpert, 2019; Johnson et al., 2019). I attempted the following response in the fall of 2018.

> As of October 13, 2018, there have been 756 fatal police shootings. Blacks comprise 138 of people killed in police shootings from January 1, 2018 to October 13, 2018, while some 288 whites were killed by police shootings. If one stops here without continuing the math logic, "Bobby" might convince her/him that #BlackLivesMatter is founded upon false pretenses. However, one must further consider the likelihood of being killed by the police by racial identity group.
>
> This math is particularly important to further analyze, since Black Americans comprise only approximately 13% of Americans in 2017 Census data, whereas non-Hispanic white Americans still comprise over 60% of the population (U.S. Census Bureau, 2017).[5] Given those proportions, one can calculate that approximately 98 Blacks would be killed by the police (13% of 756) and 461 whites would be killed by the police (61% of 756) during the observed time period. Instead, more Blacks have been killed by police than should be expected

> (138 actually killed vs. 98 expected by chance), while fewer whites have been killed by the police than could be expected by chance (288 actually killed vs. 461 expected by chance).

A second attempt to respond to Bobby's first claim reflects relevant Interpretation Violations #1, #3, & #4. To address all three violations, data was reinterpreted from scholarly sources (Tregle et al., 2018; Mapping Police Violence;[6] Ross, Winterhalder, & McElreath, 2020) using more thorough statistics. Seven benchmarks were applied by Tregle et al. (2019) to analyze the following data from 2015 to 2017: (a) US Census population data, (b) Police-Public Contact Survey's police-citizen interaction data, and (c) the Uniform Crime Report's arrest data (p. 18). Black citizens were observed to be more likely than white citizens to be shot fatally by police officers from 2015 to 2017, when population, police-citizen interactions, or total arrests were used as a benchmark (Tregle et al., 2019, p. 18). Black citizens were observed as less likely than white citizens to be shot fatally by police officers during that time period, when violent crime arrests or weapons offense arrests were used as a benchmark. Mapping Police Violence (MPV, 2019) database is also recognized by scholars as one of the most comprehensive accounts of US citizens that are killed by police since 2013. MPV (2019) indicates that from January 2013 to December 2019, some "**47% of unarmed people killed** by the 100 largest city police departments were **black.** These police departments killed unarmed black people at a rate of **4 times higher** than unarmed white people" (MPV, 2019, n.p.).

Johnson et al., 2019 apply hierarchical linear modeling to understand how neighborhoods matter in fatal matter in fatal interactions with police (FIPs) in one of the most comprehensive studies on the topic to date. The research team triangulated data sources from Killed by Police, and Fatal Encounters. These databases were "supplemented by publicly accessible information about each case from local news reports, obituaries, coroner reports, and court records" (Johnson et al., 2019, p. 228). FIPs data was merged with the Bureau of Justice Statistic's Law Enforcement Management and Administrative Statistics (LEMAS) to locate police agency characteristics, avoid some biased reporting, and information on a nationally representative sample of agencies (Johnson et al., 2019, p. 228).

A second data merge used "ARC GIS (Geographical Information Systems) and near table analysis to match" each of the FIPs "to the closest zip code found in the LEMAS database using 2013 shapefiles downloaded from the US Census Bureau" (Johnson et al., 2019, p. 228). Johnson et al. (2019) calculate odds ratio (OR) statistics and find that "the odds of a FIP for Black males are relatively greater in large cities" (OR = 2.12:1, $p < .001$). However "the relative odds of a FIP for black males is reduced significantly (OR = 0.29:1, $p = .042$)" in areas that have a lower percentage of Black residents (p. 231). The "measure related to FIPs for Black males from areas high in inequality" (OR = 1.35:1, $p = .052$) and from "the top third of percentage of black residence" (OR = 1.77:1, $p = .059$) approached statistical significance, but not at the industry standard level of $p \leq .05$ (Johnson et al., 2019, p. 231). A reduction in the "relative odds of a FIP was reduced significantly when their mental illness/drug use was considered" (Johnson et al., 2019, p. 223). The team also found that "Black males were nearly 5½ times as likely as non-Black males to have a civil suit alleging that the deadly force was unjustified" (Johnson et al., 2019, p. 233) with significantly greater odds that a civil suit was filed ($p < .001$) after a Black male died from a FIP (Johnson et al., 2019, p. 231).

Another team of researchers found "strong statistical biases that mask true racial disparities, especially in the killing of unarmed noncriminals by police" (Ross, Winterhalder, & McElreath, 2020, n.p.). Moreover, their reanalysis of 2015–2016 data using "formally derived criminality-correcting benchmarks identifies strong and statistically reliable evidence of anti-Black racial disparities" in police killings of unarmed Black people (Ross et al., 2020, n.p.). A third research team led by members of the Division of Violence Prevention, at the US Centers for Disease Control and Prevention found that "Most victims were reported to be armed (83%); however, black victims were more likely to be unarmed (14.8%) than white (9.4%) or Hispanic (5.8%) victims" (DeGue, Fowler, & Calkins, 2016, p. S173).

The racial identity of the responsible officer(s) often cannot be connected to each fatality as noted in the thorough research of (Johnson et al., 2019). However, a fourth research team was able to gather data indicating that Black people's FIP rates may not improve, even when sharing the racial identity of the police officers who killed them. Nonwhite police officers were found to kill Blacks at about the same rate as their white colleagues (Menifield, Shin, & Strother, 2018, p. 56). In sum, the ELF data interpretation finds Bobby's first claim to be misleading, at best.

Claim #2: Do Blacks Kill More Police than Police Kill Blacks?

Initially, I used only one main source (Interpretation Violation #2) and relied on population proportion (Interpretation Violation #1) as a benchmark. In short, the available data often "does not address whether officers of color are more directly responsible" for some of these homicides (Johnson et al., 2019, p. 223). Similar to Johnson and his team foreshadowed, I located only one reputable data source on the topic of Blacks killing police, as evident below in my initial attempt to respond to Claim #2.

> White police officers killed in the line of duty are less likely to be killed by a Black offender than a white offender from 1980 to 2013 (Lee, 2015). Moreover, while over 100 police officers are killed on duty each year, accidents often match or even exceed the number of officers who are murdered each year (Lee, 2015). According to the *Washington Post* database, when I initiated work for this chapter, more Blacks were killed by police already in October of 2018 than police officers have been killed by Blacks and whites, which refutes claims like the one Bobby proffers. However, Bobby does have a good point when considering that relatively weak population benchmark. The Black population ranged from 11.6% to 13% between 1980 and 2013, and given those population percentages, the percentage of Black offenders who killed police officers is disproportionately higher than would be expected by chance (Lee, 2015). Bobby did not interpret the data on Blacks being exposed more to police officers due to overpolicing (Hinton et al., 2018). Furthermore, Bobby fails to note the math indicating that over 51% of police killings occurred in the South and cities and counties with a population of less than 250,000, again where Blacks within are concentrated and overpoliced (Lee, 2015).

Hence, Interpretation Violations #1 and #2 are most relevant to consider when revising the response to this claim. An equity literate fact checking attempt to respond to Bobby's second claim would consider either augmenting the population benchmark or dropping it altogether in favor of locating or developing a more robust statistical analysis.

It is important to note that although Lee (2015) was the only recent data source initially located on the topic, the data did reflect one of the most reputable databases (i.e., Fatal Force of the *Washington Post*). Still, researchers using an ELF approach requires considering additional relevant sources that become available (e.g., from the FBI, 2019, Mapping Police Violence, and journals that adhere to the blind peer review process). For example, according to the FBI database, some 89 law enforcement officers were killed in line-of-duty incidents in 2019. Of these deaths, some 48 officers died as a result of felonious acts, and 41 died in accidents (FBI, 2019). The FBI (2019) reports that some "28 of the alleged offenders were white, 15 were Black/African American" (n.p.). The same year, 259 Blacks were killed by police, including 28 unarmed Blacks (Mapping Police Violence, 2019). In sum, even without the population benchmarking, the addition of the recent FBI and Mapping Police Violence data enhances the initial ELF data interpretation. Ultimately, the triangulation of sources provided only one source to support Claim #2. However, that one source is rather trivial and problematic for because it: (a) relies on population proportions, and thus (b) fails to consider potential influences like Blacks' overexposure to police officers due to overpolicing (Hinton et al., 2018). In sum, ELF data interpretation produced findings that largely disconfirm Bobby's second claim.

Claim #3 All Lives Matter: We Don't Need BLM If Blacks Are Killing their Own and Whites

My initial attempt to respond to Claim #3 is in the block quotations below. While most of the initial responses withstood the scrutiny of an ELF approach to data interpretation, the initial work on encounter rates, intra-racial, and interracial crimes reflected blatant Interpretation Violations.

> *Encounter Rates and Interracial Crimes.* Using equity literacy alongside math logic involving encounter rates might provide a bit more clarity on the issue of interracial crime (Wise, 2013). Wise (2013) uses the former *Wall Street Journal* (*WSJ*) database to draw three central conclusions from 2010 data that essentially corroborates the math assembled from the other sources cited here.[7] The math supporting a large part of his argument begins with interracial encounter rate estimates. It was estimated that only about 3% of people encountered by Whites are Black, while about 57% of people encountered by Blacks are White (O'Brien, 1987). Using 2010 data, and applying the rates of interracial encounter noted above (3% and 57%), Wise (2013) calculates: "Of 4,765 victims of black killers, random chance would have predicted 2,716 white victims (4,765 × .57); and,

> of 3,896 victims of white killers, random chance would have predicted 117 black victims (3,896 × .03)" (n.p.). Given relative racial homicide offending rates and rates of interracial encounter (i.e., factors determining the probability of interracial homicide victimization), "random chance would predict that there should have been about 2000 *more* black-on-white homicides in 2010 than there actually were, and about 300 *fewer* white-on-black murders than actually occurred" (Wise, 2013, n.p.). In other words, when considering interracial encounter rates, more Blacks were killed by Whites than should have been expected by chance, and fewer Whites were killed by Blacks than should have been expected.

Interpretation Violations #1, #3, and #4 were discovered through the ELF process (including a dated, Black-white encounter rate benchmark from O'Brien [1987], used by Wise [2013]). Wise (2013) does admit that the Black-white encounter rate was a bit dated, but he suggests that the rates "have not likely changed dramatically, given ongoing patterns of white/black housing isolation from one another" (Wise, 2013, n.p.). Still, without updated data on this crucial benchmark, the entire section formerly titled: "Encounter Rates and Interracial Crimes" is informative, but insufficient. A response to Claim #3 with the ELF approach necessitates working toward an understanding of at least: (a) differences in punishment/sentencing according to the racial identity of the victim versus the accused, (b) influence of implicit racial bias on policing, in addition to (c) interracial and intraracial crime data.

Punishment/Sentencing According to the Racial Identity of the Victim

The triangulation of inferential statistics-based studies nationwide reveals consistently that the "murder of Whites results in capital prosecution in far higher percentages than murders of people of color" (Turner & Dakwar, 2014, p. 7). These racial disparities among victims increase in cases with Black defendants (Turner & Dakwar, 2014, p. 7). The racial identity of victims and offenders even seems to determine which juvenile offenders are sentenced to life without parole (LWOP). Black youth with a white victim are far more likely to be sentenced to LWOP than white youth with a Black victim (Turner & Dakwar, 2014, pp. 4–5). The percentage of Black juvenile offenders serving LWOP for the homicide of a white victim (43.4%) is more than 12 times the percentage of white juvenile offenders sentenced to LWOP (3.6%) for the homicide of a Black victim (Turner & Dakwar, 2014, p. 5). The research team concludes that such disparate outcomes seem to be the result of not only racial biases influencing "who receives the harshest punishments," but also "who is arrested and who is detained" (Turner & Dakwar, 2014, p. 5). Beckett & Evans (2014) use statistical modeling on data representing key counties in the state of Washington and found that race matters in death penalty cases. More specifically, the team reports that "the size of the black population in the county in which the case was adjudicated significantly impacts the likelihood that prosecutors will file a death notice in aggravated murder cases generally" (Beckett & Evans, 2014, p. 28).

Implicit Bias Effects

Several research teams use statistical modeling to study the influence of implicit racial bias on sentencing. For example, Eberhardt, Davies, Purdie-Vaughns, and Johnson (2006) found that if a defendant had a stereotypically Black appearance, then appearance became an important predictor of the imposition of a death sentence in cases involving Black defendants and white victims. Another research team's work augments the findings of Eberhardt et al. (2006) by reporting that only the implicit prejudice of whites was associated with disproportionate lethal force of Blacks (Hehman, Flake, & Calanchini, 2017). Hehman et al.'s (2017) research team is credited for developing "the first macropsychological" predictive statistical models of lethal force by "integrating crowd-sourced and fact-checked lethal force databases with regional demographics and measures of geo-located implicit and explicit racial biases collected from 2,156,053 residents across the United States" (p. 1). Their team's results found "implicit racial prejudices and stereotypes of white residents, beyond major demographic covariates, are associated with police officers" disproportionately higher use of lethal force with Blacks "relative to regional base rates of Blacks in the population" (Hehman et al., 2017, p. 1). In other words, "as the implicit prejudice of Whites increased, so too did disproportionate use of lethal force with Blacks" (Hehman, Flake, & Calanchini, 2017, p. 4). In a second regression model, Hehman et al., 2017, found that implicit threat stereotypes (involving Black-weapon association) better predicted disproportionate lethal force, $p < .001$, than the implicit racial prejudice of whites. Moreover, this model explained a substantial 34% (as compared to 14% in the first regression model) of the variance in disproportionate lethal force (Hehman, Flake, & Calanchini, 2017, p. 5). This research indicates that the racialized context in which police officers work is associated significantly with disproportionate use of lethal force (Hehman, Flake, & Calanchini, 2017, p. 1).

Intraracial Crime Math Facts

Black leaders developed the phrase "Black-on-Black crime" to raise awareness of the need to decrease violent crimes in their communities. The term has been co-opted by opponents of #BlackLivesMatter to advance the following paraphrased logic: "If Black lives do not matter to them (citing Black-on-Black crime and killings), then Blacks should not matter to us, when considering fatal incidents with police." However, the math from reputable sources does not support this argument. First, a recent US Department of Justice-Bureau of Justice Statistics (DOJ-BJS) report indicates that all racial identity group members experience victimization most at the hands of intraracial criminals (i.e., criminals sharing their own racial identity grouping) in the US (Morgan, 2017, pp. 1, 4). Second, in the majority of violent crimes, white victims' perpetrators were white (57%) and Black victims' perpetrators were Black (63%) (Morgan, 2017, pp. 1, 4). Third, intraracial violent victimizations, the Black-on-Black violence rate (16.5 victimizations per 1,000 Black persons) was higher than the white-on-white violence rate (12.0 per 1,000 white persons). And, the Black-on-Black serious violence rate (6.7 per 1,000 Black persons) was higher than the white-on-white serious violence rate (3.7 per 1,000 white persons) (Morgan, 2017, pp. 1, 4). However, the Black-on-Black simple assault victimization rate (9.8 per 1,000 Black persons) was not statistically different from the white-on-White rate (8.4 per 1,000 white persons) (Morgan, 2017, pp. 1, 4). Fourth, in 2016, the number of homicides (2,570) involving a Black victim and black offender actually represents a dramatic decline from 7,361 in 1991 (Morgan, 2017, pp. 1, 4). Moreover, Black-on-Black and white-on-white nonfatal violent crime rates decreased 78% and 79%, respectively, between 1993 and 2015 (Morgan, 2017, pp. 1, 4). Fifth, "there were no differences among white, black, and Hispanic intra-racial victimizations reported to police" from "2012–15 (Morgan, 2017, p. 7).

Interracial Crime Math Facts

Another common rhetorical technique used to oppose #BlackLivesMatter involves the citing of misleading math suggesting the need to fear Black stranger danger (Wise, 2013). Again, math from reputable sources like the BJS and SPLC bring us closer to detailing more accurate experiences of victimization across the color line (vs. the perception of threat). According to Morgan (2017), a DOJ-BJS statistician, stranger violence accounts for the largest proportion of interracial violence (p. 5). A deeper look into the math using previously published logic (e.g., Liu, 2002; Wise, 2013) reveals more important complexity to consider.

When considering strangers only, whites were found to experience a higher percentage of violence committed by Black strangers (64.4%) than by white strangers (27.2%). However, these percentages in isolation can be misleading, because whites are also victimized by white domestic offenders (30.7%), and white offenders who are well-known/casual white acquaintances (41.4%). In other words, Morgan (2017) indicates that whites are victimized most often by white offenders they know (72.1%).

When considering strangers only victimization, Black victims experience a higher percentage of violence committed by white strangers (49.9%) than by Black strangers (36.7%). Similar to whites, Black victims experience more Black domestic offenders (26.5%) than white domestic offenders (8.4%). However, Blacks are victimized more often by white offenders who are well-known/casual white acquaintances (41.7%) and white offenders who are strangers (49.9%) than by Black offenders in those categories with percentages of 32.3% and 36.7%, respectively. This data reveals that Blacks are victimized at similar rates by known (41.7%) and unknown (49.9%) white offenders. In sum, this equity literate approach to data interpretation provides more counterevidence to the All Lives Matter claim than evidence to support it (Morgan, 2017).

Discussion: Clarifying Claims about BLM

The equity literate fact-checking was driven by a central research question: "What key claims about the BLM movement are supported or refuted by an equity literate fact-checking (ELF) approach to data interpretation?" This section returns to the question and related claims in table 1 in an attempt to offer a clarifying summary of the key findings related to the observed claims about the BLM movement. The complexity of data for Claim #1, #2, and #3 suggest the requirement of more complex data interpretation. The complexity is perhaps, highlighted most, when reframing each claim into a Q&A short-answer dialogue format.

> **Q:** Are more whites than Blacks killed annually by the police in the US?
>
> **A:** Yes and No. The "No" involves a crucial non-media-related reason—robust findings from an equity literate fact-checking approach to data interpretation. The ELF approach is important to avoid confirmation bias, to move beyond population proportions for benchmarking, to triangulate data sources, and include statistical analysis, like hierarchical linear modeling for the most defensible answer.
>
> **Q:** Are white police officers killed by Blacks more often than they kill Blacks?
>
> **A:** No. Not when applying the ELF approach to interpreting reliable nationwide data sets.
>
> **Q:** Do all lives matter?
>
> **A:** Yes. However, the ELF approach to interpreting reliable data on implicit bias, sentencing practices, and lethal force, suggests that white lives matter most of all.

Just because a higher proportion of the Black population is killed by the police than the proportion of the white population does not mean the case is closed, so to speak. However, such interpretations of data also offer misleading information, as population proportion benchmarking assumes similar lived experiences to make a valid and reliable comparison. The move toward published peer-reviewed journal articles and reports applying inferential statistics seemed to provide the most defensible interpretations of data regarding all three claims. Table 1 shares the complexity of confirming and disconfirming findings that emerged from the ELF approach.

An assemblage of research reveals limited evidence to confirm Claims #1, #2 and #3.

Table 1. Summary of Key Findings Related to Observed Claims about BLM

Claim	Disconfirming Findings	Confirming Findings	Relevant Sources
More whites are killed by police than Blacks	• Black citizens were observed to be more likely than white citizens to be shot fatally by police officers from 2015 to 2017, when population, police-citizen interactions, or total arrests were used as a benchmark.	• Of the nearly 1,000 people killed by police, whites comprise the largest number of FIP's.	Hehman et al. (2017)
	• January 2013 to December 2019, some 47% of unarmed people killed by the 100 largest city police departments were Black; these police departments killed unarmed Black people at a rate 4 times higher than unarmed white people.	• Black citizens were observed as less likely than white citizens to be shot fatally by police officers (2015–2017) when violent crime crime arrests or weapons offense arrests were used as a benchmark.	(Johnson et al., 2019) Mapping Police Violence (2013–present)
	• The odds of a FIP for Black males are greater in large cities ($p < .001$).		
	• There are anti-Black racial disparities in police killings of unarmed Black people. Black victims were more likely to be unarmed (14.8%) than white (9.4%) or Hispanic (5.8%) victims.	• Relative odds of a FIP for Black males is reduced significantly ($p = 0.42$) in areas that have a lower percentage of Black residents.	Tregle et al. (2019)
	• The measure related to FIPs for Black males from areas high in inequality ($p = .052$) and from the top third of percentage of Black		

	residence (p = 059) approached statistical significance, but not at the industry standard level of $p \leq .05$. • Black males were nearly 5½ times as likely as non-Black males to have a civil suit alleging that the deadly force was unjustified. There are significantly greater odds that a civil suit will be filed ($p < .001$) after a Black male died from a FIP • Non-white police officers were found to kill Blacks at about the same rate as their white colleagues (Menifield, Shin, & Strother, 2018, p. 56).	• Relative odds of a FIP reduced significantly when the mental illness/drug use of Black suspects was considered by the police.	
Blacks kill more police than police kill Blacks	• White police officers killed in the line of duty are less likely to be killed by a Black offender than a white offender from 1980 to 2013. • Moreover, while over 100 police officers are killed on duty each year (1980–2013), accidents often match or even exceed the number of officers who are murdered each year.	• Given a US Black population at 11.6% to 13% between 1980 and 2013, the percentage of Blacks killing police officers is higher than would be expected by chance.	(Lee, 2015) Fatal Force of the *Washington Post* (2015–Present)

continued on next page

Table 1. Continued.

Claim	Disconfirming Findings	Confirming Findings	Relevant Sources
	• In 2019, some 48 officers died as a result of felonious acts, and 41 died in accidents; 28 of the alleged offenders were white, 15 were Black/ African American. The same year, 259 Blacks were killed by police, including 28 unarmed Blacks.		FBI (2019) Mapping Police Violence (2013–present)
	• Population benchmarking is critiqued by researchers as potentially informative, but often insufficient for making defensible claims about Black vs. white data on crime and FIPs.		
All Lives Matter: We don't need BLM if Blacks kill their own & whites	• Black juvenile offenders serving Life without Parole (LWOP) for the homicide of a white victim (43.4 percent) is more than 12 times the percentage of white juvenile offenders sentenced to LWOP (3.6 percent) for the homicide of a Black victim.	• Black-on-Black serious violence rate (6.7 per 1,000 Black persons) was higher than the white-on white serious violence rate (3.7 per 1,000 white persons).	Morgan (2017) Turner & Dakwar (2014)
	• As the implicit prejudice of whites increased in a police district, so too did disproportionate use of lethal force with Blacks.	• When considering strangers only, whites experience a higher	Beckett & Evans (2014)

- Implicit threat stereotypes (involving Black-weapon association) predicted disproportionate lethal force, $p < .001$, better than the white implicit racial prejudice, per se.

- Racial identity group members experience victimization most at the hands of intraracial criminals (i.e., criminals sharing their own racial identity grouping); in the majority of violent crimes, white victims' perpetrators were white (57%) and Black victims' perpetrators were Black (63%).

- Black-on-Black simple assault victimization rate (9.8 per 1,000 Black persons) was not statistically different from the white-on-white rate (8.4 per 1,000 white persons).

- In 2016, the number of homicides (2,570) involving a Black victim and Black offender actually represents a dramatic decline from 7,361 in 1991.

- Black-on-Black and white-on-white nonfatal violent crime rates decreased 78 percent and 79 percent, respectively, between 1993 and 2015.

percentage of violence committed by Black strangers (64.4%) than by white strangers (27.2%).

- Black-on-Black violence rate (16.5 victimizations per 1,000 Black persons) was higher than the white-on-white violence rate (12.0 per 1,000 white persons).

continued on next page

Table 1. Continued.

Claim	Disconfirming Findings	Confirming Findings	Relevant Sources
	• There were no differences among white, Black, and Hispanic intraracial victimizations reported to police between 2012 and 2015. • When considering all offenses, whites are victimized most often by white offenders they know (72.1%). • When considering strangers-only victimization, Blacks are victimized more by white strangers (49.9%) than by Black strangers (36.7%). • Blacks are victimized more often by white offenders who are well-known/casual white acquaintances (41.7%) and white offenders who are strangers (49.9%) than by Black offenders in those categories with percentages of (32.3%) and (36.7%), respectively. • Black-on-Black serious violence rate (6.7 per 1,000 Black persons) was higher than the white-on-white serious violence rate (3.7 per 1,000 white persons).		

- When considering strangers only, whites experience a higher percentage of violence committed by Black strangers (64.4%) than by white strangers (27.2%)

- Black-on-Black violence rate (16.5 victimizations per 1,000 Black persons) was higher than the white-on-white violence rate (12.0 per 1,000 white persons).

In fact, there was two times the amount evidence disconfirming this claim, particularly in larger cities and predominantly Black neighborhoods. The latter finding is crucial to consider FIPs in racially desegregated and resegregated neighborhoods. Neighborhoods with relatively small populations of Black residents had "largest reduction in the odds of a FIP for Black males," in fact the "largest reduction in the analysis for any neighborhood or agency quality considered" (Johnson et al., 2019, p. 234). The racial distribution of FIPs for Black males was linked to resegregation and "the economic inequality within neighborhoods" (Johnson, 2019, p. 219). Yet, changes in neighborhood characteristics would not necessarily change FIPs without addressing any racial identity group bias among police officers. There was also overwhelming evidence to disconfirm Claims #2 and #3. I found four times the amount of data to disconfirm rather than confirm Claim #2, that more police are killed by Blacks than Blacks are killed by police. Moreover, I found over three times the amount of evidence to disconfirm the multiple terms of the All Lives Matter logic of Claim #3. One key data interpretation disconfirming Claim #3 supports previous interpretations about Black-on-Black crime. To the degree that it occurs, it is imperative to remember that it occurs comparably to white-on-white crime, except, it can be "better understood, as a function of structural racism" (Hinton et al., 2018, p. 4). Evidence from all three claims considered in tandem, suggests that white lives seem to matter more than Black lives, particularly regarding victimization, criminal justice, and fatal interactions with police.

Findings and questions raised by this chapter ultimately "will require a robust and institutionalized data collection effort to pursue" the most defensible responses (Johnson et al., 2019, p. 234). Moreover, the painstaking assemblage data collection technique underscores the "need for the institutionalization of data collection efforts about police-related injuries and fatalities among third-parties" (Johnson et al., 2019, p. 234). One effort at medical centers produced early signs of the potential to provide breadth and depth of the data in a centralized database that is beyond what currently exists (e.g., Feldman et al., 2016; Johnson et al., 2019).

Statisticians like Morgan (2017) at the DOJ-BJS provide invaluable information for deeper analysis and fact-checking on interracial crime. Moreover, DOJ-BJS math data can be assembled alongside other databases like New York City's Vera Institute of Justice for checking facts regarding the myth of Black-on-Black crime. "This [interracial crime] myth is fostered at least in part by the way that crime is measured," stated a recent brief from the Vera Institute of Justice (Hinton, Henderson, & Reed, 2018, p. 4). The Federal Bureau of Investigation's (FBI's) Uniform Crime Report "is considered the official measure of the national crime rate" (Hinton et al., 2018, p. 4). Unfortunately, this database is not only incomplete due to underreporting (Loftin, McDowall, & Xie, 2017), but also may offer a skewed view of the intersection of racial identity, social class, and offenders, because it "has always emphasized street crime to the exclusion of organized and white-collar crime" (Hinton et al., 2018, p. 4). This exclusion could mean that the FBI data used by white supremacist/nationalist groups, and criminal justice and law enforcement could actually serve to reinforce the deemphasizing of white-collar crimes, while overemphasizing crimes committed by the impoverished. Impoverished families in the US are disproportionately Black and Brown, largely because of structural racism inequities, and thereby, they disproportionately experience extreme poverty and crime (Clear, 2008, p. 97; Stemen, 2017).

Concluding Thoughts: Implications and Imagination

Hidden and explicit racialized understandings fuel the whiteness curriculum left unchecked by too many HPWIs. The curriculum is comprised too often of misleading evidence that can harm Black lives (Grant, Brown, & Brown, 2015; Watkins, 2001; Winfield, 2007). This chapter revisited three key claims about #BlackLivesMatter and addressed data interpretation violations that undermine the strength of those claims. In particular, this chapter addressed: (a) data on fatal interactions with police), (b) data on interracial and intraracial crime, and (c) data on differences in punishment for crimes according to the racial identity of the victim in relation to those claims.

Implications

There are at least six implications for researchers looking to apply the equity literate approach to interpreting data related to claims about BLM: (a) researchers are encouraged to consider equity literate fact-checking as a theoretical framework; (b) researchers are encouraged to be skeptical of the use of one data set due to issues of incompleteness and underreporting—

any claim about BLM using population/proportions with limited to no cited data sources should also be approached with a healthy skepticism; (c) researchers are encouraged either to triangulate data sources where possible, or to pursue the more comprehensive assemblage process of collecting available data; (d) researchers are encouraged to seek evidence from sources that adhere to the blind, peer-review process, published in reputable journals; (e) Researchers are encouraged to avoid misspecification of data (i.e., note whether data reflects police killings vs. police shootings); and (f) researchers are encouraged to take heed to the four interpretation violations and how they may apply to the observed database.

Imagining Curriculum as a Racialized Text at HPWIs

It is "difficult to paint a precise picture of what an equity literacy curriculum looks like because, like all curriculums, it will look different" (Gorski & Swalwell, 2015, p. 39). It relies on researchers' "abilities to cultivate . . . robust understanding about how people are treated by one another and by institutions, in addition to a general appreciation of diversity" (Swalwell, 2011; Gorski & Swalwell, 2015, p. 36). Its central tenet relies more on researchers' understandings of equity and inequity and of justice and injustice than on their understanding of this or that culture (Gorski, 2013). The findings of this chapter support a move to begin imagining implications for curriculum as racialized text at HPWIs.

1. Imagine HPWIs as central sites for developing the space(s) to disseminate information on potential interpretation violations via coursework and other enrichment activities.
2. Imagine HPWIs as central sites for equity literate fact-checking, so institutional stakeholders embrace the notion that not all lives matter equitably, until Black lives matter equitably.
3. Imagine HWPIs as central sites for calling into question how biased observers can easily misinterpret race-related data, thereby sabotaging the robustness of their claims.
4. Imagine HPWIs as central sites for adding transparency and clarity to various forms of race-related data, including how misinterpretations of data can normalize texts of a hidden curriculum[8] of racial inequity (Pinar, 1993; Gillborn, 1992, p. 57; Alsubaie, 2015, p. 125).

5. Imagine HPWIs as central sites for revisiting how racial epistemologies are hidden within the HPWI curriculum at large, as it was built and maintained within a social context where claims about #BlackLivesMatter can be easily dismissed or distorted by misinterpreted data or even (dis)interpreted data (unethically, purposefully shared misinterpretation).

This chapter demonstrates how equity literacy, as an existing construct, can become a theoretical framework for enhancing interpretations of a race-related database and for *clarifying the vision* (Bethune, 1938) of its usage. The ELF data interpretation (findings summarized in table 1) concurs with Johnson et al. (2019) about the need to consider more carefully the "neighborhood, and institutional circumstances in which the odds of having FIPs becomes greatest. . . ." (p. 234). It supports an equity literacy curriculum for teaching and learning how to cultivate and sustain bias-free and discrimination-free interpretation of data on all communities, with a particular focus on marginalized communities (e.g., Black, Latinx, and Native/Indigenous/First Nations communities). It supports an equity literacy curriculum for recognizing, responding to, and redressing bias and inequity during data collection, interpretation, and reporting. Ultimately, the ELF approach also led me to consider new questions about how the vast majority of recent media attention, civil lawsuits, and public attention about FIPs have been about Black males (Johnson et al., 2019, p. 234). And, I was led to consider whether data on white FIPs may be underreported. The data were revisited to gather some preliminary responses to these new questions. A more in-depth analysis of these questions is beyond the scope of this chapter.

Perhaps, readers may agree for now that while white FIPs may be underreported in the media, many white crimes are also underreported (e.g., hate crimes), and the current media attention to Black FIPs may be inflated, but so may be the negative media attention (van Doorn, 2015; Pezzella, Fetzer, & Keller, 2019). Media attention and race are important as "research consistently demonstrates that negative media representations of Blacks have a detrimental effect on whites' intergroup attitudes" (Tukachinsky, 2017, p. 1). Such negative representations are "likely contributing to the endurance of [Black] stereotypes" (van Doorn, 2015, p. 142). Conversely, research suggests that "positive representations" have "the potential to improve intergroup attitudes" (Tukachinsky, 2017, p. 1).

As usual, future research is necessary for ELF responses to these new questions that might withstand the scrutiny of a vast majority of critics.

Notes

1. "Bobby," 2018, White Lives Matter T-shirts. https://www.amazon.com/White-Lives-Matter-Large-T-Shirt/productreviews/B00WD4PY2U/ref=cm_cr_dp_d_srvw_btm?ie=UTF8&reviewerType=all_reviews&sortBy=recent#R16QLQTQ8A-RW6Y. The website is defunct as of June 18, 2020.

2. White Lives Matter Is on the Southern Poverty Law Center's List of White Supremacist Hate Groups. https://www.splcenter.org/fighting-hate/extremist-files/group/white-lives-matter

3. The ACLU was known for most of its 100-year-old history as a non-partisan defender of the constitutional rights of citizens, including offering legal representation to every American from Blacks to neo-Nazis. It was criticized more recently (i.e., 2018) for alleged contributions to candidates in opposition to the Trump-led Republican Party. This chapter only cites work from the ACLU's 2014 report, which was developed prior to the alleged partisan actions.

4. Information from a *Washington Post* website regarding the database indicates: "The Post is documenting only those shootings in which a police officer, in the line of duty, shot and killed a civilian—the circumstances that most closely parallel the 2014 killing of Michael Brown in Ferguson, Mo., which began the protest movement culminating in Black Lives Matter and an increased focus on police accountability nationwide. The Post is not tracking deaths of people in police custody, fatal shootings by off-duty officers or non-shooting deaths. The FBI and the Centers for Disease Control and Prevention log fatal shootings by police, but officials acknowledge that their data is incomplete. In 2015, The Post documented more than two times more fatal shootings by police than had been recorded by the FBI. Last year, the FBI announced plans to overhaul how it tracks fatal police encounters. The Post's database is updated regularly as fatal shootings are reported and as facts emerge about individual cases." https://github.com/washingtonpost/data-police-shootings

5. The US Census Bureau data from 2017 estimates Blacks comprising 13.4% and non-Hispanic Whites comprising 60.7% of the population. https://www.census.gov/quickfacts/fact/table/US/PST045217

6. The Mapping Police Violence (https://mappingpoliceviolence.org/cities) database is considered so reputable, because its data triangulates the "three largest, most comprehensive and impartial crowdsourced databases on police killings in the country: FatalEncounters.org, the U.S. Police Shootings Database and KilledbyPolice.net" (MPV, 2019, n.p.). Moreover, the planning team of the database

explains on the website how it continues working to "improve the quality and completeness of the data; searching social media, obituaries, criminal records databases, police reports and other sources to identify the race of 90 percent of all victims in the database" (MPA, 2019, n.p.).

7. Part of the data assembled, draws from antiracist author/activist Tim Wise (2013), who is widely considered a reputable source in the academy. Wise (2013) studied 2012 math data once available via a *Wall Street Journal* (*WSJ*) database. Prior to the *WSJ* database being shut down due to the discovery of hacking, it was once described by Wise (2013) as the most comprehensive data set ever compiled regarding homicides in America, because of the way it broke down offenders and victims by racial and ethnic identity grouping.

Wise (2013) further summarizes his findings: (a) "Although interracial homicide in either direction is quite rare, the fact is, any given black person in the U.S. is almost three times as likely to be murdered by a white person as any given white person is to be murdered by someone who is black," and (b) "Black-on-white homicide happened only 26 percent as often as random chance would have predicted, and the ratio of black-on-white to white-on-black homicide was only one-fourteenth as large as should have been expected."

8. The hidden curriculum refers to the "unspoken or implicit values, behaviors, procedures, and norms that exist in the educational setting" (Alsubaie, 2015, p. 125).

References

Alsubaie, M. A. (2015). Hidden curriculum as one of current issue of curriculum. *Journal of Education and Practice*, *6*(33), 125–128.

Beckett, K., & Evans, H. (2014, January 27). The role of race in Washington State capital sentencing, 1981–2014http://www.deathpenaltyinfo.org/documents/WashRaceStudy2014.pdf

Berman, M., Sullivan, J., Tate, J., & Jenkins, J. (2020, June 8). Protests spread over police shootings. Police promised reforms. Every year, they still shoot and kill nearly 1,000 people. *Washington Post*. Retrieved fromhttps://www.washingtonpost.com/investigations/protests-spread-over-police-shootings-police-promised-reforms-every-year-they-still-shoot-nearly-1000-people/2020/06/08/5c204f0c-a67c-11ea-b473-04905b1af82b_story.html

Bethune, M. M. (1938). Clarifying Our Vision with the Facts. *Journal of Negro History*, *7*(2), 10–15.

Campbell, B. A., Nix, J., & Maguire, E. R. (2018). Is the number of citizens fatally shot by police increasing in the post-Ferguson era? *Crime & Delinquency*, *64*(3), 398–420. https://doi.org/10.1177/0011128716686343

Carter, P. (2018). The multidimensional problems of educational inequality require multidimensional solutions. *Educational Studies*, 54(1), 1–16.

Clear, Todd R. (2008). The effects of high imprisonment rates on communities. *Crime and Justice*, *37*(1), 97–132. https://perma.cc/5L73-2DG

DeGue, S., Fowler, K.A, & Calkins, C. (2016, November). Deaths due to use of lethal force by law enforcement: Findings from the National Violent Death Reporting System, 17 U.S. States, 2009–2012. *American Journal of Preventive Medicine*, *51*(5 Suppl 3): S173–S187. doi:10.1016/j.amepre.2016.08.027

Denshire, S. D., & Lee, A. L. (2013). Conceptualizing autoethnography as assemblage: Accounts of occupational therapy practice. *International Journal of Qualitative Methods*, *12*, 221–236.

Denshire, S. D., & Lee, A. (2014). Conceptualising autoethnography as assemblage: Accounts of occupational therapy practice. PowerPoint presentation, University of Technology, Sydney.

Eberhardt, J. L., Davies, P. G., Purdie-Vaughns, V. J., & Johnson, S. L. (2006). Looking deathworthy: Perceived stereotypicality of Black defendants predicts capital-sentencing outcomes, *Psychological Science*, *17*, 383.

Feldman, J. M., Chen, J. T., Waterman, P. D., Krieger, N. (2016). Temporal trends and racial/ethnic inequalities for legal intervention injuries treated in emergency departments: US men and women age 15–34, 2001–2014. *Journal Urban Health: Bulletin*. New York Academy of Medicine. https://doi.org/10.1007/s11524-016-0076-3

FBI (2018, October 13). *Federal Bureau of Investigation, uniform crime reporting statistics: UCR offense definitions*. Retrieved from https://perma.cc/2ZTB-ASCK

FBI (2019). *Federal Bureau of Investigation, law enforcement officers killed and assaulted*. Retrieved from https://ucr.fbi.gov/leoka/2019/topic-pages/officers-feloniously-killed

Gallagher, R. J., Reagan, A. J., Danforth, C. M., Dodds, P. S. (2018). Divergent discourse between protests and counter-protests: #BlackLivesMatter and #All LivesMatter. *PLOS ONE*, *13*(4). e0195644. https://doi.org/10.1371/journal.pone.0195644

Gillborn, D. (1992). Citizenship, 'race' and the hidden curriculum. *International Studies in Sociology of Education*, *2*(1), 57–73.

Gorski, P., & Swalwell, E. (2015, March). Equity Literacy for All. *Educational Leadership,34–40.*

Hehman, E., Flake, J. K., & Calanchini, J. (2017). Disproportionate use of lethal force in policing is associated with regional racial biases of residents. *Social Psychological and Personality Science*, *XX*(X), 1–9.

Hinton, E., Henderson, L., & Reed, C. (2018). *An unjust burden: The disparate treatment of Black Americans in the criminal justice system*. New York: Vera Institute of Justice.

Hughes, S. A. (2007). "The only thing left for the whites is a couple of coaching jobs": Revisiting the discursive influence of pre- and post-*Brown* media on desegregation and resegregation in collegiate sports. *Journal for the Study of Sports and Athletes in Education*, Winter, *1*(1), 45–66.

Hughes, S., & Pennington, J. (2017). *Autoethnography: Process, product, and possibility*. Thousand Oaks, CA: Sage.

Hughes, S. A., Thompson-Dorsey, D., & Carrillo, J. F. (2016). Causation fallacy 2.0: Revisiting the myth and math of affirmative action. *Educational Policy*, *30*(1), 63–93.

Johnson, S. L. (2007). Litigating for Racial Fairness after *McCleskey v. Kemp*. *Columbia Human Rights Law Review*, *39*(1), 178–186.

Johnson, O. J., Jr., St. Vil, C., Gilbert, K., Goodman, M., & Johnson, C. A. (2019). How neighborhoods matter in fatal interactions between police and men of color. *Social Science & Medicine*, 220, 226–235.

Khan-Cullors, P., & Bandele, A. (2018). *When they call you a terrorist: A Black Lives Matter memoir*. New York: St. Martin's Press.

Lartey, J. (2018, January 28). "We've ignited a new generation": Patrisse Khan-Cullors on the resurgence of Black activism. *The Guardian*. Retrieved from https://www.theguardian.com/us-news/2018/jan/28/patrisse-khan-cullors-black-lives-matter-interview

Lee, M. Y. H. (2015). Are Black or white offenders more likely to kill police? *Washington Post*, Fact checker analysis. Retrieved from https://www.washingtonpost.com/news/fact-checker/wp/2015/01/09/are-black-or-white-offenders-more-likely-to-kill-police/?utm_term=.0e64c8ebf27a

Loftin, C., McDowall, D., & Xie, M. (2017). Underreporting of Homicides by Police in the United States, 1976–2013. *Homicide Studies*, *21*(2), 159–174. https://doi.org/10.1177/1088767917693358

Liu, G. (2002). The causation fallacy: Bakke and the basic arithmetic of selective admissions. *Michigan Law Review*, 1045–1107.

Mapping Police Violence. (2019, June 20). Police accountability tool. Retrieved from https://mappingpoliceviolence.org/cities

Menifield, C. E., Shin, G., Strother, L. (2019, January–February). Do white law enforcement officers target minority suspects? *Public Administration Review*, *79*(1), 56–68.

Morgan, R. E. (2017). Race and Hispanic Origin of Victims and Offenders, 2012–15. Washington, DC: *Bureau of Justice Statistics*, 2. Retrieved from https://perma.cc/4XNR-3DKX

Moskowitz, G. B., Gollwitzer, P. M., Wasel, W., & Schaal, B. (1999). Preconscious control of stereotype activation through chronic egalitarian goals. *Journal of Personality and Social Psychology*, *77*(1), 167–184. http://dx.doi.org/10.1037/0022-3514.77.1.167

Moskowitz, G. B., & Salomon, A. R. (2000). Preconsciously controlling stereotyping: Implicitly Activated egalitarian goals prevent the activation of stereotypes. *Social Cognition*, *18*, 151, 155.

O'Brien, R. (1987). The Interracial nature of violent crimes: A reexamination. *American Journal of Sociology*, *92*(4), 817–835. Retrieved from www.jstor.org/stable/2780040

Pezzella, F. S., Fetzer, M. D., & Keller, T. (2019). The dark figure of hate crime underreporting. *American Behavioral Scientist*. https://doi.org/10.1177/0002764218823844

Pinar, W. (1993). Notes on Understanding Curriculum as Racialized Text. In Cameron McCarthy and Warren Crichlow (Eds.), *Race, Identity and Representation in Education* (pp. 60–64). New York: Routledge.

Pitofsky, M. (2018, July 23–July 25). What is the alt-right? And how is it using social media to spread its message? *USA Today*. Retrieved from https://www.usatoday.com/story/news/2018/07/23/alt-right-philosophy-white-identity-civil-rights/800232002/

Rachlinski, J. J., Johnson, S., Wistrich, A. J., & Guthrie, C. (2009). Does unconscious racial bias affect trial judges? *Cornell Law Faculty Publications*. Paper 786. http://scholarship.law.cornell.edu/facpub/786

Ross, C. T., Winterhalder, B., & McElreath, R. (2020). Racial disparities in police use of deadly force against unarmed individuals persist after appropriately benchmarking shooting data on violent crime rates. *Social Psychological and Personality Science*. https://doi.org/10.1177/1948550620916071

Ryan, J. (2016). "This is a whitelash": Van Jones' take on the election results. *CNN Politics*. https://www.cnn.com/2016/11/09/politics/van-jones-results-disappointment-cnntv/index.html

Schatzki, T. (2002). *The Site of the Social: A philosophical account of the constitution of social life and change*. University Park: Pennsylvania State University Press.

SPLC (2017). The alt-right on campus: What students need to know. *Southern Poverty Law Center*. Retrieved from https://www.splcenter.org/20170810/alt-right-campus-what-students-need-know#alt-right-targeting

SPCL (2018). White Lives Matter. *Southern Poverty Law Center*. Retrieved from https://www.splcenter.org/fighting-hate/extremist-files/group/white-lives-matter

Stemen, D. (2017). The prison paradox: More incarceration will not make us safer. New York: Vera Institute of Justice, 2–12. Retrieved from https://perma.cc/5TBR-WSDC

Tanaka, G. (2003/2007). *The intercultural campus: Transcending culture and power in American higher education*. New York: Peter Lang.

Tregle, B., Nix, J., & Alpert, G. P. (2019). Disparity does not mean bias: Making sense of observed racial disparities in fatal officer-involved shootings with multiple benchmarks, *Journal of Crime and Justice*, *42*(1), 18–31. DOI: 10.1080/0735648X.2018.1547269

Tukachinsky, R. (2017). Media portrayals and effects: African Americans. *Oxford Research Encyclopedias: Communication*. DOI:10.1093/acrefore/9780190228613.013.453

Turner, J., & Dakwar, J. (2014). Racial disparities in sentencing hearing on reports of racism in the justice system of the United States submitted to the Inter-American Commission on Human Rights 153rd Session, *American Civil Liberties Union*. October 27, 1–15. Retrieved from https://www.aclu.org/sites/default/files/assets/141027_iachr_racial_disparities_aclu_submission_0.pdf

U.S. Census Bureau (2017). QuickFacts UNITED STATES. *U.S. Census Bureau*. https://www.census.gov/quickfacts/fact/table/US/PST045217

U.S. News & World Report. (2013, September 12). *National University Rankings*. Retrieved from http://colleges.usnews.rankingsandreviews.com/best-colleges/rankings/national-universities/data

van Doorn, B. W. (2015, February). Pre- and post-welfare reform media portrayals of poverty in the United States: The continuing importance of race and ethnicity. *Politics & Policy*, *43* (1), 142–162. DOI: https://doi.org/10.1111/polp.12107

Watkins, W. H. (2001). *The white architects of Black education: Ideology and power in America 1865–1954*. New York: Teachers College Press.

Wilcher, S. W. (2018, May). Coping with the proliferation of hate and bias on college campuses. *INSIGHT into diversity*, 1–5.

Wise, T. (2013, August 25). *Nazis can't do math: Reflections on racism, crime and the illiteracy of right-wing statistical analysis*. Retrieved fromhttp://www.timwise.org/2013/08/nazis-cant-do-math-reflections-on-racism-crime-and-the-illiteracy-of-right-wing-statistical-analysis/

Woodson, C. G. (1990). *The Mis-education of the Negro*. Washington, DC: Associated Publishers. (Original work published 1933.)

From the Mouths of the Lives that Matter

Ngozi Williams

My race defines very little about me. I have been privileged in that I feel it has had no reflection on my social class or my grades or my aspirations. It is not indicative of any biological difference between me and any other human being on the planet, and it holds almost no anthropological significance (Smedley & Smedley, 2005). At the same time, my race colors everything about me in the ways that I am identified (Varenne & McDermott, 1998). Every person I have ever met has seen the color of my skin before they have noticed anything else about me. Their preconceived notions of how they identify me—favorably or unfavorably—shape our interactions. This skew comes out in job applications, in classrooms, and even at temple, when a man assumed that I was a babysitter instead of a member. In turn, these interactions color how I interact with myself. It is why I tell people at Starbucks my name is "Nicole," or why I shy away from wearing certain clothing colors, and especially why I take great care in how I present myself to new people.

While this parallels my experience as an LGBTQ+ person, race is visible in a way that sexual orientations are often not (Spack, 1997). I have never felt the need to explain my sexuality, and since I am someone who performs my gender (Butler, 1990) in a traditionally feminine way; I have never had to be open about it unless I wanted to share this aspect of my life. I have almost always had the option of safely coming out to people who I wanted to know about my sexual orientation. Further, I have absolutely always had the opportunity to define what it means for me to experience my sexuality, rather than having it defined by others.

I have never had to come out as Black. It is something I literally wear on my sleeves. I have never had the opportunity to define for other people what it means for me to experience my race as it is usually done for me by others. People see my race before they meet me, and they judge me based off my race before they know me. As many times as I have felt marginalized or alienated for my sexuality, I have a thousand more experiences of the same feeling about my race. In this way, my race is a defining characteristic of my life in a way that my sexuality is not, because people generally know me and then my sexuality, but I feel as though personality is always playing catch-up to *their* expectations of *my* race.

I am the eldest daughter of proud Guyanese immigrants. My sisters have never wondered about the degrees to which they identify as Guyanese or American; they are simply American. I am the bridge between my parents and my sisters, and I am both Guyanese and American—even though I am often asked to choose. I am forever the girl with one foot in each culture: half soca music and cook-up rice, half country music and peach cobbler. Save for the boxes on forms that ask me to define myself as one thing, and to stay that thing forever, I would never have felt the need to be anything but the mosaic I am. For me, walking the tension between how I see myself and conforming to broader social standards of who I should be has become a lifelong and dangerous method of self-destruction. Whether it is my relationship with my weight or my nose or my hair, the way society has impressed on me that the way I am naturally is incorrect or undesirable has irreversibly changed my self-image. Even the act of choosing to be proud is a conscious one to combat years of fatigue (Smith et al., 2007) sparked by a kind of shame that I could not initially name. I only knew that I wanted to have narrower hips, a smaller nose, and "good" hair.

As I write the most recent iteration of this chapter, I have gone from a high school student to a young Black woman entering her fourth year of college in a dual STEM undergraduate degree program. I am on an endless adventure of self-discovery, and I walk this path by critically examining the steps I have taken to grow into the woman I am, and the influences that guided my steps on this journey. The point of this chapter is to examine one possible way of being a Black woman—as I recognize the ways to be a Black woman are endless—through the lenses of being a Black, first-generation woman. This chapter is an intentional braiding of some of the marginalizing experiences that have defined my life. I begin with my childhood, explicating what it meant to me to relax my hair at a young age and then find my power through agency over my own hair as a young adult. I continue by exploring the role of the media in my perception of myself and my Blackness and how the media's obsession with white beauty has managed to overlook health disparities found in Black communities. Next, I discuss how, aside from wrestling with questions of beauty, I also feel fatigue when my even my name is inadequate for white culture. Finally, I map out some of the many ways one can "be" Black, and the inherent tension I felt growing up as an immigrant youth before explicating my specific experiences with schools and systems of schooling. I conclude with a call to action on behalf of all of those voiceless individuals for whom we, those with the privilege of a platform, are responsible. It is our duty to put our very selves on the line to advocate for those in need, and I hope that I have been able to play some small part in the battle to build a better world.

Hair, Social Expectations, and Agency

I got my hair relaxed for the first time at ten years old. For many Black women, one's hair is her crowning glory. Having "nappy" hair, or hair that was unmanageable and kinky—the way most Black women's hair grows naturally out of their scalps—was unthinkable. For many Black women, "good" hair—smooth, frizz-free hair that has well-maintained edges—was the ultimate goal in my childhood. I can still remember the smell of the lye, and the way it felt burning the skin on my scalp. The sores oozed for a week; the sticky, clear liquid matted my hair for weeks after that until my mother patiently soaked my scalp in oil and combed out the knots. Nevertheless, I bore it because I wanted to have "good" hair. I continued this practice every six weeks for almost a decade: a relaxer, a blowout, and a flat iron. It cost my mother $60 and four hours out of our Saturdays. It took me years to realize that I was participating in a form of ritualistic self-mutilation designed to meet white standards of beauty. I hated everything about it, from the rawness of my scalp to the pointless hours spent in the chair, to the inevitable fight when my roots starting growing in. However, I continued to participate in this process because it felt like a rite of passage, as I saw every female member of my family, from my sisters to my cousins, go through it in the same way that I did. I considered it to be a generational trauma (Byrd & Tharps, 2014) that our mothers inflicted on us because their mothers inflicted it on them, and eventually we would inflict it on our daughters. It was a special price of being a Black woman, of never having "good hair," despite what the hair actually looks like and whether the owner of the hair was happy with it.

I cut my hair two weeks after the movie *Black Panther* was released. When I saw Danai Gurira and Lupita Nyong'o, I knew exactly what I wanted to do. I was terrified walking into Great Clips, an inexpensive hair salon that is common in the Midwest part of the United States. I was afraid because, to begin with, I had never actually set foot in a Great Clips and, second, because I did not know how this experience would impact my sense of self. For years I cut my hair into all sorts of trendy and crazy styles; I dyed it purple, got an undercut, shaved the side of my head, because, well, it was just hair and it would grow back. This, somehow, this felt more significant. Inches of chemically straightened hair fell from my head, and my short, natural hair that had grown in became visible. In this moment, I started to see myself again. I had been afraid of losing myself, but, in fact, I found myself. I still looked exactly as I had as a child, the same wide eyes staring over my father's nose, but I looked more powerful. I felt more powerful. Seeing my hair and realizing that, despite what everyone had ever told me, there was nothing wrong with my hair. I was suddenly more aware of how much violence I had done to myself and how many years I had followed someone else's vision of who I wanted to be. In so many ways, reclaiming my hair has been a way of reclaiming myself.

Media and Me: Discovering Beauty between, by, and because of Advertisement

Media subtly—and in cases like the recent Dove and Nivea commercials, not-so-subtly—tells us that who we as Black women is inferior to white standards of beauty (Coleman et al., 2019; Schooler et al., 2004). It is in the absence of positive depictions of Black individuals in fashion and cosmetic campaigns that drives home the societal preference for light skin (Reed, 2019). I used to feel out of place going shopping. For me, stores were places where "nude," and other beige colors, were the only shades available, none of which blended with my skin tone. The mall was a space where every poster depicted a corn-fed, blonde-haired woman, and not a single body deemed "beautiful" enough to be a model was an image of someone I could be someday. I lived with and in the fact that I looked nothing like these women and that the products they represented were not made for me.

I know that I am far from alone in this feeling. For example, Beyonce's own father theorized that she might not be the icon that she is today if she were dark-skinned (Sharma, 2018). I am dark-skinned. I am so dark that that there is not a contour shade for me at beauty stores like Sephora, and, in fact, there are barely foundation shades for me. I am also not particularly dark-skinned compared to other people of African descent. For example, if I struggle to find foundation shades, they do not exist for my mother. The world, in general, and the United States, in particular, does not cater to dark-skinned Black people. The *Guardian* examined 312 shows and over 8,000 casting calls for the fall 2016 fashion season, and found that fewer than 25% of models were people of color (Andrews, 2016). The cosmetic and fashion industries do not highlight the excellence and beauty of people of color, and as a person of color it is easy to believe that means I am neither excellent nor beautiful.

I am "pretty for a Black girl" or "too pretty to be fully Black," according to some of the boys I have met in college. I haven't always had the vocabulary to articulate why that was an insult, but I have never liked the way that statement made me feel. I am pretty, and I am a Black girl. My Blackness does not disqualify me from being pretty, nor does the fact that I am pretty become more extraordinary because of my race, and certainly no one is doing me a favor by thinking I'm attractive despite my race. Colorism is an issue that runs deep within minority communities (Nakray, 2018). Yet, this narrative is not solely perpetuated by minority communities, it is a narrative that is reinforced through whiteness—the ideal that being white, or as close to it as one can get, is preferable.

I used to be ashamed of how dark my skin is. I used to be horrified at the brown ring left in my bathtub after I had exfoliated because it looked so filthy. I knew, of course, that the skin that came off my body would be the same color as the skin on my body, and that the ring in my bathtub was probably just skin cells and not actual dirt, but all I could see was that my skin had made something dirty. This is probably not unique. After all, one only needs to recall the racist images of African Americans portrayed in Pears soap advertisements from the turn of the 20th century to understand why this imagery is so ingrained in American culture. As a result, I also used to buy skin-lightening soaps and lotions for my body and face. Although they were probably designed to treat hyperpigmentation caused by acne scarring, I had some small and unnamed hope that I might someday become lighter because I used those special products on my skin. This is also probably not unique. I wanted to be lighter because I thought that lighter meant prettier. After all, every "pretty" person on TV was lighter than me, even when they were people of color. All the girls who got the boys, or the girls who got the other girls, were still lighter people than I was, and I wanted that. I didn't see it at the time as a rejection of my Blackness even though it certainly was. I didn't realize that I was acting out the internalized racism I had absorbed from the media. I just wanted to be pretty.

My desire to be pretty did not stop at my skin color. I also found myself struggling with other body image questions as beauty in my youth was always synonymous with "skinny." Most of the girls I went to school with were taller and thinner than I was. No matter what they ate, and no matter what I ate, the width of my hips was unmatched in middle school, and I was ashamed of it. Being a Black woman means having a body that is policed, whether too muscular, too fat, or not curvy in the "correct" places (Appleford, 2016). I struggled and continued to struggle with my body image because of the images of impossible-to-obtain bodies presented by models—from those on television to those on posters and billboards. Fashion companies cater to and promote a body type that is not what most women look like, with Victoria's Secret models standing at a minimum of 5-foot-8 and weighing, in general, between 110 and 130 pounds. I have not weighed under 130 pounds since I was 12 years old. While I was consistently shamed for this fact, it's important to remember that the average woman in the United States wears a size 16 dress size, is 5-foot-3, and weighs between 160 and 170 pounds (Christel & Dunn, 2017). This obsession with measurements—which stems from the measuring of people commonly found in the eugenics movement—is not related to health, in fact, it often requires us to put health aside and follow restrictive diets and cleanses in order to attempt to reach an unattainable beauty standard (Talleyrand et al., 2017).

I was always healthy, maybe a bit shorter than average, but my diet was rich in nutrients and our air and water were clean. I was allowed to take my health for granted because I have never lacked the resources to take care of it. I have 19 houseplants, all with labeled pots, because they clean the air in my home, and I buy soy wax candles because they release don't release air toxins like paraffin wax when they burn. I aspire to a low-waste lifestyle and I live fifteen minutes away from a Whole Foods. On an average shopping trip, I'm bulk-buying organic brown rice and shredded coconut flakes, and either chia seeds or steel-cut oats for breakfast.

Not only do I have access to healthful food, I can afford to buy it. I buy jalapenos and organic baby spinach at the grocery store every week and I meal-prep on the weekends with my roommates. Not only do I have the resources to live a healthy lifestyle, but I have the time to do so. Access to these items are a matter of privilege, because many individuals within the Black community lack the same opportunities (Sadler, 2016). The health consequences of these luxuries are clearly illustrated in the health disparity between the Black and white communities. This next section is meant to think through some of these disparities in order to think not just about body image but how bodies are negatively impacted by racial injustices across the United States.

Healthy Living: Analyzing Food and Health Disparities across Community Contexts

Marginalized communities contain more food desserts than majority-white communities, meaning that the healthy options I am accustomed to are not universally available. It is no wonder then why the incidence of lifestyle or environmentally related disease is higher among minority populations than among white populations. A 2013 paper published by the US National Library of Medicine found that "Racial/ethnic minorities are 1.5 to 2.0 times more likely than whites to have most of the major chronic diseases" (Price et al., 2013). By major chronic diseases, the paper refers to obesity, diabetes, asthma, and hypertension, among others. For asthma alone, the paper reports that Black children are less likely to receive consistent treatment from health care providers, be prescribed medication for prevention or treatment, and have 7.6 times the death rate (Price et al., 2013). The paper also finds similarly increased results for the incidence of other noncommunicable diseases among Black populations, such as 19 per 100,000 rate of type 2 diabetes among Black youth, as opposed to 3.7 per 100,000 for white youth. Despite these known health risks to Black and other minority individuals due to their environments and socioeconomic positions, the barriers to proper health care are largely socioeconomic. This encompasses everything from a lack of physical or financial access to preventative measures to a lack of physical or financial access to the tools that make a healthy life possible (Cuevas, O'Brien, & Saha, 2016).

A 2012 study by the CDC found that four out of five Black women in America are overweight or obese (Friday, 2012), but despite that, *Essence* magazine, which caters primarily to Black women, dedicates countless articles to having laid edges instead of how to ensure one's physical health. Overweight or obese individuals are often associated with slovenliness and looked at with disgust in society (Hart, Sbrocco, & Carter, 2016), but the factors that contribute to that obesity are rarely addressed across social media, in the communities they impact, and, sometimes, across health professions. In fact, by driving Black women to focus on white beauty standards, all too often I feel as though the underlying heath disparities are lost through the distraction of the beauty industry. Twitter, for example, has focused more on comparing Serena Williams to a gorilla, despite her status as one of the most prominent tennis players in the history of the sport, than spreading awareness about the blood clots she developed after her cesarean section, which nearly took her life after her daughter's birth. Despite the statistic that Black women are three to four times more likely to die in childbirth than white women in the United States (Chawla, 2017), the focus still remains largely on questions of beauty rather than health and safety. Along these lines, the state of Texas reports that, although they make up just 11% of the birth rate, Black women contribute 29% of maternal deaths (Chuck, 2017). Many Black women of childbearing age have preexisting conditions that compound potential pregnancy complications, as well as many facing the inability to take time off from work to receive proper pre- or postnatal care, all of which contribute to maternal death rates and emotional distress.

Instead of focusing on necessary health care and attempting to right the structural wrong done to Black people by the health care industry, the focus is on aesthetic. Plastic surgeons have reported a rise in minorities seeking cosmetic procedures, including both surgical and nonsurgical options. In fact, minorities now constitute 22% of the 11.7 million cosmetic procedures performed across the United States, with a 129% increase in African American populations (Wimalawansa et al., 2009). While it cannot be assumed that all of the people undergoing cosmetic procedures are seeking to conform to current beauty standards, it would also be foolish to assume that people would not seek to change things about themselves in order to be seen as "beautiful" in the court of public opinion. An easy and visible example of this is that the culture around dieting focuses much less on individual health than adherence to an arbitrary aesthetic standard. In other words, people generally don't work out with the sole purpose of lowering cholesterol, but, generally, because people want to look like the models. Unfortunately, even clothing lines are not generally built for a Black woman's body (Hackett & Rall, 2018) and even the ideal of beauty within clothing styles becomes unattainable. This cultural standard of beauty pushes anyone who does not meet it and encourages a fundamental dissatisfaction with curvy bodies, a dissatisfaction that manifests itself in internalized racism and colorism, as well as through seeking to change one's identity to adhere to the white standards. The loss of identity stretches from the loss of one's physical looks—whether due to hair relaxing or body modification—to the normalized denial of one's heritage. We perform whiteness (Fordham & Ogbu, 1986; Matias, 2016) in every arena from our social behavior to our physical appearance. Yet, in order to participate in American society, we must deny nearly every intrinsic part of ourselves. This next section will argue just how implicitly and explicitly Black people deny their identities and, in turn, how those identities are discounted by white community members.

#SayOurNames: Social Exclusion by Every "Othered" Name

Names in the Black community are subject to discrimination as much as hair texture or the size of one's hips (Edelman, Luca, & Svirsky, 2017). Names with apostrophes, multiple syllables, or unusual consonant blends such as my own name are scrutinized and seen as "ghetto." Employers are less likely to call back individuals with "black-sounding" names as opposed to "white-sounding" names (Ge et al., 2016). This discrimination crosses all industries and occupations sampled in the survey, including so-called equal opportunity employers and federal contractors (Francis, 2020). Researchers found that white applicants received 36% more callbacks than equally qualified Black individuals, with no evidence in a change in the anti-Black hiring discrimination over time (Quillian et al., 2017). Social mobility is inaccessible without access to work and education, yet job opportunities across all fields, and access to education, are often limited simply by having a "black-sounding name." In fact, prominent business schools, like Harvard, have urged students to "whiten" their résumés by removing all reference to their races in applications (Kang et al., 2016). Studies have found that students who engage in this whitening process are twice as likely to receive callbacks, even from companies that claim to value diversity (Gerdeman, 2017). This consistent devaluing of names exists across communities. Only one example can be found in an article written about the discrimination Tran Loan faced after acting as Rose Tico in *Star Wars: The Last Jedi* (Martinelli, 2018). In the article, she describes how common it is for Asian Americans to change their names entirely in order to fit into a world not otherwise prepared to accommodate and accept their birth names.

My name is the gift my parents gave me. It is the name by which my god knows me. It is a link to my family and to my culture. It is the second thing people notice about me, after my race. Actress Uzo Aduba's mother told her as a little girl, "If they can learn to say Tchaikovsky and Michelangelo and Dostoevsky, they can learn to say Uzoamaka" (Dickerson, 2014). I believe, then, that they can learn how to say Ngozi. It is not rude or difficult to correct people who pronounce my name incorrectly, and even if it temporarily embarrasses or inconveniences the people around me, I am working on no longer being afraid to exist.

The Many Ways to "Be" a Black Girl

I have been told to smile more because otherwise I seem aggressive. In reality, I am not aggressive. I hover around corners at parties because I feel too shy to talk to people and I never ask salespeople for help because I hate the feeling of being inconvenient. I grew up afraid to take up space, because otherwise I would be accused of being rude or brash or difficult. In my mind, women who fulfilled the cultural idea and ideal of the loud Black girl (Annamma et al., 2019)—the women I rolled my eyes at in Tyler Perry films—were the opposite of who I wanted to grow up to be. Yet these stereotypes are not just imbricated with white media. Rather, they are often perpetuated even by Black media. As Woodson (1933) argued, it is the combination of both communities that often force some to become alienated from our own race, to be afraid to "act Black" as if there were only one way to be Black. Those stereotypes reduce Black women to caricatures, exaggerations of one type of personality that exists across racial lines and contribute to the idea that everyone of a particular race is the same way.

I say that I am a Black woman. As I mentioned, I am a first-generation American, transplanted from the tropical ground of Georgetown, Guyana, to the wintery Medina, Ohio. There are coconut trees in my blood, even if I live in a county that grows corn. As such, I have never felt at home with the term *African American*. It simply never felt wide enough for me and my heritage. I sometimes feel alienated by what is traditionally described as African American culture because I didn't grow up in a traditional African American environment. My mother's kitchen bumps with Maxi Priest's *Close to You* album and my favorite food is curried chicken with mango sour and roti. My experience of being Black is shaped by this cultural difference between me and many American-born Black people, and, growing up, it was easy to distance myself from much of the Black American experience because at home and in my parents' community, we were Black but we were not African American.

The particularly insidious part of the racial and cultural alienation, however, is that it almost felt like a virtue to me. In the same way that some girls proclaim, "Oh, I'm not like other girls" as a way to appeal more to people who look down on those who wear leggings, drink iced coffee, and like the color pink, I was almost proud to be "not like other Black people." It was internalized racism of the highest order. In many ways, I felt as though I had some sort of special leg up because I didn't listen to rap music, speak in African American Vernacular English, or have a complicated relationship with my ancestry. It took me years to learn that not only was there no virtue in missing those experiences but that there was also no deficit in those experiences. For years this mental trap kept me from empathizing with my counterparts, forever blaming the poor for their poverty or looking down on those who were educationally disenfranchised without holding accountable the unfair system that actively kept them in those positions. The truth is that I was and am privileged, and the insulation of my class privilege kept me from that truth.

Growing with Whiteness

I attended a large, suburban high school in the Midwest that was 93% white, with only 15% of the families in the district qualifying for free and reduced lunch programs (US Census Bureau, 2018). This is in comparison to the state average, where 45% of students qualify for free and reduced meals and the percentage of white students is 71% (US Census Bureau, 2018). This was a school where taxpayer money bought class sets of Chromebooks and kept current editions of textbooks for most departments. This was a place where even the parking lot was repaved every two to three years. Our library was well stocked, and we never lacked for enrichment opportunities. These are broad generalizations because, to be sure, there was poverty in Medina County. However, for the most part, students in Medina County were assured a quality education and, if students fit into the norm, a good chance at graduating with a district graduation rate of 93% (US Census Bureau, 2018). Although I certainly benefited from the use of property taxes to fund the school system, I recognized the deep flaws in this system, as schools from the next county over were often underfunded and struggled to maintain buildings and staff that fell under the state's "highly qualified" category.

Turner et al. (2016) argue that segregation through property-tax funded schools leads to schools that are rural and urban suffering disproportionately compared to their suburban counterparts. Some towns, like Medina, boast economic wealth and many thriving local businesses. However, some neighborhoods, like the Ridge neighborhood in Chicago, have fewer resources that generate less revenue in taxes (Turner et al., 2016). The well-documented laws and policies like redlining that has caught national and international attention only continues to show that such inequities are based in historical and contemporary realities for people of color (Castro et al., 2020). Economically disenfranchised people and communities will continue to struggle under this system because they will remain under systemic oppression through schools and systems of schooling. This socially and politically engineered poverty is a violence that impacts not only Black students but also Latinx, Indigenous, Asian, and immigrant students, many of whom are also learning English as a second language while attending underfunded schools.

I'm recognize the privilege that I received by growing up where I did. My parents chose to settle in Medina County specifically because of the quality of the schools, and they had the privilege of making that choice. Other parents don't have the opportunity to give their children the same leg up in life that I had. My experience of my race is tailored by Medina County, which is 95.8% white (Census Bureau, 2018). However, I also recognize the difficulty this created as a Black woman growing up in an overwhelmingly white place. I was able to count my Black classmates on my two hands at graduation. This trend continued at my current institution, Cleveland State University (CSU), where there are only 63% white students and a faculty that is 72% white (College Factual, 2019). This race and ethnic diversity is apparently above average for universities of similar standing in the area. However, in the district that surrounds my institution, Cleveland Metropolitan School District (CMSD), students are approximately 65% Black, non-Latinx, and 16% Latinx (Cleveland Metropolitan School District, 2019). I wonder—how could a university continue to be overwhelmingly white while being located in the middle of a generally Black and Latinx school district? Part of the issue is that the vast majority of CSU students don't matriculate from CMSD, but instead come from the first and outer ring suburbs of Cleveland, wealthier areas like Beachwood, Bay Village, and Seven Hills. Like many urban-located institutions, CSU is a place that serves the suburbs and not the community in which it is located.

This issue of overwhelming whiteness among the student body extends to the faculty that I encounter. I recently complained to a professor that I was tired of having faculty who didn't look like me, and that our lack of diversity in the engineering department could be related to the fact that the majority of CSU faculty was male and white. After all, who wouldn't feel alienated knowing that they would be the only Black female in any civil engineering class they would take up after three years in college? I will also note that in the physics department, I am currently the only Black physics major, of any gender. Despite this tension between feelings of isolation as the only Black person, I am still cognizant of the privilege it took to arrive in this place.

It is a privilege to receive the education I am receiving, and there was no barrier to entry for me, that I perceived. Further, I recognize that I stand on the shoulders of my parents, who went to college and always emphasized the importance of education, and high school thoroughly prepared me for the academic challenges of college. I also had no financial hardship to distract from my education. My only real problems in college have been unspiced dining hall food and late public transit. I know that this stage of life must be harder without college-educated parents, without solid prior education, and without financial stability, and so I know that I, with all the discomfort caused by the intersection of my race, gender, and sexual orientation, am still having a comparatively easier time than my counterparts who struggle without the privileges I often take for granted.

Conclusion: It's Up to Us: What We Do with Our Privilege

It is a privilege to have a voice, but it is most often those who need, and deserve, the opportunity to be heard who have the least access to a platform. It is important to discuss the differences in the Black experience while being transparent about questions of privilege. My experience as a cisgender Black, queer woman is different from those of a transgender Black woman. As a college-educated Black woman, my experiences are also different from Black women who might not have access to education, and so on. I cannot represent the entire Black community, because my way of being Black is not universal. It is important to represent the entire spectrum of the Black experience and every intersection of being Black, because we are made of those intersections of race and class and gender and sexuality and culture.

Representation matters because seeing icons who look like us gives Black youth the space and care to know that it's okay to be who we are. Danai Gurira was that for me. It is also important to show ourselves in our authentic form, whatever that looks like, to others so they can understand who we are. The children I work with, despite my fears, behaved no differently toward me after my haircut. In fact, they barely seemed to notice. One girl, meeting me for the first time, asked if I was a boy or a girl, because she couldn't tell due to my "small, curly hair." Up to that moment, I hadn't realized that representation was as important for people of other races as it was for me. Representation normalizes differences between people, showing the world that some people have small, curly hair, and that that's perfectly alright. As a child, I wish I had known that. Now, as an adult, I wish I had known then that it was alright to be exactly who I already was. I wish I had known to be proud of my hips and my nose and my hair and my name and everything else about me that I tried to work out of existence.

My race is the truest thing about me. It is one of the only things about myself that I cannot change, and it is one of the things that I sometimes find hardest to love about myself, but, like Laverne Cox who started the hashtag #TransisBeautiful as a reminder to herself that she was beautiful, it is something that I am always working at loving. Some days I fall into resenting my race, and truly, most of the things in my life that I deeply struggle with would be easier if I were not Black. I would not be afraid of police officers. I would have countless models through history of successful individuals whose paths were open to me. I would be able to eat fried chicken in public without worrying that someone would dismiss me as a stereotype. I wouldn't have to watch my grammar and my manners to avoid being labeled "poorly raised" and "classless." I would be able to just be.

Sometimes being a marginalized person is a burden. It is burdensome to correct my friends when they say things that are racist, when they argue with me about whether something is racist, or to choose to ignore what they have said that is racist. It is exhausting to know that I will always be underestimated and underpaid. It is draining to comfort my white friends who are shocked by witnessing the racism I experience, and the fact that I'm used to racist encounters is problematic to say the least. The truth is that being a Black woman in the United States sometimes is ugly work, yet I am still privileged enough to be insulated from much of it.

While we stand on the histories of parents, it is also true that so many of our traumas are inflicted on us by our parents. Whether intentionally or unintentionally given on us, we live with the scars of our ancestors. Epigenetics research has shown that the traumas inflicted on a generation fundamentally alters their genome, and those altered genes, holding that trauma and those illnesses, continue on in their children (Krippner & Barrett, 2019). This coupled with the knowledge that poverty propagates itself through generations means it is no wonder that so many generations of Black Americans have remained locked out of the American Dream: to be successful, to have "good" and stable homes with clean water and healthy food, and to raise children who will grow up in a better world—those are the things my parents came to this country to find, and I am lucky that they found them here.

It is up to us, those who are privileged enough to have voices, to identify and break the cycles that keep minority individuals disadvantaged and downtrodden. I am my sisters' keeper. I have been responsible for them since the days they were born. I have fought for them, I have cried with them, and I have celebrated every triumph they have ever had. We are all the keepers of our brothers and sisters, and everyone in the world is our brother and sister. We are responsible for doing whatever we can to make this world into the best one for everyone by increasing education, teaching acceptance, and demanding diversity in voice and perspective across contexts. We can build a better world than the one we have, and we are all responsible for doing so. We owe it to our ancestors who gave their voices, their blood, and even their lives for the rights we have today. We owe it to our children who should never have to know or suffer the things we have suffered in our lives. We owe it to our brothers and sisters whose voices are never heard but whose lives matter as much as everyone else's.

References

Andrews, J. (2016). Runway Diversity Report Fall 2016—theFashionSpot. Retrieved from https://www.thefashionspot.com/runway-news/685109-runway-diversity-report-fall-2016/

Annamma, S. A., Anyon, Y., Joseph, N. M., Farrar, J., Greer, E., Downing, B., & Simmons, J. (2019). Black girls and school discipline: The complexities of being overrepresented and understudied. *Urban Education*, *54*(2), 211–242.

Appleford, K. (2016). "This big bum thing has taken over the world": Considering Black women's changing views on body image and the role of celebrity. *Critical Studies in Fashion & Beauty*, *7*(2), 193–214.

Butler, J. (1990). *Gender trouble*. New York: Routledge.

Byrd, A., & Tharps, L. (2014). *Hair story: Untangling the roots of Black hair in America*. New York: Macmillan.

Castro, A. J., Cuenca, A., & Williamson, J. (Eds.). (2020). *Teaching for citizenship in urban schools*. Charlotte, NC: IAP.

Chawla, S. (2017). Black women are 3.5 times more likely to die from being pregnant. *Vice*. Retrieved from https://www.vice.com/en_us/article/mb7j4p/black-women-are-3-times-more-likely-to-die-from-being-pregnant

Christel, D. A., & Dunn, S. C. (2017). Average American women's clothing size: Comparing national health and nutritional examination surveys (1988–2010) to ASTM international misses & Women's Plus Size clothing. *International Journal of Fashion Design, Technology and Education*, *10*(2), 129–136.

Chuck, E. (2017). Why does Texas have the highest maternal death rate in the developed world? *NBC News*. Retrieved from https://www.nbcnews.com/news/us-news/texas-has-highest-maternal-mortality-rate-de veloped-world-why-n791671

Cleveland Metropolitan School District. (2019). Fast facts about CMSD and Cleveland. Retrieved from https://www.clevelandmetroschools.org/domain/24

Coleman, M. N., Reynolds, A. A., & Torbati, A. (2019). The relation of Black-oriented reality television consumption and perceived realism to the endorsement of stereotypes of Black women. *Psychology of Popular Media Culture*, *9*(2), 184–193.

College Factual (2019). How diverse is Cleveland State University? Retrieved from https://www.collegefactual.com/colleges/cleveland-state-university/student-life/diversity

Cuevas, A. G., O'Brien, K., & Saha, S. (2016). African American experiences in healthcare: "I always feel like I'm getting skipped over." *Health Psychology*, *35*(9), 987.

Dickerson, J. (2014). Why Uzo Aduba wouldn't change her Nigerian name for acting. Retrieved from https://www.huffpost.com/entry/uzo-aduba-name_n_5534112

Edelman, B., Luca, M., & Svirsky, D. (2017). Racial discrimination in the sharing economy: Evidence from a field experiment. *American Economic Journal: Applied Economics*, *9*(2), 1–22.

Fordham, S., & Ogbu, J. U. (1986). Black students' school success: Coping with the "burden of 'acting shite.'" *The urban review*, *18*(3), 176–206.

Francis, D. (2020). Employers' replies to racial names, *National Bureau of Economic Research*. Retrieved from https://www.nber.org/digest/sep03/w9873.html

Friday, L. (2012). Exploring the causes of Black women's obesity, *BU Today*. Retrieved from http://www.bu.edu/articles/2012/exploring-the-causes-of-black-womens-obesity

Ge, Y., Knittel, C. R., MacKenzie, D., & Zoepf, S. (2016). Racial and gender discrimination in transportation network companies. *National Bureau of Economic Research*. Retrieved from https://www.nber.org/papers/w22776

Gerdeman, D. (2017). Minorities who 'whiten' job resumes get more interviews, *Working Knowledge*, *1*(2), 1–4.

Hackett, L. J., & Rall, D. N. (2018). The size of the problem with the problem of sizing: How clothing measurement systems have misrepresented women's bodies, from the 1920s to today. *Clothing Cultures*, *5*(2), 263–283.

Hampton, D. (2018). How trauma can damage the brain for generations and can be reversed: The best brain possible. Retrieved from https://www.thebest brainpossible.com/epigenetics-trauma-brain-reversed-mental-health/

Hart, E. A., Sbrocco, T., & Carter, M. M. (2016). Ethnic identity and implicit anti-fat bias: Similarities and differences between African American and Caucasian women. *Ethnicity & disease*, *26*(1), 69–75.

Kang, S. K., DeCelles, K. A., Tilcsik, A., & Jun, S. (2016). Whitened résumés: Race and self-presentation in the labor market. *Administrative Science Quarterly*, *61*(3), 469–502.

Krippner, S., & Barrett, D. (2019). Transgenerational trauma: The role of epigenetics. *Journal of Mind & Behavior*, *40*(1), 59–62.

Martinelli, M. (August, 2018). Kelly Marie Tran's defiant response to racist harassment: "My

real name is Loan. And I am just getting started." Retrieved from https://slate.com/culture/2018/08/loan-tran-a-k-a-kelly-marie-pens-nyt-op-ed-about-harassment-that-drove-her-off-instagram.html

Matias, C. E. (2016). *Feeling white: Whiteness, emotionality, and education*. Boston, MA: Brill.

Nakray, K. (2018). The global beauty industry, colorism, racism and the national body, *Journal of Gender Studies*, *27*(7), 861–863.

Price, J., Khubchandani, J., McKinney, M., & Braun, R. (2013). Racial/ethnic disparities in chronic diseases of youths and access to health care in the United States. Retrieved from https://pubmed.ncbi.nlm.nih.gov/24175301/ Quillian, L., Pager, D., Hexel, O., & Midtbøen, A. H. (2017). Meta-analysis of field experiments shows no change in racial discrimination in hiring over time. *Proceedings of the National Academy of Sciences*, *114*(41), 10870–10875.

Reed, J. (2019). Cosmetic counter connotations: Black Millennial women and beauty. In M. L. Damhorst (Ed.), *The meanings of dress* (pp. 162–169). Ashland, OR: Bloomsbury.

Sadler, R. C. (2016). Strengthening the core, improving access: Bringing healthy food downtown via a farmers' market move. *Applied Geography*, *67*, 119–128.

Schooler, D., Ward, L. M., Merriwether, A., & Caruthers, A. (2004). Who's that girl: Television's role in the body image development of young white and Black women. *Psychology of Women Quarterly, 28*(1), 38–47.

Sharma, R. (2018). What is colourism? Beyoncé wouldn't be successful if her skin was darker, says her dad. Retrieved from https://www.ibtimes.co.uk/what-colourism-beyonce-wouldnt-be-successful-if-her-skin-w as-darker-says-her-dad-1659474

Smedley, A., & Smedley, B. D. (2005). Race as biology is fiction, racism as a social problem is real: Anthropological and historical perspectives on the social construction of race. *American Psychologist, 60*(1), 16.

Smith, W. A., Allen, W. R., & Danley, L. L. (2007). "Assume the position . . . You fit the description": Psychosocial experiences and Racial Battle Fatigue among African American male college students, *American Behavioral Scientist, 51*(4), 551–578.

Spack, R. (1997). The (in)visibility of the person(al) in academe. *College English, 59*(1), 9–31.

Talleyrand, R. M., Gordon, A. D., Daquin, J. V., & Johnson, A. J. (2017). Expanding our understanding of eating practices, body image, and appearance in African American women: A qualitative study. *Journal of Black Psychology, 43*(5), 464–492.

Tran, K. (2018). Kelly Marie Tran: I won't be marginalized by online harassment. The *New York Times*. Retrieved from https://www.nytimes.com/2018/08/21/movies/kelly-marie-tran.html

Turner, C., Khrais, R., Lloyd, T., Olgin, A., Isensee, L., Vevea, B., & Carsen, D. (2016). NPR Choice page. Retrieved from https://www.npr.org/2016/04/18/474256366/why-americas-schools-have-a-money-problem

U.S. Census Bureau QuickFacts: Medina County, Ohio. (2018). Retrieved from https://www.census.gov/quickfacts/medinacountyohio

Varenne, H., & McDermott, R. (1998). *Successful failure: The school America builds.* Boulder, CO: Westview.

Wimalawansa, S., McKnight, A., & Bullocks, J. M. (2009). Socioeconomic impact of ethnic cosmetic surgery: Trends and potential financial impact the African American, Asian American, Latin American, and Middle Eastern Communities have on cosmetic surgery, *Seminars in Plastic Surgery, 23*(3), 159–162.

Woodson, C. G. (1933). *Miseducation of the negro.* New York: Tribeca Books.

The Summer of 2016 in Baton Rouge

Riots, Levees, and Community Uplift When Black Lives Matter Comes to Town

Roland W. Mitchell

The charge that I was given in this chapter—discuss how the Black Lives Matter movement impacts your day-to-day work—parallels, in my opinion, the paradox that many professionals from underrepresented groups experience across the arc of their careers in majority white contexts. People of color are taught that to be "part of the team"; you must leave home behind. However, the incidents that sparked the Black Lives Matter movement provide a sobering view that even if a person of color wanted to perpetrate an assimilationist's position, plainly stated—Jim Crow ain't having it. Moreover, history provides numerous illustrations that there is a greater sense of safety in numbers. For example, consider the experiences of Hmong immigrants clinging to 5,000 years of collective wisdom to survive physical and cultural genocide (Chang & Rosiek, 2003), when they migrated to the US at the conclusion of the Vietnam War, as well as the infusion of seeds of resistance in the artistic expressions (Bolden, 2003; Baraka, 1999; Mitchell, 2010) and faith beliefs (Thurman,1975; Mitchell, Mitchell, & Mitchell, 2017) of enslaved Africans in the Americas to endure 400 years of bondage. In the end, the very act of being forced to make the decision—assimilate or resist—and then act as if the binary choice ever really existed, is on page one of white supremacy's *How to Handbook of Alien*ation.

Although I work in higher education, I believe that regardless of whether one works in K–12 education, banking, real estate, medicine, or numerous other professions, the paradox exists. On the one hand, the fabled "American Dream" celebrates the virtue of working hard, going to school, and by the sheer strength of one's singular effort—and the support of your Western-sanctioned Judeo-Christian god—anyone can pull themselves up out of poverty. While, on the other hand, individuals from underrepresented populations are often attuned to the value of community but are often aware of how such relations are the antithesis of the rugged individual simulacra undergirding this peculiar American Dream. Moreover, fully actualizing the dream is often predicated on white understandings concerning rising out of tribalism and ignorance to emerge as an *enlightened* democratic citizen. However, this vision of affiliation to the United States has been so radically shaped by white supremacy that American-style enlightenment comes at the cost of racial (Obadele), linguistic (Nieto, 2002), ethnic (Rushdie, 1991), and cultural genocide (Spring, 2009). Even for those willing to pay the devastating costs, the proposed benefits of achieving this white supremacist American Dream have never been fully assessable to people of color.

There is nothing particularly insightful or new about this characterization of what others have colloquially referred to as "Living while Black in America" (Higginbotham, 2018). However, there are those particular moments when these tensions move from being media stories broadly covered by historians, talking heads, and social theorists to moments that directly impact day-to-day living—events in which members of an underrepresented group's professional facade of being so fabulously gifted as to effortlessly tap dance the tightrope of appealing to their indigenous community and their majority white workplace is completely shattered. For me that moment occurred in the summer of 2016, when Alton Sterling was killed by the East Baton Rouge Police Department (EBRPD) in June. This was followed by a 500-year flood in August, and the retaliatory killing of three EBRPD officers by an African American man, Gavin Eugene Long, in September. Long, a decorated Marine veteran form Missouri, was said to be motivated by the rhetoric of Black Lives Matter to come to Baton Rouge to seek retribution for the murders of Sterling in Baton Rouge, Sandra Bland in Texas, Philando Castile in Minnesota, and countless other people of color who had lost their lives in altercations with the police.

The metaphor that I will use to contextualize this chapter is one of floods and hurricanes that are all too common to the Gulf region of

Southern Louisiana. In this metaphor, the Sterling case represents a deluge—a flood surfacing century-old distrust between law enforcement and the Black community. In the midst of the flood I will refer to instances where I felt my range of possible actions were seriously constrained, as contraflow—a term typically referencing transportation routes in which all traffic is funneled in one direction for public safety. When an evacuation is occurring—in this case the water is rising—one must choose to either shelter in place with no support from the authorities or be shepherded in a state-approved direction. Finally, in the midst of the flood there are deep-rooted protests traditions pushing back against the deluge. In the chapter I will refer to these deep-rooted protest traditions as levees that were strained by the immense tension associated with international interests and outrage concerning the Sterling case. And finally, with the levees under extreme pressure and the waters rising, I will seek to provide insight gleaned from occupying the liminal space as a Black educational administrator working in an unapologetically white context.

The Water Is Rising

I moved to Louisiana in June of 2005, just weeks before Hurricane Katrina poured in excess of 250 billion gallons of rain on New Orleans. Prior to the move, because I had lived 27 of my 33 years in a landlocked state, I had no idea what a levy was, much less their importance. Nor did I understand what it means when the department of transportation initiates contraflow traffic as a result of a public emergency. However, I quickly learned how critical it would be for my survival to understand what at the time seemed like large mounds of dirt was the only thing holding back the mighty Mississippi River. Further, when these dirt mounds, or levees, are at risk of being breached and the announcement is made that all lanes of traffic must flow in one direction, not having a well-tested plan to shelter in place or a full tank of gas for heading to higher ground can be life threatening.

Consequently, Hurricane Katrina set the stage for me to learn not simply how to transition into the professoriate as a Black man, but the true importance of having a comprehensive understanding of the environment you are entering. So for me, coming to Louisiana meant learning to recognize that as long as the river of white supremacy has shaped the institutional coastline, so to speak, there have also existed levees of resistance in communities of color. Despite the proven power of the river of white supremacy to create industry, generate revenue, and ultimately structure institutional practices, one should not let the simplicity or substance for which the levee is composed cause them to overlook a levee's profound strength. As it relates to Black protest traditions, and their levee-like ability to counter white supremacy, these levees are composed of the same stuff that Black people depended on to strategically organize the US civil rights movement. Consequently, through these levees of resistance, the US civil rights movement was able to rewrite the laws and history of the most powerful nation that the world has ever seen (Anderson, 1998).

On the way to Louisiana, I studied at a historically Black college (HBCU), Fisk University; an elite private institution, Vanderbilt University; and a large public research institution, the University of Alabama. The most profound commitment of who I am as a complete person today was shaped during my HBCU years. My time at Fisk allowed me to begin my engagement in the majority white educational context of Vanderbilt grounded in the Black intellectual traditions of thinkers like Lisa Delpit (1995), Manning Marable (1998), and Audre Lorde (1984). I had grappled with the one philosopher Cornel West described as the crucible that all US Black intellectuals must endure—W. E. B. Du Bois (1903). I appreciated the vast resources, world-class facilities, and access to the market that the majority white institutions that I attended afforded, but this access came at a cost and I was far from in awe at what I received. Let me be clear the ideas that I was introduced to during my doctoral studies at the University of Alabama blew my mind! From Gramsci (1982) and Freire (1970) I learned the structural and systemic nature of resistance and oppression. Dewey (1934) challenged me to think about the limitations and the possibilities of the uniquely American approach to philosophy and schooling. Contemporary thinkers like William Watkins (2001), Vanessa Siddle-Walker (1996), Marimba Ani (1994), and James Anderson (1988) provided the ideas to help me understand race and schooling in a manner beyond the aspirational color-blind rhetoric that was gaining ground in my college years.

Similar to today's enrollment statistics, in the late 1990s the US higher education system was achieving never before seen success at enrolling a more diverse student population. However, we were still struggling to provide meaningful services associated with retention, academic success, and overall wellness to combat the ongoing legacy of Jim Crow schooling once they arrived on campus. My personal experiences of these struggles included constantly being tokenized as a scholarship athlete while enduring the now infamous posting of a crime occurring on campus. A posting that is often followed by a public announcement, "Black, male suspect, average height, average build," committed this act. This vague and all but useless description could be read to include 95% of every Black man on campus and, subsequently, led to a community-wide sigh of Black folks saying, "I can't deal with this again . . . They gotta do better!" The insight gained from these and similar oppressive encounters caused me to quickly learn to: (a) stay focused on the reason I was on campus; (b) find my happiness elsewhere and not expect validation; and, above all, (c) never let them see me sweat. Over the course of my 13 years of postsecondary study, for better or worse, I stuck to these simple ideas; although they evolved and became more nuanced, they still guided my thinking when I started my first professorship.

I started the position as an instructor because I had not yet completed my dissertation. As one of two Black men in my department and three in the entire college, I was quite aware that I was hypervisible to faculty, staff, and students. This visibility took many forms. In committee meetings my voice was often ignored but my presence was highly monitored. Students of color and Black students in particular were interesting because they often either wanted 24/7 access and mentoring or assumed that I had somehow slid passed the gatekeepers and could not possibly be as qualified as the white faculty that they typically engaged. Staff members of color were also interesting because they did not hesitate to tell me how proud they were of me, but they also watched me closely and would give me the, "Don't mess this up for the people who are coming behind you," lecture. My read on all of this was consistent. Know who you are, control what you can, and stay focused. Finish the dissertation, write the articles to get tenure, and along the way look for sources of sustenance for the journey.

At the university, that sustenance came from the Black students and staff who were experiencing similar aspects of toxic whiteness. Although initially the ways that I encountered their responses to toxic whiteness felt patronizing, as we built more profound relationships their support was indispensable to my professional success and mental well-being. This support came in the form of an endless supply of voluntary teaching and research assistants, brilliant minds to write and think alongside of, and some of the best racquetball matches and weightlifting sessions I have experienced to date. As a result of this approach to traversing my new white educational context, I was able to move from instructor to dean in fourteen years—along the way earning the distinction of being the college's first Black dean, the first Black person to earn the rank of full professor, and the first Black endowed professor, of which today I am the holder of two professorships.

Now, it would be easy to end the story here, but this is actually the moment where my true learning began. In 2016, the year of the Alton Sterling shooting, I earned the rank of professor and was promoted to associate dean of Research Engagement & Graduate Studies. My career had taken off, and already discussions were swirling across campus, "He's just an affirmative action appointee," or "Now that he is on the rise, is he still going to be as vocal an advocate for Black folks." Against this backdrop, I was president of the university's Black Faculty and Staff Caucus, and my entire presidential platform focused on the exodus of Black women professionals from the university as a result of the absence of opportunities to move into upper-level administrative positions. Specifically, in my college, the fact that my job oversaw community engagement and research afforded space for a focus on studies and outreach in traditionally marginalized communities. But even as I felt as if I were staying consistent to the foundation I had gained in my grounding in the Black community, questions of my authenticity or commitment were constantly raised.

For better or worse, this characterization of the tension professionals of color face working in white spaces is common. For example, consider the significance of authenticity or *keeping it real* to your home community for African Americans. This pressure for continued allegiance—"not forgetting where you come from" (Woodson, 1933)—is so pervasive that specialized and particularly virulent insults are reserved for members of minority communities who cross this perceived line. In the Black community these individuals are referred to as *Oreos*—people who are perceived as Black on the outside and white in the middle. In the Asian community they are referred to as *Bananas*—Yellow on the outside but white on the inside. In each case these supposed race turncoats are shunned by their indigenous community for their perceived adoption of the norms of a majority community. It is particularly noteworthy that no similar pressure exists among majority communities to make a choice between the options to pursue the American Dream, stay allegiant to their home community, or live schizophrenically in the in-between (Du Bois, 1903). In majority communities, it is simply viewed as a taken-for-granted life goal to vigorously pursue the rewards in economic, political, and social status associated with the American Dream. From this perspective, as multinational financial services corporation American Express boast, "Membership has its privileges."

Consequently, even if you do not take account of the Sterling storm, I suppose it will not be news to individuals reading this volume that US universities can be challenging places for people from historically marginalized communities. However, in times of crisis the historic facade between the town and gown is shattered. I can outflank 21st-century Jim Crow with the best of them. From "You are surprisingly articulate" to "You are lowering the standards by letting in too many of those students," I have had these and similar discussions so many times I cannot be rattled. But the summer of 2016, in Louisiana's capitol city was something different. The civic unrest caused by the events surrounding Sterling's killing, the BLM-movement-led protests, and the fact that the unprecedented 500-year flood in the Red Stick disproportionately impacted Black neighborhoods was unnerving and honestly, to this day, are still impossible for me to adequately convey. However, despite these challenges, these devastating circumstances did provide a framework for me attempt to come to terms with the all-too-familiar tensions associated with being a person of color working on a majority white campus, as well as the increasing tension of the flagship postsecondary institution of the state lacking the racial, ethnic, and cultural diversity of the contentions that is charged with serving. This disruption to the traditional function of the university as a result of the Sterling case constitutes the water rising beyond the traditional race-based town-and-gown boundaries.

Contraflow

In 2016, Louisiana universities, similar to other public higher education institutions across the nation, were coming to terms with the fact the state was no longer willing to invest public dollars into higher education at the same levels it had in the past (Marcus, 2019). Proof of this historic divestment was the fact that over a five-year period from 2011 to 2016, the level of state appropriations to my institution had dropped from 70% of our operating budget to less than 27%. In response to this state divestment my university invested heavily in what we referred to as variable revenue streams—ways that the university could generate revenue that were not dependent on state appropriations. Key among these variable revenue streams were the growth of online programs and increased grant and sponsored research activity. However, arguably, the greatest of these approaches to financial independence was growing the student enrollment with a particular focus on out-of-state and international students who are charged more for tuition than their in-state counterparts.

As the flagship university of the state, we typically outperformed our instate peer institutions in recruitment of out-of-state and international students, primarily based on our national name brand recognition, more diverse academic offerings, and world-class facilities. Despite the fact that we are in a relatively poor state, because of the beauty of our campus, a common refrain at our university is, "If we can get a potential student, staff, or faculty on campus for a visit—we got 'em!" Against this backdrop, in 2016, we were much more aggressive in our recruitment efforts, unveiling an entirely revamped approach to data-driven recruitment with the aim of growing our freshman class by 25% and increasing the overall student population by 7,000 students.

Our enrollment projections, based on the number of applications and the number of campus visits, caused us to be extremely confident that we would recruit a record-setting freshman class. But then it occurred; the floodwaters hit with the Sterling incident and our recruiting plans were wrecked! Sterling is killed, protest break out across the state, a 500-year flood of biblical proportions occurs, and then Long slays the EBR police officers, leading to even more intense riots, all playing out for an international viewership. Keep in mind our data-driven approach to recruiting confirmed that the white middle- to upper-class 18- to 21-year-old college-going population that we traditionally recruited is rapidly declining. Consequently, we like numerous other institutions, took up the flag of diversity because if we did not, we simply would not be able to keep the doors opened.

We were working hard to move beyond the specter of Jim Crow that impacts everything from the names of the buildings on campus to the racial and gender makeup of the faculty and staff. We did everything that the most successful of our peer institutions did facing the countervailing forces of historic student demographic shifts and state divestment. We created publications with the notorious overrepresentation of students of color engaging in cultural activities. University administrators and faculty were advised to build relationships with affinity groups geared toward students from underrepresented populations. Contrastingly, the 24-hour news coverage, complete with the grainy images from the officer's body cameras documenting the last moments of Sterling's, life paired with the resulting images of citizens of color and their allies going toe to toe with officers in riot gear, cut through this liberal revenue-driven "ode to diversity" like a the proverbial hot comb through natural Black hair.

As a resident of a city for which the storm clouds were gathering, I was overwhelmed and I felt a similar level of anxiety that I felt when coming to terms with the fact that during a hurricane the laws of traffic change, cellular communication is spotty at best, and even necessities like fast food or big box store shopping are limited. There was no insulation as a result of being an administrator at a school that functioned like a city within the city. For example, I recall during Katrina trying to find housing. Places that rented for $800 a month before the hurricane skyrocketed to $1,400 a month days after the storm. Another not-so-subtle change occurred as I recall trying to lease a home. While my discussion over the phone and the process of electronically filling out the form were fairly straightforward, the moment I met the landlord in person, it all changed. He saw from the application that I worked at the university, but when we met he insisted I get my "boss" on the phone to confirm that I was who I claimed to be—a professor at the university.

As a result of the storm, there was an influx of displaced people; primarily Black people from New Orleans. The media largely portrayed these displaced citizens as potential criminals, gang members, and rapist. Given that I was a new Black man in town, looking for a place to live at the same time that many Katrina survivors were moving to the area, there was a sense of hypervisibility that could not be surmounted by terminal degree, or even working at the university. As a result of this overtly racist treatment I refused to lease a house from this person, so I moved on. However, the insight gained from being a transplant trying to find housing in this context taught me that even in the midst of a natural disaster or the civil upheaval associated with instances like the Sterling shooting, your terminal degree, tenure-track position, or institutional affiliation cannot protect you from white supremacist contraflow.

Where the university was concerned after Sterling, those precious white middle- to upper-class students that we fought to bring to campus, as well as the growing demographic of first-generation students from historically underrepresented groups, both agreed on one thing: they, and particularly their parents, had no interests in sending their kids to start their college years in the middle of a race riot. Baton Rouge in the summer of 2016 looked nothing like the slick publications and tightly filmed social media advertisements they had observed. Neither the allure of Southeastern Conference athletics, brand-new disciplinary-themed living and learning residential halls, or even a lazy river swimming pool were enough to make a city at war seem appealing. Consequently, the difference between the out-of-state enrollment in freshman who paid deposits and those that actually showed up in the fall cost the university millions of dollars in lost revenue that even four years later we are still struggling to recoup. So I return again to the concept of contraflow. The student demographics that the university was depending on to address the severe budget shortfall were distinct in many ways. However, the common denominator for each was they uniformly decided Baton Rouge was not safe in 2016.

Levees

> Hurricane Katrina was a true disaster; an unprecedented crisis that the university was unprepared to address. However, a month later when Hurricane Rita arrived, it was devastating but, we cannot truly refer to it as an unexpected crisis. Rita instead, provided an opportunity for us to test if the measures we put in place during Katina were effective.
>
> —John Lombardi, LSU system president, 2007–2012

To this point I have attempted to parallel my experiences of entering the academy and moving to a new city in a time of never-before-seen civil upheaval, due to Katrina against a backdrop of later experiencing civil upheaval due to the Sterling case. Just as a natural disaster and a race riot are different, a decade later my response was different. Having learned the lessons of navigating the university and the community through my experiences of Katrina, I knew where the high ground was and had provisions to shelter in place, as opposed to being herded in a singular direction. In this last section, I want to attribute this increased wisdom from Katrina to Sterling, as the direct result of building community in and outside the academy to weather the storm. This community is what I will refer to as the levees—historic structures that often go unnoticed but actually shape the course of history. A particularly meaningful example of a levee in my adopted community highlights that fact that history may not document their names, but I would not be on campus to tell this story today, had it not been for the masses of working-class Black women that civil rights icon attorney A. P. Tureaud depended on to successfully integrate Louisiana higher education (Durant, 2015).

I vividly recall starting my Sunday morning zooming past the Airline Road exit on Interstate 12 headed to the university. I had the classic unhealthy, *I can do it all* approach to the academy. Rise early on the weekends, before my family is out of bed, get to the office while nobody is there and I can work for three hours, meet my family for worship and brunch, and then back to the office. But on this morning things would change. The exact moment when I was heading to the office, Gavin Long arrived in Baton Rouge. The city was ready to erupt in response to the Sterling killing, and word on the streets was that representatives from the Black Lives Matter movement would be arriving in town to help organize a community response. Consequently, when Long opened fire on local law enforcement, Baton Rouge tapped into familiar racist tropes concerning outside agitators firing the first shots at the new Harper's Ferry, signaling the start of the 21st-century Civil War.

The difference in reaction I observed on campus along racial lines was striking. At the time I was president of our Black faculty and Staff Caucus, and the membership was greatly troubled by the Sterling killing and the later Gavin ambush. The Caucus meets at noon on the first Wednesday of every month, with 25 to 30 members typically in attendance. The meeting after the Gavin incident, however, was standing-room only, with nearly 100 people in attendance. During the meeting several caucus members discussed their befuddlement that many of their white colleagues arrived at work as if it were just another day. The general sentiment in the room was that even if it was just an hour out of their workday, the traumatized people of color on campus needed some time for a reprieve from white folks—to be in a community that they did not have to explain that Black lives matter.

A unique aspect of the Caucus on our campus is that it receives no funding from the university and is constitutionally mandated by its bylaws to be an independent body with the expressed interests of advocating for its predominantly African American membership. The independent nature of the Caucus was particularly relevant in this moment, because the university's diversity office was mobilized to gauge the mood of Black folks on campus and ensure the racial tension in the community did not spread to the campus. In the end, during the engagements between the Caucus and the Office of Diversity in these turbulent times, the most damaging critiques of institutionalized diversity efforts on campuses surfaced, and six decades after *Brown*, the university is still ill-equipped to comprehensively meet the educational needs of diverse populations (Mitchell et al., 2018).

Despite the university's best efforts, the racial tension in the city could not help but breach the artificially imposed town-and-gown boundaries. One place that I personally found inspiration and hope in these bleak times was my volunteer service to an organization called the Baton Rouge Youth Coalition (BRYC). BRYC's mission is to "prepare high-achieving, under-resourced high school students to enter, excel in, and graduate from college so they can become full participants in society" (Baton Rouge Youth Coalition, 2020, n.p.). I first started serving as a BRYC volunteer shortly after arriving in Baton Rouge because I felt isolated. My professional career was going well, but I was convinced there had to be more. One night I called my mother complaining about how lonely I was, and she provided sage advice tempered with tough love reminiscent of Black mothers. Momma said, "I realize the transition can be hard, but keep in mind you are blessed in ways in this early part of your life many people will never experience across their entire career." She went on to suggest that "Sometimes the best way to shake off the blues is to stop concentrating on yourself and go and do something for someone else." Shortly after I got over myself and fully accepted her advice, I received an email that heralded how participants in this local college preparation program gained admission into prestigious institutions like the University of Wisconsin, Stanford, Morehouse, Colby, and Spellman. Students from the most impoverished parts of Baton Rouge were excelling in college, and I simply wanted to provide any service that I could to help them succeed. Not as a person who studied universities as an area of scholarly inquiry; not simply as a person in the community who wanted to see kids in difficult circumstances make it.

The events of 2016 provided the perfect opportunity for the BRYC fellows to get an early start on being "full participants in society," as stated in their mission. There was significant discussion within the organization about how the fellows should express their feelings about the riots that were taking place in their community. One vein of the conversation suggested that due to safety concerns, and the fact that they were primarily Black youth from working-class neighborhoods who had historically had negative interactions with law enforcement, the fellows should focus on their academics and stay out of the fray—in other words shelter in place. While, on the other hand, a contrasting view for the very same reasons felt it was critical that the BRYC fellows join with their communities as full participants in the protest concerning Sterling's killing. In the end, I was so incredibly inspired by the fellows because not only did they stage a march but they actually went to the legislature, met with policy makers, and made a compelling case about how allowing these historic injustices to go unchecked will limit their possibilities in the world they will inherit. Additionally, I commend the policy makers for meeting with the fellows because it was a very public and emotionally charged meeting—the true definition of the often-used idiom *speaking truth to power*.

Finally, the last and arguably most personally impactful event of the summer of 2016 in Baton Rouge that I want to consider occurred during a rally on campus titled Justice for Alton. It was sponsored by a student organization, thus providing the opportunity to host it in the campus's African American Cultural Center. The scheduled speakers included a well-respected African American State Representative, several student speakers, and me. However, as the environment became more emotionally charged, the number of participants outgrew the capacity of the scheduled venue. Further, as the crowd spilled over into the street, the formal schedule of events was thrown out and it became a more organic community rally. I was very tense as I considered my message. I was used to academic conferences, but this event had a totally different feel. I remember discussing how the images that we consumed daily on the five o'clock news; story after story of Black male suspects created an image of broken homes and Black criminality. While the commercials during that same news hour, rife with ad after ad of adolescent white children proclaiming, "Buy a car from my paw paw," created contrasting images of wholesome generational stability. As far as I was concerned, my tone and content were appropriate and I was just hitting my stride when someone from the crowd shouted, "What are you talking about? And why are we even meeting here? Everybody knows this university doesn't care about Black folks or North Baton Rouge."

I was totally caught off-guard and had no response. Don't get me wrong, I grew up in Black schools and in a Black church where you were not doing your job if the crowd was not talking back to you (Asante, 1993). But this was not the type of talking back or call and response I expected. After a short pause I ultimately rambled through the remainder of my talk, and continued on at the rally more as community member than university representative. After a few more speeches and several moments of self-reflection the woman who made the remarks—or better yet *Kanye'd* me during my speech—I walked up and started a conversation.

In our one-on-one, I started by sharing about a program we had started in North Baton Rouge associated with reducing truancy and increasing educational success among Black male fourth-graders. She seemed somewhat interested in the program, but she followed by asking, "Oh, if you are doing work on those issues in North Baton Rouge you must know . . ." and you fill in the blank—every name she mentioned was a foreign to me. As this line of discussion progressed, she subtly (and surgically) proved her overarching point: If you are not connected to the community and familiar with the existing network of resources, how can you effectively serve the community? Therefore, let's be clear; she and I both new that these remarks about university outreach were little more than self-defense for a wounded ego and, in the end, her critique was well founded.

After I got over my initial embarrassment, we started a much deeper conversation in which she shared that she was a native of Baton Rouge who had pastored a church in the most impoverished parts of the city for nearly three decades. She went on to describe how the Sterling killing actually galvanized her constituents and that they had recently started a community-based initiative to provide educational enrichment to students who have traditionally had low levels of higher education participation. As she discussed her work in these regards, I could not help but be energized because her excitement about the students and their increased possibilities was contagious. It also became apparent to her that despite our initially bumpy start, collaboratively we could make a real difference for populations we both cared about deeply. She went on to invite the person who had a deep commitment to Black educational uplift to participate in her program, as opposed to the university researcher. In the end she and her church's efforts functioned like a levee, and I had been invited to play a role in strengthening the fortification.

High Water, Contraflow, and Levees: So What Have I Learned?

Returning to my original charge, simply put—the Black Lives Matter movement deeply impacts my day-to-day work because it served as a flashpoint, surfacing the volatility of the liminal space that I occupy as a Black administrator on a white campus in a predominantly Black city. Natural disasters, race riots, and unprecedented higher education budgetary instability brought these issues to the forefront. However, one should not overlook the fact that there are deeper endemic issues rooted in white supremacy that may be more subtle, but still, similarly reap mass devastation on communities of color. In Louisiana these issues are typically characterized as racial disparities in access to education (US Department of Education, 2017), health care (Schott Foundation, 2017), and incarceration rates (Fasching-Varner et al., 2017). But what is often overlooked is the way these quality of life indicators are markers of the deeper onto-epistemological assault on communities of color (Fasching-Varner et al., 2015) that led to the need for a Black Lives Matter movement in the first place.

As I have become more familiar with these issues I would now like to reframe the three-point mantra that I depended on when I started my academic career, which was informed by the wisdom gleaned by weathering the storm. My first point was to simply, *Know who you are.* This point is still critically important, because as my dear brother and colleague T. Elon Dancy, the Helen Faison chair and director of the Center for Urban Education at the University of Pittsburgh, often tells me about the academy, "As a Black person if you do not define yourself, this field will." Based on my experiences and reminiscent of Dr. Dancy's comments, I now know hypervisibility is a reality for Black folks in these spaces. So own it, and through that ownership, push back against the flood of rugged individualism that is rampant in the US academy. Particularly pernicious examples of this individualism include racial stratification that establishes boundaries between the mostly Black custodial and clerical staff and the limited Black faculty on majority campuses, as well as the artificially imposed racial town-and-gown boundaries in schools that are often located in communities of color. We are stronger together and we should not let less than 60 years of limited access to majority institutions dictate who matters in communities of color.

Next, *Control what you can.* For me controlling what I can was directly related to my ability to not simply gain a deeper appreciation for who I was as an individual, but more importantly, to understand who I am in relation to my responsibility to my new community. More profoundly, it involved recognizing that I gained strength and had greater control of my environment by becoming more knowledgeable about and connected to a broader community. This growth in connection started on campus with my participation with the Black Faculty and Staff Caucus, but it was not fully realized until I started volunteering with BRYC. This was my opportunity not only to find the high ground but to actually accept my position on the levee.

Finally, *Stay focused*, not letting the trappings of success as defined by the academy (i.e., tenure, administrative appoints, etc.) cause me to lose track of the fact that what was most needed in my work with BRYC, as well as the challenge I encountered at the rally, was not a person who studied universities as an area of scholarly inquiry. Instead, I was both most personally satisfied and more useful to the cause when I was a person in the community who simply wanted to see kids in difficult circumstances succeed. Clearly my university affiliation and training were assets, but it did not necessarily have to be my leading qualification. Consequently, I have learned that as opposed to burying myself day and night in academic work, both my community and my work as a scholar are enhanced when they are guided by passions beyond my own self-interests. So I suppose Dr. Patricia Mitchell, Mom, got it right after all.

References

Anderson, J. (1988). *The education of Blacks in the South 1860–1935*. Durham, NC, Chapel Hill: University of North Carolina Press.

Ani, M. (1994). *Yurugu an African-centered critique of European culture thought and behavior.* Trenton, NJ: Africa World Press.

Asante, M. (1993). *Malcolm X as cultural hero and other Afrocentric essays*. Trenton, NJ: Africa World Press.

Baraka, Amiri (1999). *Blues people: Negro music in white America*. New York: Harper Perennial.

Bolden, T. (2003). *Afro-blue: Improvisations in African American poetry and culture.* Champaign, Urbana: University of Illinois Press.

Chang, P., & Rosiek, J. (2003). Anti-colonial antinomies: a case of cultural conflict in the high school biology curriculum. *Curriculum inquiry*, *33*(3), 251–290.

Delpit, L. (1995). *Other people's children: cultural conflict in the classroom*. New York: The New Press.

Dewey, J. (1934). *Art as experience*. New York: Perigee Books.

Du Bois, W. E. B. (1903). *The souls of Black folk*. Chicago, IL: A. C. McClurg.

Durant, T. (2015). *A view from the inside . . . thirty-six years of desegregation*. Chula Vista, CA: Aventine Press.

Fasching-Varner, K., Hartlep, N., Mitchell, R., Hayes, C., Martin, L., & Mitchell Allen, C. (Eds.). (2015). *The assault on communities of color: Reactions and responses from the frontlines*. Lanham, MD: Rowman & Littlefield.

Fasching-Varner, K. J., Martin, L. L., Mitchell, R., Bennett-Haron, K., & Daneshzadeh, A. (Eds.). (2017). *Understanding, dismantling, and disrupting the prison-to-school pipeline*. Lanham, MD: Rowman & Littlefield.

Freire, Paulo. (1970). *Pedagogy of the oppressed.* New York: Continuum.

Gramsci, A. (1982). *Selections from the Prison Books.* London: Lawrence and Wishart.

Higginbotham, H. (August 2018). Living while Black in America. *New York Amsterdam News.* Retrieved from http://amsterdamnews.com/news/2018/dec/06/living-while-black-america/

Lorde, A. (1984). "The master's tools will never dismantle the master's house." *Sister outsider: Essays and speeches.* New York: Ten Speed Press.

Marable, M. (1998). *Black leadership.* New York, NY: Columbia University Press.

Marcus, J. (2019). Most Americans don't realize state funding for higher ed fell by billions. Retrieved from https://www.pbs.org/newshour/education/most-americans-dont-realize-state-funding-for-higher-ed-fell-by-billions

Mitchell, R. (2010). Cultural aesthetics and teacher improvisation: An epistemology of providing culturally responsive service by African American professors. *Urban Education, 45,* 604–629.

Mitchell, R., Mitchell, C. A., Whitmore, J., & Fasching-Varner, K. J. (2018). The chief diversity officer purpose and preparation. In Joy Blanchard (Ed.), *Controversies on campus: Debating the issues confronting American universities in the 21st century.* Santa Barbra, CA: Praeger. Mitchell, R., Mitchell, N. E., & Mitchell, C. A. (2017). Spirituality and education: Humanities timeless search for certainty and security. In Matthew Harris (Ed.), *Oxford Research Encyclopedia of Education.* New York: Oxford University Press.

Nieto, S. (2002). *Language, culture and teaching: Critical perspectives for a new century.* Mahwah, NJ: Lawrence Erlbaum Associates.

Obadele, I. (1984). *Free* the land*! The true story of the trials of the rna-11 in Mississippi and the continuing struggle to establish an independent Black nation.* New York: House of Songhay Commission.

O'Donoghue, J. (2018, June, 29). 8 reasons why Louisiana's prison population hit its lowest point in 20 years. *NOLA.com.* https://www.nola.com/politics/index.ssf/2018/06/louisiana_prison_population.html

Rushdie, S. (1991). *Imaginary homelands: Essays and criticism 1981–1991.* New York: Granta Books.

Spring, J. (2009). *Deculturalization and the struggle for equity: A brief history of the education of dominated cultures in the United States,* 6th ed. New York: McGraw-Hill.

The loving cities index framework. The Schott Foundation. Retrieved from The Schott Foundation. https://lovingcities.schottfoundation.org/the-loving-cities-index/

Thurman, H. (1975). *Deep river and the Negro spiritual speaks of life and death.* Richmond, IN: Friends United Press.

U.S. Department of Education, National Center for Education Statistics. (2017). *Status and Trends in the Education of Racial and Ethnic Groups 2017* (NCES 2017-051), Degrees Awarded. https://nces.ed.gov/pubs2017/2017051.pdf

Walker, V. S. (1996). *Their highest potential: An African American school community in the segregated South*. Chapel Hill: University of North Carolina Press.

Watkins, W. (2001). *The white architects of Black education ideology and power in America 1865–1954*. New York: Teachers College Press.

Woodson, C. (1933). *The mis-education of the Negro*. Washington, DC: Associated Publishers.

Black Theory Matters

AntiBlackness, White Logics, and the Limits of Diversity Research Paradigms

Kirsten T. Edwards

> "there w[ere] various projects of Western empire and colonialism, where slavery etc. were in a sense guiding the science. So that made the science have the wrong questions. And when you ask the wrong questions you're bound to get the wrong answers, right? . . . So you know, maybe that's—I don't want to discard science at all, but I want to say that maybe we need to look at what forces are directing the kinds of questions our scientists are asking.
>
> —Chenjerai Kumanyika, *Seeing White*, 2017

Introduction

Research on race in higher education has been of increasing interest in the field of higher education for almost three decades. Early publications such as Altbach and Lomotey's (1991) *The Racial Crisis in American Higher Education*, and Gurin et al.'s (2002) "Diversity and Higher Education: Theory and Impact on Educational Outcomes" charted the course for intellectually rigorous explorations into the ways in which race impacts postsecondary education. These publications also gave credence to the long-lamented, but rarely attended to voices of the unheard—students, faculty, and staff of color. Following the example of these early studies, scholars concerned with the experiences, and more specifically the survival of racially minoritized peoples on college campuses, have explored various dimensions of higher education at the intersection of race.

For example, researchers have now been able to move beyond general/izable examinations of progression along standard measures of academic success, such as retention, graduation, promotion, tenure, and career advancement (Bradley, 2005; Brown & Davis, 2001; Cooper, 2006; Hurtado et al.,1998). Contemporary publications explore cognitive and affective contours of racialized higher education (Bowman, 2010; Dancy, 2012; Edwards, 2015; Pascarella & Terenzini, 2005). Scholars have also analyzed race at the intersection of multiple identity categories and systems of power, including but not limited to gender, sexual orientation, class, religion, and nationality (e.g., McCarty, 2009; Stewart & Lozano, 2009). As research has uncovered the numerous challenges racialized subjects face on college campuses, various interventions have been proposed and applied, which themselves have received considerable research attention.

Examples of specific interventions include culturally responsive mentoring programs, Black male leadership programs (and in rare cases Black female spinoffs), diversity and intergroup dialogue facilitation, and the integration of Black student organizations into the official institutional frame. While these efforts have facilitated some advancement, scholars of race and justice have aptly noted the perennial challenges faced by Black and Brown collegians and professionals. After more than three decades of rigorous research, diversity scholarship has yet to deliver us to the educational Promised Land. Questions about this lack have also been taken up in the literature.

Some scholars have argued that many of the interventions that emerge from current diversity research focus on direct supports to people of color without challenging the fundamental configuration of white institutions (Cabrera, Franklin, & Watson, 2016; Chun, 2012). Frankly stated, researchers have attempted to best position people of color to reap the rewards of higher education previously only available to their white counterparts. More radical race thinkers have noted the colonial, antiBlack design of postsecondary institutions, a design predicated on the dehumanization of people of color and antiBlack labor exploitation (Dancy, Edwards, Davis, 2018; Edwards, 2010; Kelley, 2016; Wilder, 2013). This line of scholarly critique reveals the reverberations of the racial contract evidenced in the ethos and practices of contemporary higher education (Mills, 1997). Whether one takes a conventional or unconventional position, the ongoing crises of justice in higher education should give pause. Why does higher education scholarship continue to encounter limits/limitations in its ability to positively alter the experiences of people of color on college campuses? Why has the preponderance of literature related to race and justice seemingly produced little to no impact on higher education's colonial project? How might expectations regarding standard research practice within the field inhibit productive lines of inquiry? After all of these years of research and practice, why does Black life still not matter on college campuses? I argue that these questions and others are fundamentally connected to the liminality of philosophical paradigms undergirding research design in higher education.

The purpose of this chapter is to consider research paradigms often applied to scholarship on race in higher education. More specifically, I will explore the ways traditional conceptual approaches limit Afrocentric inquiry and Black revolutionary methodologies, and therefore ultimately participate in the production of interventions that support or fail to disrupt white supremacy and antiBlackness. My analysis will take as an example research on Black spaces within historically white campuses (e.g., Black cultural centers, Black Greek letter organizations [BGLOs], and Black activist communities). Much of the higher education and student affairs literature concerning these types of communities recognize them as "safe spaces" of solace for students of color amid an educational environment plagued by systemic racism (e.g., Patton, 2006). However, I question whether there are particular elements of Black space-making that are made visible through the application of theoretical and methodological analyses that center Afrocentric and other radical Black logics. If this is the case, what are the implications for Black higher education research and what do these more radical analyses reveal about institutional responses to and with regard for Black life? Put more plainly, this project explores the tethered relationship between Black lives and Black theory in higher education.

Black Collegiate Spaces in Review

White Theory in Black Face

Since the campus protests that led to the creation of ethnic studies programs, institutions of higher education have struggled with the integration of nondominant intellectual traditions (T'Shaka, 2012). Much of this struggle is the result of white resistance. While institutions may have found it prudent to pursue an additive approach to diversity in order to avoid further revolt, structural change that disrupts normative practices—changes that decenter white interests—have been ferociously thwarted. Institutional efforts often go as far as white comfort will allow. Higher education administrators and the general public often consider the idea of reparations as radically absurd. The necessity of affirmative action is a perennial "debate." The removal of exploitative revenue-generating sports (almost exclusively occupied by Black male bodies) from collegiate settings is a nonstarter. These are just a few areas where white interests trump Black life.

The centering of white comfort is also evident in the theoretical and conceptual models that are legitimized in higher education diversity research. Often scholars will take up conceptual frames such as the "multiple identities" framework (Abes, Jones, & McEwen, 2007) and/or "sense of belonging" (Tinto, 1993) to support the maintenance of these spaces within white institutions. Unfortunately, while acknowledging the challenges Black students endure within institutionalized racism, sense-of-belonging literature does not engage radical Black resistance, and the multiple-identities frame decenters Black feminist thought along with its explicit analysis of systemic power and domination (Collins, 1990; Crenshaw, 1989). Both of these frames also assume the validity and value of white higher education for Black collegians (Ani, 1994; Woodson, 1933). The aforementioned paradigmatic dispositions have implications for the solutions that arise from these research studies.

For instance, many of the studies in the field of higher education and student affairs offer programmatic and curricular solutions that follow familiar disciplinary themes such as enhanced mentoring strategies, curricular adaptations, culturally responsive programming, and directed advising (Bimper, 2017; Brooms, 2018; Domingue, 2015; Karkouti, 2015). While these solutions are important and commendable, they seem to have produced incomplete results, which border on ineffective, insomuch as they have not fundamentally altered the challenges Black students, faculty, and staff encounter as occupants of historically white institutions (HWIs). For example, the concerns Black student activists in the 21st century express are strikingly similar to their 1960s counterparts: limited hiring and retention of Black faculty, scholarships and financial assistance for Black students, supportive programming, and Black presence at the executive-level of the administration (Anderson, 2007; Creager, 2017).

The continuance of the aforementioned struggles reflects structural flaws embedded within the foundation of HWIs that are unresponsive to the measures of change often suggested by higher education diversity literature. Said differently, much of the scholarly inquiry that emerges from the field about Black people seems ill-equipped to contend with the reverberations of oppression rooted in enslavement and antiBlackness that formed not only the nation, but also its institutions of higher learning (Mills, 1997; Wilder, 2013). While the available literature cogently argues that there are major challenges in regard to race and racism on college campuses and targeted action is needed, the actions suggested reveal an understanding of HWIs as permanent and essential, and therefore spaces that must/can be made safe for Black people. This view makes "unvisible" HWIs' creation and emergence as colonizing instruments within already occupied lands and civilizations (McKittrick, 2006). It also erases the practices of education that existed in freedom before they were destroyed and reengineered to enslave and exterminate (Ani, 1994). In very real ways, the conceptual frames of inquiry that direct contemporary scholarship about Black people in higher education participates in the seduction of forgetting African indigenous ways of knowing in order to normalize whiteness and white frames of reference (Dillard, 2012).

Some might argue that the challenge is not the inquiry or the implications for practice that emerge from said scholarship, but instead the lack of implementation. Such a response fails in two ways. First, since the emergence of significant research on the experiences of Black people at HWIs, there have been attempts to implement suggested strategies to improve campus racial climate. Black male leadership initiatives (BMLIs), Black cultural centers, TRIO programs, faculty and staff mentoring, and the like have seen a modicum of success but not the wholesale change needed to support an equitable, free future. Black people continue to experience marginalization, isolation, and macro-/microaggressive violence on college campuses (Dancy et al., 2018). These ongoing experiences reveal the saliency of white supremacy and systemic dominance within higher education, and the futility of nonstructural programmatic approaches. Second, if one supports the presupposition that HWIs have not effectively implemented proposed strategies, then it further substantiates the argument made in this essay that these institutions are resistant to and therefore undermine educational practices that take seriously the humanity and thriving of Black people.

Tokenization of Black Thought: Critical Race Theory and Intersectionality

> Black people will never gain full equality in this country. Even those herculean efforts we hail as successful will produce no more than temporary "peaks of progress," short-lived victories that slide into irrelevance as racial patterns adapt in ways that maintain white dominance. This is a hard-to-accept fact that all history verifies. We must acknowledge it, not as a sign of submission, but as an act of ultimate defiance.
>
> —Derrick Bell, *Faces at the Bottom of the Well*, 1992, p. 12

While much of the higher education scholarship that examines the experiences of Black people employs dominant theoretical and conceptual frames, there are two frames that have emerged out of radical Black consciousness that have gained much traction in the field within the past few decades. These traditions are critical race theory (CRT) and intersectionality. The revolutionary history of both traditions is undeniable. Scholars of race and racial domination owe a great debt to these early Black theorists. Their work opened up pathways to thinking and action that have made indelible marks on theorizing about Black life in higher education and beyond.

However, as Derrick Bell, foundational CRT thinker, warned us, the shape-shifting capacity of white domination in this country is infallible. Even the most radical Black positions are either relegated to the realm of the unscientific, unscholarly, fictious, and therefore treated as disposable folklore in academic dialogue; or diluted, stripped of their radical power and assimilated into institutional discourse. The latter is often the case when scholars deploy CRT and intersectionality in higher education research.

CRT and intersectionality have stood the test of academic time, but not without battle scars. For instance, scholars regularly invoke the five tenets of CRT in research, yet the disruptive core of the ideas are often muted. Take for example one of CRT's central ideas, interest convergence. This concept suggests that race progressive initiatives—efforts put forward by Black people for the benefit of Black communities—are only successful when they converge with white interests. Bell's (1980) classic example of interest convergence is *Brown v. Board of Education*. Several scholars have taken up interest convergence in research to describe the success or lack thereof of diversity initiatives on campus. However, many of these research reports ignore an important companion to the interest convergence dilemma first explored by Lani Guinier (2004): interest *divergence*. Interest divergence suggests that while certain gains may be made on the part of certain Black people (usually the more enfranchised) when those gains further the larger interests of upper- and middle-class whites, the centering of white interests simultaneously forecloses access to resources for other (less enfranchised) peoples, while also deepening structural inequalities across a variety of scales. Not only is interest divergence a decidedly austere analysis of whiteness and white psychology, it is also a warning about the futility of developing programs and policies that in any way appease white interests. Interest-convergence and its corollary interest-divergence remind Black scholars of the utterly radical idea that we must, at all cost, keep our eyes and intentions laser focused on freedom; a freedom that will not be found in relationship with whiteness. This message is often not evidenced in higher education research focused on Black people.

Similarly, the field has not always fully engaged the radical contours of Kimberlé Crenshaw's Intersectionality theory. Intersectionality is definitively focused on the intersections of *systems* of power that come to bare on the lives of specific *populations* of people who share similar social identities, namely, Black women (Crenshaw, 1989, 1991). Unfortunately, Crenshaw's structural framing is often reduced to an analysis of intersecting identities (e.g., Davis, 2008). The reduction of systems to discreet identities has several implications, one being a distraction from the structural changes needed for Black people to survive and thrive. By focusing on the individual identity, analyses locate the problem and solution within the individual student, faculty member, or staff, as opposed to the recognition that the individual identity emerges in response to a system dependent on domination. These analyses lead to discussions about the importance of thinking about students "intersectionally," instead of thinking about institutions as structurally violent via mechanisms of intersecting systems of oppression.

The individualization of Intersectionality works in tandem with its morphing into a buzzword in popular culture (Robertson, 2017). Now scholars and laypersons alike deploy the term at their individual conveniences to describe events and issues that bare very little relevance to intersectionality's theoretical and critical aims. The dilution of CRT and intersectionality in higher education research often translates into less-than-radical analyses of phenomenon with resulting subpar solutions.

These solutions do not recognize white institutions as irreparably flawed and they often do not equip Black students, faculty, and staff with the information needed to fugitively respond to an institution committed to their enslavement.

Collegiate Marronage

Reconceptualizing Black Spaces

In an effort to concretize the present discussion concerning radical Black conceptual alternatives and their application in higher education research, I take as an example the study of Black collegiate spaces within HWIs. Specifically, in this section, I situate Black collegiate spaces within Roberts's (2015) notion of *marronage*, "a group of persons isolating themselves from a surrounding society in order to create a fully autonomous community" (p. 4).

When higher education scholars apply traditional conceptual frames to analyze the practice of Black space-making in white collegiate settings, the subsequent research reports often propose programmatic and curricular solutions that follow familiar disciplinary themes such as enhanced mentoring strategies, curricular adaptations, culturally responsive programming, and directed advising (e.g., Bimper, 2017; Brooms, 2018; Domingue, 2015; Karkouti, 2015; Museus & Ravello, 2010). While the aforementioned vein of research provides practical and targeted solutions to perennial diversity challenges, they often offer limited nuanced analyses that situate contemporary racism within a history of deep-structure antiBlackness and the simultaneity of white colonial preoccupations. These research projects are often predicated on an implicit understanding of unintended institutional harm resulting from the residue of a discriminatory past—collective bad habits that can be rectified—or a minority of unchecked racists who can be mitigated through effective policies. The underlying proposition being that a sense of belonging for the oppressed is possible, if higher education sufficiently adapts to respond to the "unique" needs of Black students through changes in institutional policies and practices.

Alternatively, marronage places antiBlackness and the perpetual assertion of white dominance at the crux of its analysis, recognizing these constructs as central to the Black global experience. If a scholar is theorizing from a conceptual frame that takes seriously Afrocentric and radical Black propositions, offering suggestions to white institutions on ways to create more inclusive programming in an effort to promote Black student "safety" and "engagement" would be at best internally inconsistent and at worst illogical. Such a project fails to recognize that white civil society and its supporting institutions are predicated on Black enslavement (Mills, 1997). These assumptions belie the project of white dominance through colonization, while simultaneously subduing the radical instincts of Black students.

To better understand the paradigmatic rifts between marronage (or Afrocentric and radical Black thought) and traditional postsecondary conceptual frames, it is important to take a more focused look at marronage as a concept. The term *marronage* is drawn from the freedom practices of Black enslaved populations in the Caribbean and parts of the Americas. Maroons retreated to the mountains, wildernesses, and jungles of colonized lands in order to escape their white enslavers. Risking the dangers of a harsh, unfamiliar natural environment, they cultivated uninhabited terrain and/or cooperated with Indigenous Peoples, eventually establishing autonomous, free communities *within* colonized territories. Maroon settlements did not provide the freedom once available on the African continent, but instead offered liberation that was predicated on constant fugitivity, and the inability of white enslavers to navigate the terrain. Roberts describes "maroons" as "resid[ing] in liminal suspension between slaves on a plantation and colonizers dictating standards of normativity," who established "zones of refuge" (Roberts, 2015, p. 5) within the context of enslavement.

By examining Black space-making on college campuses through this conceptual frame, scholars might view Black students as contemporary maroon resisters who are subconsciously, if not consciously, attuned to the project of enslavement facilitated by higher education. They are not simply creating places of undisruptive comfort but are "Maroons . . . cultivating freedom on their own terms within a demarcated social space that allows for the enactment of subversive speech acts, gestures, and social practices antithetical to the ideals of enslaving agents" (Roberts, 2015, p. 5). If one proceeds from a place of Black knowing and resistance, then an analysis of fugitivity becomes central to any programmatic intervention. The maintenance of white (institutional) unknowing would also be a paramount concern. Instead of focusing on assimilative priorities such as perceived safety and engagement, researchers invested in an Afrocentric or radical Black paradigmatic position, which recognizes the college campus as a reincarnation of the plantation, might invest in strategic imperatives that support an awareness of lack of safety, a separatist agenda that simultaneously navigates the siphoning of resources for survival, while also supporting Black community and revolutionary action.

Reconceptualizing Implications

One of the most potent possibilities available when situating Black spaces within the marronage frame is the opportunity for researchers to shift conceptions of Black students away from a normalized white student pattern with its underlining interests and goals. By applying a radical Black lens to Black student practices, the essay situates Black spaces as examples of fugitivity and Black reimagination. Furthermore, it highlights the ways qualitative research paradigms control what inquiry is possible, particularly when studying Black people within white higher education. In effect, I argue, available/acceptable diversity research paradigms work as antiBlack blockades to radical Black and Afrocentric inquiry, which has deleterious implications for research design and methodological process, fundamentally altering the way the field understands the lives and experiences of Black human beings understudy.

The present project identifies various implications that address the commitments outlined in the previous section. First, a marronage conceptual analysis recognizes the revolutionary as opposed to the assimilationist dispositions of Black students. A radical Black analysis, which offers a substantive critique of white social and cultural dispositions, understands the ways Black students are situated as enslaved within white supremacist dictates for economic and social survival in a capitalist society. The creation of Black spaces within collegiate settings, therefore, enables the survivance of Black students in a physical context that demands their objectification. In this vein Black students are conspirers for freedom as opposed to simply victims of discrimination. Marronage also highlights the fallacious assumption that Black spaces are maintained to mitigate Black students' intellectual and cultural deficiencies.

Second, a marronage investigation recognizes HWIs as colonial projects. As such, they are committed to white supremacy, genocide, and enslavement. This recognition necessitates a rejection of policies that seek institutional reform. White US higher education is unreformable insomuch as the purpose of the institution, since its inception in 1636, is first and foremost the perpetuation of white dominance and the maintenance of a colonizing and colonized class.

Third, this analysis rejects policy proposals that situate Black spaces as "safe spaces" or learning opportunities for white institutions. Instead these maroon projects provide a context for subversion that supports ideas and practices that are necessarily "antithetical to the ideals of enslaving agents" (Roberts, 2015, p. 5). While much of higher education research notes the benefits of Black spaces for increasing Black student persistence, retention, and sense of belonging, a marronage analysis of Black spaces might illuminate efforts at dissent, resistance to institutional measures of success, promotion of Afrocentric educational models, and macro-/micro-attacks on the institution that undermine the social order and the power of colonial agents.

An investigative approach prioritizing policies that are attentive to the above listed implications would also compel different programmatic responses, as well as radical questions. Would research that supports and nurtures the revolutionary practices of Black students necessarily promote persistence and retention within a context of white domination? Are white university partnerships with Black student groups or an increase in Black students' GPAs markers of success? Do these markers evidence movement toward Black freedom or white normativity? These questions may trigger discomfort in some higher education researchers, but is that discomfort reflective of an inherent flaw with the questions or the field's socialization toward a particular (white) agenda?

The Power of Revolutionary Inquiry

The above section offers a brief example of the potential impact radical Black thought could have on higher education research. The present treatise invites critical Black scholars to imagine higher education research that centers radical Black and Afrocentric paradigms such as: Afro-futurism, Afro-pessimism, Africana womanism, Black feminism, Yurugu, endarkened feminist epistemology, Black Atlantic consciousness, and marronage, to name a few. I contend that these paradigms offer the anecdote to seductive educational narratives that conscript Black scholars into research practices that sustain white dominance (Dillard, 2012).

In her book, *Learning to (re)member the things we've learned to forget*, Dillard offers a reflection on her experience at an academic conference, which reveals the paradox many Black scholars contend with in white academe. She writes,

> As consecutive panels gathered on the podium and presented their conference papers, I became more disconcerted, recognizing the deeply entrenched and global nature of the meaning of being a "researcher," . . . Although those in attendance represented diverse countries and were predominately of African heritage, it was clear that we'd all been trained in Western theories and notions of research, with little resistance or critical examination of how such training had shaped our pedagogies and approaches to research. We'd literally been trained away from ourselves. (Dillard, 2012, p. 18)

Dillard's reflection exposes the weight of the colonial project on Black thought. It is important for observers to note that her critique does not focus on the topics or subject matter understudy, but instead the "theories" that frame said subject matter and the controlling ideas that dictate what the research process should encompass. She makes clear that dependence on Western pathways to knowing are central to colonization insomuch as it displaces a commitment to our own Black ways of knowing and therefore our humanity. Stated differently, one can simultaneously study Black people and participate in the denial of Black humanity.

Drawing on Franz Fanon, Denise Baszile and I, similarly, describe the process of white occupation in the Black imagination:

> It is epistemic violence when you must seek validation from those who have a stake in your not speaking for yourself. It leaves you no choice but to give in, to follow the rules and codes of academic presentment, to participate in the perpetuation of your own lack of voice, your own invisibility. As Fanon surmises, "it is implicit that to speak is to exist absolutely for the other." (Edwards & Baszile, 2016, p. 17–18)

What both Dillard and Baszile and I expose is a method of Black containment (enslavement) facilitated through normed conceptual standards. To be sure, patterns of conceptual objectification translate into very real forms of physical labor and bodily control for Black occupants in higher education (Dancy et al., 2018).

While these challenges are endemic to the academy broadly, I note a particular investment in white normed practices in the fields of higher education and student affairs. As a young, and in many respects, striving field, scholars of higher education and student affairs have displayed an acute commitment to identifying and adhering to a canonical scholarship. Conference proposal acceptance and publication in the field's preeminent journals require situating one's scholarship squarely within an established line of inquiry, and subsequently citing the recognized sources (Stanley, 2007). Again, this is not an assessment of topic. A quick perusal of any of the major conference programs or journal tables of contents in the field will reveal a plethora of "diversity"-related topics. As social justice becomes vogue and allyship avant-garde, the subjects that consume these pages are often related to issues of identity. However, as mentioned previously, if identity is taken as a benign unit of analysis without a substantive investigation into power, specifically antiBlackness and white dominance, then the project only serves to maintain hegemony. Furthermore, it is unreasonable to assume that a liberatory critique of the white episteme and its subsequent cultural project can also emerge from the white psyche. Instead, even as Black scholars endeavor to produce scholarship that attends to their community's needs, in order to maintain space within a field predicated on white supremacy, said scholarship must comport to standards of civility and logic defined by whiteness. As Fanon writes,

> All colonized people—in other words, people in whom an inferiority complex has taken root, whose local cultural originality has been committed to the grave—position themselves in relation to the civilizing language: i.e., the metropolitan culture. The more the colonized has assimilated the cultural values of the metropolis, the more he [sic] will have escaped the bush. The more he [*sic*] rejects his blackness and the bush, the whiter he [*sic*] will become. (Fanon, 2008, p. 2)

For Black people in the colonial state, our bodies become occupied land. And for the Black intellectual, our minds are the most fertile soil. It is imperative that we resist the appropriation of our minds for the service of the Empire. This requires active retreat to the intellectual "bush" to apply Fanon's language. The bush, or place of Black intellectual origin, are those ideas that emerge in the Black consciousness. As marronage teaches, these ideas can also manifest in the context of Black fugitivity. While the ideal may be to produce research in the context of freedom, in light of global white imperialism and antiBlackness, this option may be presently impossible. Afrocentric and radical Black conceptual frames provide scholarly maroons conceptual spaces of refuge to envision freedom in the context of epistemic enslavement and institutional colonization.

There is emerging evidence of this retreat among many Black scholars within and beyond the fields of higher education and student affairs. An example is Cooper's *Beyond Respectability*. She encourages scholars to pursue an unapologetic retreat to Black women's intellectual thought, or the early writings of "race women." This retreat will require giving the philosophical positions of Black women the same, if not more, intellectual credence as the writings of established white male scholars. As she notes,

> Most academics have been trained to *trust* that white males of all varieties are capable of "deep thoughts." *Beyond Respectability* requires that we approach Black women's long history of knowledge production with this same kind of trust. If I were aiming to show (and was successful at showing) how Black women's ideas dovetailed the ideas of Michel Foucault or Gilles Deleuze and Feliz Guattari or Louis Althusser or Judith Butler, this book would be deemed sufficiently rigorous and, dare I say, "original." That I aim for a different goal, namely to show that we should take Black women, from Fannie Barrier Williams to Mary Church Terrell to Pauli Murray, as theoretically serious as we take the work of French white males, requires a different inclination. (Cooper, 2017, p. 2; emphasis in the original)

She goes on to cogently argue that Black women's intersectional analyses; analyses that emerge from the complexity of Black womanhood engaging the relationship between multiple systems of oppression, are best positioned to chart the course for the kinds of intellectual inquiry that produce freedom for a multiplicity of peoples. However, a project of this kind requires an epistemic and ontological resistance to the compulsion to define one's humanity and the value of one's scholarship within the norms of whiteness. As Cooper notes, standard academic gatekeepers would accept a project that links Black thought to established white thinkers. Radical Black scholars must not be seduced into such benign ventures. Instead, like Cooper, we must chart new Black pathways that center the Black experience and Black liberation.

A Logical Conclusion: Black Divestment in Research Design and Practice

> Now that we have broken the power of their ideology, we must leave them and direct our energies toward the recreation of cultural alternatives informed by ancestral visions of a future that celebrates our Africanness and encourages the best of the human spirit.
>
> —Marimba Ani, *Yurugu: An African-centered Critique of European Cultural Thought*, 1994, p. 570

In many ways this essay asks the same question, Carter G. Woodson posed to the Black intellectual almost a century ago: are "these 'educated' persons . . . actually equipped to face the ordeal before them or unconsciously contribut[ing] to their own undoing by perpetuating the regime of the oppressor" (Woodson, 1933/2000, p. xvii). I believe radical Black scholars of higher education are equipped to respond to Woodson's invocation. However, we must boldly reject notions of inquiry that are rooted in antiBlackness. We must draw on the strength of our critical, dexterous, Black curiosity to escape the plantation and retreat to the bush.

In our pursuit toward fugitivity, we can take direction from the intellectual abolitionists who have gone before us. In his foundational text, *The Mis-education of the Negro*, Woodson warns,

> Negroes who have been so long inconvenienced and denied opportunities for development are naturally afraid of anything that sounds like discrimination. They are anxious to have everything the white man has even if it is harmful. The possibility of originality in the Negro, therefore, is discounted one hundred percent to maintain a nominal equality . . . [Education] has been worked out in conformity to the needs of those who have enslaved and oppressed. (Woodson, 1933/2000, pp. xvii–xviii)

In order to break free of the anxiety of white domination Woodson describes, Black scholars must abandon the desire for educational models and ambitions that continue to enslave and oppress. But how do researchers who have been trained exclusively within white frames of logic pursue social, spiritual, and epistemic freedom?[1] In a previous essay, I with my colleagues, argue that

Black educational liberation will be facilitated by Black divestment (Dancy et al., 2018). For us, Black divestment is a, "project that abandons attempts at liberation that do not take seriously the centrality of the racial contract and anti-Blackness to the current social order [and therefore] would constitute radical self-determination" (Dancy et al., 2018, p. 190). In this section of the present treatise I imagine what Black divestment might look like in the work of Black scholars studying higher education.

Taking heed to the admonition of the Combahee River Collective (1982), I recognize that any substantive response to the perpetual and interlocking systems of oppression experienced by marginalized peoples in this nation and across the globe, must begin with a recognition that the political system, and its attending institutions, is "a system of white male rule" (para. 3). Any conceptual analysis or subsequent research project that obfuscates that reality is fundamentally not in service to the needs of Black people. Research design that is intended to support the progression of Black people must clarify the oppressive realities that define our condition within the nation-state.

In regard to the positionality of Black students in the context of HWIs, radical Black research might shift analyses of their relationship to higher education from one of (grateful, un/deserving) recipient to investor due a return. If researchers take seriously the unpaid labor enslaved Black people invested into institutions of higher education, then it seems fitting that their descendants would benefit from its profits and resources in a more generous measure than their collegiate counterparts who are white legacy admits.

I also question programmatic efforts that attempt to prepare Black students in becoming more "competitive" in the educational and professional marketplace. Such solutions do not fundamentally disrupt the imperialist white supremacist capitalist patriarchal social order (hooks, 2015), but instead conscript Black students into participating in its maintenance. These solutions also do not take seriously the capitalist marketplace's dependence on antiBlackness and the continuation of a permanent (Black) slave caste ("Combahee River Collective," 1982; Marx & Engels, 2005; Mills, 1997). Instead, programmatic and policy solutions that emerge from a commitment to radical Black divestment might encourage the creation of collectivist educational and professional models. They might detail the design of antiinstitutional programs for the preparation of Black student activists who are equipped to quickly identify, organize against, and resist discriminatory practices on the white campuses they presently occupy. As radical Black scholars, it may also become necessary to consider solutions that equip students to escape HWIs in a way that does not disrupt their intellectual development or economic solvency when the racist violence has become untenable.

These are just a few proposals that might emerge in the context of radical Black divestment. While the limits are virtually immeasurable, the process must begin within a radical Black frame. This is one of the greatest challenges before Black scholars, but it's not impossible. In a world where the freedom of Black lives matter, Black theorizing must be the guide.

Note

1. To be clear, I do not assume white frames of logic only exist and are perpetuated by HWIs. As others have cogently argued (see Njoku, Butler, & Beatty, 2017), minority serving institutions, and specifically historically Black colleges and universities, often are significant enforcers of white logic and norms because they are the most policed by white supremacy. Therefore, Black scholars who are educated within these institutions are still susceptible to white intellectual enslavement.

References

Abes, E. S., Jones, S. R., McEwen, M. K. (2007). Reconceptualizing the model of multiple dimensions of identity: The role of meaning-making capacity in the construction of multiple identities. *Journal of College Student Development, 48*(1), 1–22.

Altbach, P. G., & Lomotey, K. (Eds.). (1991). *The racial crisis in American higher education*. Albany: State University of New York Press.

Anderson, J. (2007). Past discrimination and diversity: A historical context for understanding race and affirmative action. *Journal of Negro Education, 76*(3), 204–215.

Ani, M. (1994). *Yurugu: An Afrikan-centered critique of European cultural thought and behavior*. Washington, DC: Nkonimfo Publications.

Bell, D. (1992). *Faces at the Bottom of the Well: The Permanence of Racism*. New York: Basic Books.

Bell, D. (1980). Brown v. Board of Education and the interest-convergence dilemma. *Harvard Law Review, 93*(3).

Bimper, A. J. (2017). Mentorship of Black student-athletes at a predominately white American university: Critical race theory perspective on student-athlete development. *Sport, Education and Society, 22*(2), 175–193.

Bowman, N. A. (2010). College diversity experiences and cognitive development: A meta-analysis. *Review of Higher Educational Research, 80* (1), 4–33.

Bradley, C. (2005). The career experiences of African American women faculty: Implications for counselor education programs. *College Student Journal, 39*, 518 527.

Brooms, D. R. (2018). 'Building us up': Supporting Black male college students in a Black male initiative program. *Critical Sociology, 44*(1), 141–155.

Brown, M. C., II, & Davis, J. E. (2001). The historically Black college as social contract, social capital, and social equalizer. *Peabody Journal of Education, 76*, 31–49.

Cabrera, N. L., Franklin, J. D., & Watson, J. S. (2016). Whiteness in higher education: The invisible missing link in diversity and racial analyses. *ASHE higher education report, 42*(6).

Collins, P. H. (1990). *Black feminist thought: Knowledge, consciousness, and the politics of empowerment.* Boston, MA: Unwin Hyman.

Combahee River Collective. (1982). A Black feminist statement. In G. Hull, P. B. Scott, and B. Smith (Eds.). *All the women are White, all the Blacks are men, but some of us are brave: Black women's studies* (pp. 13–22). Old Westbury, NY: Feminist Press.

Cooper, B. C. (2017). *Beyond respectability: The intellectual thought of race women.* Urbana, Chicago, and Springfield: University of Illinois Press.

Cooper, T. L. (2006). *The sista' network: African-American women faculty successfully negotiating the road to tenure.* Bolton, MA: Anker.

Creager, D. (2017, January 26). OU unheard updates university on progress since SAE incident with #RollTheCredits hashtag. OU Daily. Retrieved from http://www.oudaily.com/news/ou-unheard-updates-university-on-progress-since-sae-incident-with/article_ec7511dc-e357-11e6-832f-c3f6c97cc793.html

Crenshaw, K. (1991). Mapping the margins: Intersectionality, identity politics, and violence against women of color. *Stanford Law Review, 43*(6), 1241–1299.

Crenshaw, K. (1989). Demarginalizing the intersection of race and sex: A Black feminist critique of antidiscrimination doctrine, feminist theory and antiracist politics. *University of Chicago Legal Forum*, 139–167.

Dancy, T. E., Edwards, K. T., & Davis, J. E. (2018). Historically White universities and plantation politics: Anti-Blackness and higher education in the Black Lives Matter era, *Urban Education, 53*(2) 176–195.

Dancy, T. E. (2012). *The brother code: Manhood and masculinity among African American males in college.* Charlotte, NC: Information Age Publishing.

Davis, K. (2008). Intersectionality as buzzword: A sociology of science perspective on what makes a feminist theory successful. *Feminist Theory, 9*(1), 67–85.

Dillard, C. (2012). *Learning to (re)member the things we've learned to forget.* New York: Peter Lang.

Domingue, A. D. (2015). "Our leaders are just we ourself": Black women college student leaders' experiences with oppression and sources of nourishment on a predominantly white College Campus. *Equity & Excellence in Education, 48*(3), 454–472.

Edwards, K. T. (2015). Perceptions of power and faith among Black women faculty: Re-thinking institutional diversity, *Innovative Higher Education, 40*(3), 263–278.

Edwards, K. T. (2010). Incidents in the life of Kirsten T. Edwards: A personal examination of the academic in-between space, *Journal of Curriculum Theorizing, 26*(1), 113–128.

Edwards, K. T., & Baszile, D. T. (2016). Scholarly rearing in three acts: Black women's testimonial scholarship and the cultivation of radical Black female inter-subjectivity, *Knowledge Cultures, 4*(1), 85–99.

Fanon, F. (2008). *Black skin, white masks.* New York: Grove Press. (Original work published 1952.)

Guinier, L. (2004). From racial liberalism to racial literacy: Brown v. Board of Education and the interest-divergence dilemma. *Journal of American History, 91*(1), 92–118.

Gurin, P., Dey, E. L., Hurtado, S., and Gurin, G. "Diversity and higher education: Theory and impact on educational outcomes." *Harvard Educational Review,* 2002, 72(3), 330–366.

Hartman, S. (1997) *Scenes of subjection: Terror, slavery and self-making in nineteenth-century America.* New York: Oxford University Press.

hooks, b. (2015). *Understanding patriarchy.* No Borders: Louisville's Radical Lending Library.

Hurtado, S., Milem, J., Clayton-Pedersen, A., & Allen, W. (1998). Enhancing campus climates for racial/ethnic diversity: Educational policy and practice. *Review of Higher Education, 21,* 279–302.

Karkouti, I. M. (2015). The role of student affairs practitioners in improving campus racial climate: A case Study. *College Student Journal, 49*(1), 31–40.

Kelley, R. D. G. (March 7, 2016). Black study, Black struggle. *Boston Review.* Retrieved from http://bostonreview.net/forum/robin-d-g-kelley-black-study-black-struggle

Kumanyika, Chenjerai (May 17, 2017). Episode 38: skulls and skin (Seeing white, part 8). *Scene on Radio.* Retrieved from https://www.sceneonradio.org/episode-38-skulls-and-skins-seeing-white-part-8/

Marx, K., & Engels, F. (2005). Manifesto of the Communist Party (with Friedrich Engels). *Marx: Later political writings, 1,* 1–30.

McCarty, R. W. (2009). Facilitating dialogue on religion and sexuality using a descriptive approach. *New Directions for Student Services, 125,* 39–46.

McKittrick, K. (2006). *Demonic grounds: Black women and the cartographies of struggle.* Minneapolis: University of Minnesota Press.

Mills, C. (1997). *The racial contract.* Ithaca, NY: Cornell University Press.

Pascarella, E. T., & Terenzini, P. T. (2005). *How college affects students: A third decade of research.* San Francisco, CA: Jossey-Bass.

Patton, L. (2006). The voice of reason: A qualitative examination of Black student perceptions of Black culture centers. *Journal of College Student Development, 47*(6), 628–646.

Roberts, N. (2015). *Freedom as marronage*. Chicago, IL: The University of Chicago Press.

Robertson, E. (September 30, 2017). Intersectional-what? Feminism's problem with jargon is that any idiot can pick it up and have a go. *The Guardian*. Retrieved from https://www.theguardian.com/world/2017/sep/30/intersectional-feminism-jargon

Sexton, J. (2016). Afro-pessimism: The unclear word. *Rhizomes: Cultural studies in emerging knowledge, 29*. https://doi.org/10.20415/rhiz/029.e02

Stanley, C. A. (2007). When counter narratives meet master narratives in the journal editorial-review process. *Educational Researcher, 36*(1), pp. 14–24.

Strayhorn, T. (2008). Fittin' in: Do diverse interactions with peers affect sense of belonging for Black men at predominantly white institutions? *NASPA Journal, 45*(4), 501–527.

Stewart, D. L., & Lozano, A. (2009). Difficult dialogues at the intersections of race, culture, and religion. *New Directions for Student Services, 125*, 23–31.

Thomas, S. R. (2000). *Dark matter: A century of speculative fiction from the African diaspora*. New York: Warner Books.

Tinto, V. (1993). *Leaving college: Rethinking the causes and cures of student attrition* (2nd ed.). Chicago, IL: University of Chicago Press.

T'Shaka, O. (2012). Africana Studies Department history: San Francisco State University. *Journal of Pan African Studies, 5*(7), 13–32.

Wilder, C. S. (2013). *Ebony & Ivy: Race, slavery, and the troubled history of America's universities*. New York: Bloomsbury Press.

Woodson, C. G. (1933). *The mis-education of the Negro*. Washington DC: Associated Publishers.

Education as if Black Lives Mattered

A Critical (and Crucial) Literacies Approach

Yolanda Sealey-Ruiz, Marcelle Haddix, and Cluny Lavache

> It's not who you attend school with but who controls the school you attend.
>
> —Nikki Giovanni

Black people have always known that their lives matter. Despite their existence in a society that refuses to acknowledge their humanity, throughout history there are examples of how Blacks resisted degradation, control of their destinies, and remained creative at a time when their communities were crumbling, neglected, and stereotyped as degenerate. As a nation, we've been witnessing through the Black Lives Matter movement, resistance to yet another attack on Black people's humanity—their right to live, to be educated, and create sustaining forces of happiness and well-being. The Black Lives Matter movement, incited by a rash of murders of unarmed Black women, men, and children by police, is arguably the current generation's civil rights struggle. There is also a growing intensity of anti-Blackness the world, ever since Trump began to enact his political agenda as president. The fact is, that throughout history, and as long as Black people have been in this country, their struggle has never ceased. The quintessential place where Black lives should matter most, namely school, is where the

American society has failed Black students at the most alarming rate. According to Caralee Adams (2008), "One African-American student is suspended every seven seconds of the school day, 7% of the teachers in the United States are African-American, and 91% of 8th grade Blacks are designated below proficiency in math" (p. 28). This is a mere snapshot of the inequitable education that has been purposely designed for Blacks, particularly within the American school system.

The education of Blacks have been anchored in subjugation of their bodies and an indoctrination of their minds—an essential design of their educational experiences is for them to believe they are without history, that their culture is barbaric and uncivilized, and that the success of Black people is often dependent on their ability to assimilate by accepting and/or adopting European perspectives. Historically and currently, Black people are embroiled in a perennial fight for fair treatment, justice, and a decent education. Some of the most noted philosophers and educators have theorized the role education plays in determining social success and well-being. Just as Marian Wright Edelman reminds us, "Education is a precondition to survival in America today." Therefore, it is not surprising that many Black academics and Black teacher activists have dedicated their careers to researching and challenging educational inequality in their practice. We three authors choose to dedicate our research careers to this issue because we desire to do all that is within our reach to improve educational opportunities for Blacks and other children who are marginalized because of their race and social location.

We are three Black women who are students of our own history. We acknowledge that the challenge for our people to receive a decent education traces back to the design of our role in this nation: to be chattel slaves. It was never intended for Black people to be educated, therefore it should come as no surprise that one of the most consistent battlefields of protest for equity happens on school grounds and in academic spaces. Equity has always been a contested term, reshaped by those in power who steadily manipulate the term based on their best interests. Only when equity has been of interest to those in power has there been an allowance for Blacks to participate in the democracy. As scholar activists and teachers, we seek to fully test the spirit of America's democracy and the power of education to change lives in that democracy.

Black lives have always mattered to Black people. It is the American society that continues to struggle with this idea. The struggle, failure, and disbelief of American society to admit that Black Lives Matter is as a result of fear—fear that would contradict its very premise for existing. The disbelief that we do matter is why Blacks find themselves locked out of many influential positions that can improve their lives, and the lives of other marginalized people. The highest positions in government, health care, business, law enforcement, and education, to name a few, are held by whites who lean on centuries' old single stories about Blacks and their inability to competently perform in those positions. Perhaps they cling onto those ideas because they fear the endless possibilities of Black people in our capacity to achieve greatness; or they fear retaliation on a wide scale.

America has mistreated Black lives for over 500 hundred years. Even still, when Blacks secure positions of power, as with the twice-elected President Barack H. Obama, there appears to be a national presence of anger and hostility; and indefatigable attempts to block or ridicule the executive decisions that he makes. Each time Blacks learn to play the game, the rules change and a different set of rules are implemented, and like a chameleon we adapt to our environment, to changes so we can continue to fight for what are our inalienable human rights. As Black people, our ability to remain resilient comes from our cultural capital such that, "When they go low, we go high" (former First Lady Michelle Obama, 2016), not out of weakness; but out of the need to keep fighting and giving hope to the next generation that things must get better. Our cultural capital has allowed for Blacks in America to withstand, resist, and ultimately overcome the oppression of white supremacy.

When access and opportunity to an education were nonexistent for Blacks we created our own schools. Black communities took responsibility for caring for their own out of necessity; establishing educational institutions that thrived even when resources were scarce and inadequate. The facilities that Black people occupied were not conducive to learning, yet, there was a sense of community, a sense of belonging that allowed students to succeed. Teachers who graduated from historically Black colleges and universities came back to their communities, engaging and inspiring young Black scholars about their experiences, motivating them to explore their options. Black Lives Mattered then as they matter today. Sizemore (1987) reminds us that, "Culture is the total of artifacts that a group uses in its struggle for survival and autonomy and independence" (p. 51). We have maintained, and at times adapted our culture capital to remain ahead of the constant challenges Black people continue to face. Therefore, it is a moral imperative that we continue to dig deeper into and dismantle the consistent, persistent, soporific and lethal schemes designed to ensure our continued oppression. To this extent, we must claim our place at the table, recognizing that our right to live and to be educated will not be handed to us, but that we have to demand it.

We recognize that the failure of America is not as a result of opportunities that are available, but lack of access to those opportunities. Equity for marginalized people, in particular Black people of the diaspora in America, begins with access despite the opportunities that exist. We have envisioned and at times witnessed the greater possibilities of a better America when Blacks are given access to a quality education. We understand that Blacks don't have systemic and systematic power to control or influence policy in the schools their children attend, this is the reality of what poet Nikki Giovanni lamented. Fundamentally, the lack of power to control or influence policy in our schools results in decisions that are made by others that fail to recognize the essence of Black Lives, and the experience of being Black in America and all of its facets. Access to educational opportunities becomes obscured by the guise of school choice and newly established charter schools that are in predominantly segregated neighborhoods. Seventy-three percent of these charter schools have been defined as "apartheid schools" by Kucsera and Orfield (2014). For the most part, these are schools where Black students make up 99% of the student demographics and an overwhelming majority of the teachers are white, representing another plot to maintain control by the dominant culture. Moreover, it continues to allow the castration of Black Lives, relegating the masses to believing the propaganda that equity can be achieved if we are not sitting at the table demanding what rightfully belongs to us and our students.

Black lives should matter to everyone. Educators and academics have responded to the call to teach and educate. We believe they must constantly ask themselves why they entered the field of education, and what their responsibilities are as teachers and scholars in the age of mass incarceration and a Black Lives Matter movement. We challenge ourselves as well as our fellow educators to be intentional about exposing and dismantling systematic white supremacy in education. We ask that they focus an aspect of their research and ground their teaching in support of the liberation of others. We see this approach to educational research and practice as critical and crucial toward any meaningful and sustainable positive change for all students in schools, and particularly Black students who are often pushed furthest to the margins and away from opportunity for academic success. We ask that all scholars and teachers, but particularly those whose work directly engages what happens in classrooms with Black students to (re)dedicate themselves to the fight for an equitable education for all.

We ask educators and policy makers to consider ways to reimagine educational spaces as if Black Lives Mattered, and not where tests that are not designed for Black students to be sanctioned measurements of their intelligence and academic status in schools; representing "only one dimension of a much more complex and nuanced reality" (Milner, 2012, p. 694). We ask that there is consideration to increase the racial congruency of teachers serving Black students by hiring more teachers of color; to the extent that studies have shown that racial congruency of teachers greatly impacts the academic achievement of Blacks. Additionally, for non-Black teachers, developing cultural competence and cultural awareness has the ability to positively improve the educational outcomes for Black students based on the cross-cultural communication that can occur, reducing racial and academic disparities. A 2015 *U.S. News & World Report* article citing data from several think tanks and educational-data reporting agencies remind us of the pervasive inequalities Black people endure in everyday life and in education. For example, citing statistics from the Forum on Child and Family Report, Black students entering kindergarten for the first time score lower than their white counterparts in reading, mathematics, science, cognitive flexibility, and approaches to learning—every category tested. These tests are not designed to show the strength of Black children, but to continue the status quo of "trends" that perpetuate the "inability" of Blacks to score well on these measurements. The gaps in access persist throughout schooling, at 4th, 8th, and 12th grades.

According to Child Trends, a nonprofit and nonpartisan research center that tracks data about children, disparities in discipline begin in preschool and continue through every level of schooling. The disheartening results of these metrics begin at birth for Black students and are linked to the preexisting inequities faced by their parents. Blacks are also overrepresented in special education classes and underrepresented in Advanced Placement courses. Many of their general education classes remain in the shadow of the academic rigor found in classes with white and Asian students. Despite this dismal and deficit framework from which Black Lives are perceived, the deficit framework often ignores the cultural strengths, resiliency, and fortitude that Black students walk into schools with and goes unnoticed. Black students are able to achieve academic success when a teacher's perception reflects a growth mind-set, high expectations are conveyed, and support is provided to meet expectations. When Black students are nurtured in an academic environment that respects and honors who they are, they are willing to make multiple attempts, in the face of academic and social challenges, to meet the expectations of those who believe in them. As a result, when Black students have a school experience that is uncommon (Hilliard, 2000), they are empowered and academic success is inevitable. Ultimately, when Black Lives Matter, Black Excellence is achieved and everyone benefits.

There are many scholars who study and document these disparities. In this chapter, we write to ask these scholars (as we constantly ask ourselves): How are you engaging these issues in a direct fight to eliminate them? Exposure through scholarship is important, but we must begin to envision action for the work that we publish, and use our lives to help bring about change. And for those scholars who believe that disparities in education hold no concern for their "research agenda," we implore them to reconsider that position. The Children's Defense Fund reports that there are more Black children who live below the poverty line than other children in our nation. There is a perfect formula at play: lower wealth, lower health, lesser education, more dealings with suspension in schools and the justice system out-of-school, and Black children find themselves in the predicament their ancestors have for generations when attending schools not specifically designed with them in mind: they are left without a guarantee for educational opportunities that may lead to an enhanced life and their well-being.

How we envision the lives of Black children—specifically how we define their worth—directly impacts and informs what we, as educators and scholars, do in practice. A predominant counterpoint to the Black Lives Matter movement is the argument that "all lives matter," in many ways an active refusal to acknowledge the blatant inequities and racial violences targeting a specific group of people. Such "all lives matter" ideology is akin to the kinds of color-blind methodologies and one-size-fits-all curricula and pedagogies that disadvantage Black children and that render their unique strengths and particular needs invisible. In this next section of this essay, we ask: What can a literacy curriculum that foregrounds the belief that Black Lives Matter facilitate? What can it look like? How is it enacted? Who creates it, teaches it, and how is it taught? We know all too well the results and outcomes of curricula that are predicated on constructions of Blackness as less than whiteness in ways that are devalued, and nonmattering. We conclude by imagining in real ways what this can look like and believing in the possibilities for such change.

The Invisibility of Black Voices in Literacy Education

Black voices, and particularly within white education circles, have always been excluded. For example, when one of largest English Education/literacy organizations was formed in 1911, the National Council of Teachers of English (NCTE), the plight of Blacks and their access to literacy education was not central to the mission of the organization. In fact, it was not until 60 years later, in 1971, that a Black Caucus was formed to address the concerns of the literacy education of Black children. In 1974, a group of Black scholars who were members of another literacy organization, Conference on College Composition and Communication (CCC), released the position statement, "Students' Right to Their Own Language," to argue that the verbal literacy skills of students of color, and particularly Black students, should be valued and not dismissed or degraded. The resolution, which passed in November 1974, reads as follows:

> We affirm the students' right to their own patterns and varieties of language—the dialects of their nurture or whatever dialects in which they find their own identity and style. Language scholars long ago denied that the myth of a standard American dialect has any validity. The claim that any one dialect is unacceptable amounts to an attempt of one social group to exert its dominance over another. Such a claim leads to false advice for speakers and writers, and immoral advice for humans. A nation proud of its diverse heritage and its cultural and racial variety will preserve its heritage of dialects. We affirm strongly that teachers must have the experiences and training that will enable them to respect diversity and uphold the right of students to their own language.

To emphasize how the battle for respect of Black voices in the literacy field is long-standing, a group of Black literacy and linguistic scholars upheld and reissued the resolution in 2003.

> The Conference on College Composition and Communication reaffirms the students' right to their own language and language varieties. Realizing the continued need to preserve our Nation's diverse heritage of languages and language varieties, the CCCC reaffirms and upholds its 1974 position statement, "Students' Right to Their Own Language." —November 23, 2003

This type of exclusion of Black voices in literacy education has historically been deep and wide. One only needs to look at the "literary canon" that students in schools across the nation are expected to read to see the absence of Black voices. While there are likely multiple theories and explanations for why this is so, we believe that the absence of Black voices, historically and currently in literacy organizations and school curriculum, is synonymous with the treatment of Blacks in society—they were "stamped from the beginning" to be less than human and not full participants in American society (Kendi, 2017).

What Can a Literacy Curriculum that Foregrounds the Belief that Black Lives Matter Facilitate? What Can It Look Like?

It is not enough for children to see characters in books who look like them or for Black history lessons to be summed up in tales of slavery during the month of February. Diverse representation in texts and in the curriculum is important but it is just a start. A literacy curriculum that foregrounds Black lives as mattering understands the essentiality of including multiple stories, histories, and perspectives. It does not shy away from addressing the harsh and difficult realities of the past nor the critical and sometimes controversial issues facing the Black community of present. In fact, at the core of a Black Lives Matter literacy curriculum are texts that are both mirrors of ourselves and windows out into the world (Bishop, 1990), as well as texts that incite young people to resist and act as change agents and to create and produce.

However, texts that incite young people as agents of change begin with the decision of the classroom teacher, and the commitment of administrators and educational stakeholders. The classroom teacher must have self-knowledge, an understanding of history, and perhaps most importantly, the willingness to facilitate such discourse, as they recognize their position in relation to the Black students they service. In order to interrupt the status quo and the Eurocentric perspective of the dominant culture they often belong to, the classroom teacher must self-reflect and deconstruct their white privilege.

In schools where Black Lives Matter, Black students are taught by people who believe in their success. Educators are passionate about the content they teach and their role and responsibilities as educators. Moreover, when racial congruency exists, such educators act with the intention of breaking the cycle of marginalization for Black students by encouraging and supporting academic success. In an environment where Black Lives Matter, students feel they belong to a community—a collective body of individuals that will guide them toward accomplishing their goals by believing in and supporting them, respecting who they are as the teachers, and acknowledging and honoring their uniqueness. This is significant even if they resist or fall short, as emerging young adults often do.

Black Lives Matter when schools have a culture where expectations are high and excellence is the criteria for all students. When academic expectations are high, conveyed, and supported, Black students rise to meet the expectation and standards. They begin to develop a critical consciousness, allowing them to navigate and succeed within the dominant culture's power structures. Furthermore, the development of a critical consciousness for Blacks is accomplished when access and opportunity is made available to Black students; this entails a rigorous academic program that is culturally responsive, whereby students are able to visualize not only their success but are able to challenge the status quo.

How Is It Enacted?

When educators and scholars value the lives of Black children and their communities, their practices reflect a critical stance toward presumed competence, intellectual prowess, and academic and social success. The pedagogical practices of the educator are intentional, whereby Black children are engaged and empowered. Assessments aim to illuminate the literacy strengths of learners in authentic contexts for real purposes as opposed to searching out deficits and highlighting academic gaps. Black children's abilities are not measured based on assessment norms developed within predominantly white, middle-class, and monolingual populations.

Teachers engage antiracist and culturally relevant pedagogies aimed at preparing the next generation to disrupt inequities that marginalize certain communities. Teachers draw on critical literacy approaches that empower students to read the word and the world (Freire, 1993).

Who Creates It, Teaches It, and How Is It Taught?

When Black lives matter, there is a principled intention to ensure that a diverse teaching force is available to all students. In classrooms, Black teachers are in positions of intellectual authority as curriculum builders, teacher researchers, and lead teachers, challenging the miseducation that persists when young people see predominantly white teachers in the classroom. There is a national directive to recruit, train, and retain Black teachers in classrooms across the country. Teacher education and preparation programs center the racial histories and experiences of Black students as part of their development as teachers.

We have tested America time and time again to avow that its fullest potential rests in the inclusions of Blacks. Therefore, the battlefield begins with placement of highly qualified teachers in schools with the highest needs. This does not necessarily mean such teacher candidates have the highest GPA or have graduated from the highest-ranked educational programs. Instead, it means and requires the selection of teachers to be passionate, have the ability to see greatness in the Black students they may one day service, and not only understand and theorize that Black lives matter, but believe that Black lives matter and demonstrate that through their actions, deeds, and instructional practices. These actions are crucial to the well-being of the Black child, and by extension, the Black community. If we reimagined an education as if Black lives mattered, all children would benefit from a curricular and pedagogical infrastructure that values humanity.

References

Adams, C. (2008). What are your expectations? *Instructor, 117*(4), 26–30. Retrieved from https://files.eric.ed.gov/fulltext/EJ792955.pdf

Bishop, R. S. (1990). Mirrors, windows, and sliding glass doors. *Perspectives,* 6(3), ix–xi.

Conference on College Composition & Communication. (1974/2003). Students' right to their own language. *College Composition & Communication 25*(3).

Freire, P. (1970/1993). *Pedagogy of the oppressed.* New York: Continuum.

Hilliard, A. G., III. (2000). The state of African education. Paper presented at the annual meeting of the American Educational Research Association, New Orleans, LA. Retrieved from http://citeseerx.ist.psu.edu/viewdoc/download?doi=10.1.1.608.6157&rep=rep1&type=pdf

Kendi, I. X. (2017). *Stamped from the beginning: The definitive history of racist ideas in America* (Reprint ed.). New York: Nation Books.

Kucsera, J., & Orfield, G. (2014). *New York State's extreme school segregation: Inequality, inaction and a damaged future.* Retrieved fromhttps://civilrightsproject.ucla.edu/research/k-12-education/integration-and-diversity/ny-norflet-report-placeholder/Kucsera-New-York-Extreme-Segregation-2014.pdf

Milner, H. (2012). Beyond a test score: Explaining opportunity gaps in educational practice. *Journal of Black Studies*, *43*(6), 693–718. Retrieved from http://www.jstor.org.cupdx.idm.oclc.org/stable/23414665

Sizemore, B. A. (1987). The organization—A viable instrument for progress, developing effective instructional programs. Los Angeles: University of California, Center for the Study of Evaluation.

Getting Schooled

A Curriculum of Lying, Choking, and Dying

Walter S. Gershon

All groups and individuals educate their children and do so according to specific sets of sociocultural values that establish what is normal and acceptable. What is taught is political—a choice of one idea over another as well as the weight given each possibility. Education, then, is as much about what is taught as what is overlooked and about sociocultural understandings as much as academic content—political decisions, emphases, and normalization. The field of curriculum studies conceptualizes educational ways of being and knowing as forms of curricula—pathways and trajectories for the dissemination and reception of knowledges across all forms of delivery and contexts, including, but not limited to, schooling.

Continuing an unfortunate and long-standing trend in United States education, one of the central tenets we teach our children is a curriculum of lying, choking, and dying. While this may seem deeply pessimistic, overstated, or biased, as this chapter documents, such a characterization of US curriculum at the onset of this millennia is indeed metaphorically and literally the case. For example, how we teach pedagogy to future educators, and how teachers attend to their students, is through lesson plans with measurable goals and objectives. Seeming to ring the bell of common sense on its surface, these are tools intentionally created toward specific eugenics ends by Franklin Bobbitt, a man who is in many ways the father of US education and a proud, self-avowed eugenicist. Or, as but one other example, young people of color learn every day in our nation that they can be murdered, most often without recourse or justice, because of the amount of melanin in their skin. This metaphorical choking of educational possibilities and material killing of people of color are both forms of curriculum, educational ways of being, knowing, and doing.

Part of what makes this curriculum so pernicious is its interconnective tissue; tendons, and ligaments of violence that stretch between classrooms and communities. This is because, as universally normalized as this brutality is conceptualized and expressed, its direction is focused at children, youth, and adults of color. As much as it takes a village to raise children, it takes that same village at least an equal amount of time and effort to engender aggression as normal and brutal selective consequences as natural outcomes.

There are generations of work dedicated to illuminating the viscera of violence in education (e.g., Churchill, 2004; Cooper, 1892; Morris, 2016; Watkins, 2001). This chapter is but one condensed set of connections that operates at a given layer of scale, one of many possible perspectives and levels of analysis, to consider intersections of curriculum, race, and (in)justice. Specifically, this chapter attends to how curricular understandings indicate actions as they convey content and normalize violence as they slam into Brown and Black bodies. Here I present how a curriculum of lying in schools is linked to a curriculum of choking of self, both of which are inexorably interconnected to a curriculum of dying in the streets. This lying, choking, and dying is a crushing feedback loop that gains power as each iteration flips recursively back on itself, successive generations coming to understand and accept the normalcy of such violence and, in turn, reproduce the norms and values that allow its perpetuation.

Systemic and Formal Curriculum: Narrow Imaginations and Racist Roots

The word *curriculum* first meant a racetrack, an understanding that evolved from racecourse to course of study, solidified in Franklin Bobbitt's (1918) *The Curriculum*, in which he proposes that teaching should be a series of measurable goals and educational objectives. These curricular possibilities were solidified in Ralph Tyler's (1949) *Basic Principles of Curriculum and Instruction*. So pervasive is this understanding that, in spite of claims to the contrary, teachers still are taught to write lesson plans with measurable goals and teaching objectives (e.g., Wiggins & McTighe, 2005). In addition, new teachers' success is in no small part conceptualized by their ability to translate education to a goal of attaining measurable objectives, often according to percentages of students' who can correctly parrot their teachers' spoken and unspoken intentions (e.g., Jackson, 1968; Gershon, 2017a; McNeil, 1986; Taubman, 2009).

Further, in spite of thoughtful reimaginings of Tyler's rationale (e.g., Doll, 1993) and over 100 years of educational scholarship with myriad alternate pathways for conceptualizing how public education might function (e.g., Cooper, 1892; Dewey, 1938), we arrive time and again at measurable goals and objectives as the central tool for imagining curriculum delivery (e.g., Hunter, 2004; Wiggins & McTighe 2005). The use of curriculum delivery as opposed to teaching or pedagogy here is intentional. Rather than a method for teaching, the use of measurable goals and objectives is a means for delivering curriculum, an ends-means feedback loop where what a teacher plans as a lesson's content is measured by either students' ability to parrot that prescribed content or a behavior that can be observably documented as following those instructions. It is not about either how that information should be taught to students or meant to encourage students to inquire or wonder on their own.

For example, there is a great deal of literature in teacher education dedicated to questions of "classroom management," studies that attend to how to keep students focused on the tasks that teachers set forth. It is certainly the case that a degree of order is needed to educate (imagine a class of kindergarteners where the teacher says, "Okay, everybody color!" without guidance, processes for getting and returning supplies, etc.) and students are indeed in school to spend time on information that local experts (teachers) provide. However, the notion that anything a teacher does not intend, stated or implied, is somehow not of value or educational is at best limiting to educational experiences (for more, see Au, 2008; Freire, 2000; hooks, 1994; Taubman, 2009). Where, for example, are opportunities for students to have a deep impact on choices about what they might like to study? What of moments of genuine inquiry as opposed to known information questions (Mehan, 1979)? What happens to education when there are always singular correct answers (Gershon, 2017a)?

That there has been little actual change in how we conceptualize the role of teachers in the ways that are most often enacted in public schools, as opposed to the many different possible directions for school and schooling, is deeply concerning for a variety of reasons. Yet, for the purposes of this chapter, concerning as this might be, it is not the most troubling aspect of how we construct formal curriculum in the United States, the knowledge students are intended to learn in schools (for more on formal or official curriculum, see Apple, 2000; Gershon, 2010, 2017a; Kliebard, 2004; Schubert, 1986). Instead, the biggest concerns about formal curriculum in schools are an overattention to pedagogical processes and the racism of curricular eugenics baggage at the core of Bobbitt's beliefs.

Kliebard (1970) delivered what is perhaps the most cutting critique of Tyler's rationale, one that is equally applicable to Madeline Hunter's lesson plans and Wiggins and McTighe's backward design. Tyler's curriculum design is based on four central questions that Kliebard rather directly encapsulates as "the familiar four-step process by which a curriculum is developed: stating objectives, selecting 'experiences,' organizing 'experiences,' and evaluating" (p. 260). Objectives are created from "studies of learners, studies of contemporary life, and suggestions from subject matter specialists, as well as . . . how data from these 'sources' are to be 'filtered' through philosophical and psychological 'screens' " (p. 260). Kliebard carefully documents the errors in Tyler's claims about historical precedent for objectives and the stratification of public education into forms of tracking (pp. 261–262); the difficulties of arriving on objectives based on studies of the child (pp. 262–264); and the overwhelming prevalence of local and less local sociocultural norms and values in determining "the contemporary life source."

In sum, Klibard's critique of Tyler asserts that what Tyler calls, "an acceptable educational philosophy," and a curriculum designer's "philosophical screen," is, in the end, a person's particular set of biases, the sociocultural norms and values that render their understandings sensible (pp. 266–267). Objectives are no more than what the curriculum designer thinks is reasonable after checking with sources that primarily concern the designer's own understandings. These objectives are to be checked by students' own experiences, a possibility that is again largely circumvented by, in Tyler's words, "manipulation of the environment in such a way as to set up stimulating situations—situations that will evoke the kind of behavior desired' " (Tyler as cited in Kliebard, p. 268) about which, "The Pavlovian overtones of such a solution are not discussed" (Kliebard, p. 268). Evaluation is the degree to which students match answers to objectives. These Pavlovian overtones, creating learning situations with known information questions and narrow, often singular correct answers is precisely the prescribed ends-means feedback loop noted above. In the end, the criteria for curriculum design using measurable goals and objectives focuses on how to create lessons according to what a teacher finds to be normal and valuable, understandings that most often reflect dominant sociocultural norms and values.

As Wayne Au (2011) has noted, we are indeed in another Tylerian era of curriculum (see also, e.g., Gershon, 2017; McNeil, 2000; Taubman, 2009). What is often implied but not stated, these moments of standardized normalization—replete with emphasis on English as a language for curriculum delivery, rote memorization, and skills-focused literacies—is their correlation to national influxes of immigrants and accompanying waves of xenophobia. Removing the authors from citations, consider the following dates in chronological order: 1918, 1949, 1982, and 2005. These represent, respectively, the end of World War I, the end of World War II/beginning of the space race and McCarthy-era "Red Scare," the beginning of the Reagan administration (but not the Reagan era that is arguably extended by George H. W. Bush), and the middle of the George W. Bush administration, an election where immigration was (and remains) a deeply contested issue.

The point here is not that somehow there isn't an ongoing xenophobia or that ends-means education isn't ever truly what's expected in education. Rather, the assertion is that these tendencies are overwhelmingly in the fore during periods of an uptick in immigration, an increased negative awareness of those who are characterized as being less American, and of widespread changes in national demographics in ways that threaten dominant constructions of normalcy (as opposed to social change that presses back dominant norms and values). These changes are most often noted in terms of race.

Race is made up, a social construction, something most readers of this volume will already know and take as a matter of course in their understandings. Yet, despite overwhelming confirmation, in our contemporary moment where rhetoric again falsely claims scientific evidence (in insisting a degree of Indigeneity or religious affiliation can be definitively proved through DNA results, for example, as in the recent moves by Senator Elizabeth Warren [Green, 2018]), we have arrived at a moment of measurement that is eerily familiar in a 1918 fashion. As but one counterexample, there may be perhaps no clearer indication of the fallacy of race as it relates to actual scientific evidence than noting that Jewish people, with the same level of melanin as their Russian, Eastern European, and German neighbors, were considered to be another separate, inferior race. Not just different in terms of sociocultural norms and values or religious beliefs and practices, but different kinds of animals that are not-as-human, or even inhuman. That ghetto, a term for the areas of forced settlement for Jews, was again used for the forced settlement of people of African descent is neither surprising nor accidental. To be clear, this is expressly not a comparison of oppressions, an attempt to equivocate between histories, or any other move other than to note this point about the socioculturally constructed nature of race.

But just because race isn't a fact doesn't mean that it can't be "facted" (Varenne & McDermott, 1998), made and remade significant through its use. And it is also no accident that ongoing tensions between people of African descent and Jewish descent make stating the obvious about race in this way such tenuous ground. Race is a category of Otherness, applied for the purpose of marking another as other in ways that serve those in power and/or aid the maintenance of the status quo.

Just as this is the case outside of schools, so it is the case in schools. While talk about race is much more often expressed in studies of the social and cultural everyday life of schools (e.g., Morris, 2016; Rist, 1973; Tatum, 1997), it is far less frequently documented as part of the histories of how education was constructed over the course of the previous century (e.g., Watkins, 2001; Winfield, 2007; Woodson, 1933). It is here that Bobbitt's legacy runs deep. For Bobbitt was an unabashed eugenicist, of social efficiency in education, and one of our nation's founding educational founders. As Mark Carbajal notes, in *The Curriculum*, "Bobbitt emphasizes three core concepts that were indicative of a well-designed curriculum plan: Effectiveness, efficiency, and economy" (p. 3). Toward these ends, Bobbitt proposes a curriculum divided into tracks based on students' ability. It is the combination of these factors, eugenics, effectiveness, efficiency, and economy, which is particularly pernicious.

The point about Bobbitt's eugenics is often documented through his casual use of describing "lesser" children of "lesser" races as "marred in the original making, if he springs from worm-eaten stock" (Bobbitt, 1909, p. 385). It is a description that continues.

> if the foundation of his being is distorted and confused in heredity before his unfoldment begins, then the problem of healthy normal development is rendered insoluble before it is presented. Such a child is difficult to protect against adverse influences, and he remains to the end stupidly unresponsive to the delicate growth factors of education. (p. 385)

This excerpt is from only the second paragraph of Bobbitt's (1909) "Practical Eugenics" in *The Pedagogical Seminary*, a journal now known as *The Journal of Genetic Psychology: Research and Theory on Human Development*, a point to which I will return momentarily. It is also a terrible understanding of the world that conflates social class and cultural capital with genetic superiority and does so with claims of scientific evidence. Yet there is more—connections that are central to the argument here about the racist nature of our foundational educational understandings.

In a nutshell, Bobbitt believed that once superior races were not doing their part to maintain their physical and mental superiority with which he self-identifies (e.g., "Eugenics, the newly-arising science which seeks to improve the inborn qualities of our race," p. 386), while those of inferior stock were being given too much help in spite of their inherent inability to transcend such inherent deficits (e.g., "At the present time our medicine, hygiene, and public sanitation keep alive multitudes of weaklings that were formerly weeded out by hard conditions," p. 387). This understanding is complicated by Bobbitt's acknowledgment that a mingling of the races over time has created contexts where there are a few at the top who would ever remain weaker than they should and members of lower stock that could ascend, given the opportunity and training. Therefore, Bobbitt sought to further implement what he saw as a double move, further strengthening those at the top, including those who might be salvaged in lower races, while stemming the tide of increased family size of lower races and limiting their access to tools that would ultimately prove unfruitful against their imbecility.

And what were these tools that were given to inferior races?

> Our schools and our charities supply crutches to the weak in mind and in morals, nursing them and cherishing them in every possible way, helping them to economic independence, to family life, and thus further to corrupt the streams of heredity which all admit are at present sufficiently turbid. (Bobbitt, 1909, p. 387)

Schools, then, should be retooled to promote the culling of inferior minds and the promotion of those of "sound, sane stock" (p. 385), some of whom could be plucked from inferior conditions and most of whom would arise from upper-middle-class and, more likely, upper-class families.

When read from this perspective, Bobbitt's desire for efficient, effective schooling that positively impacts the general economy through a combination of measurable goals and objectives and differentiated education, is a societal weed-whacker. This is not hyperbole for a man who firmly believed that making a better society paralleled Luther Burbank's gardening techniques for breeding superior plants and eradicating weeds: "It is the weeds that get special protection. Let one imagine . . . if Luther Burbank cherished the weeds of his garden with a more tender solicitude than he bestows upon his fruitful plants" (p. 391).

Should this combination somehow be unclear, it bears repeating that Bobbitt is also the father of educational efficiency and effectiveness in the United States. For Bobbitt, this meant that inferior and superior races can and should be separated in factory-like ways that produce superior products without wasting important energy toward those who cannot be improved on. "Education is a shaping process as much as the manufacture of steel rails," claims Bobbitt, "Man must set up standards and arbitrarily control conditions even here in order that, with the aid of the growth process, he may secure the full possible product. In education it is the same" (Bobbitt, 1913, pp. 12–13). Teacher success, Bobbitt contends, can be measured by students' ability to meet standards that are differentiated according to their "native abilities" in ways that also convey what he believes to be appropriate stratification.

> For certain classes of students, bookkeepers and accountants for example, the standards need to be high; for other classes of workers, musicians, for example, or bricklayers, the standards set may well remain fairly low and their energies expended upon matters more important for them. (Bobbitt, 1913, p. 15)

It is also of no small point of importance that Bobbitt's (1913) formal call for educational efficiency cited here is *The Twelfth Yearbook of the National Society for the Study of Education: Part I The Supervision of City Schools.*

Efficiency from this perspective is a well-ordered factory-like practice for effectively separating the wheat from the chaff and giving each group its appropriate understandings. Such differentiation exists as much in "heavenly high schools" (Page, 1991) and majority Anglo spaces (e.g., Anyon, 1980), as they do in educational ecologies that reinforce notions of white academic and intellectual superiority in schooling (e.g., Kozol, 1992; Morris, 2016; Rist, 1973). Further, the scientific tools developed in this era that Bobbitt relies on are IQ tests (Simon-Binet) and set the stage for future standardized measurements very much like the ones we utilize today across the nation.

Although we no longer utilize Simon-Binet IQ tests, in spite of claims to the contrary, our current measurement systems nonetheless continues its history of curricular discrimination of another socially constructed, racially biased construct—intelligence. Students must have their intelligence measured in order to qualify for the many resources available in what is now called "special education," a category that remains disproportionately filled with students of color. The same holds true for the efficiency of our system for measuring students' and teachers' attainment on annual standardized measurements where children of color also continue to be overrepresented below national median scores. Teachers' success is similarly not only measured by Bobbitt's assertion that teachers be measured by their students' ability to meet standards the way a factory worker is responsible for producing a correct widget. Their success is also founded on an understanding that their central role as educators is predicated on effectiveness, most often exemplified by students' success, from lesson plans to textbooks to their evaluation by administrators.

In sum, though scholars tend to turn to Tyler (1949) as the architect of modern, contemporary education, it is Bobbitt and his vision of curriculum-driven schooling as a tool for the effective, efficiency delivery of eugenics that is our systemic legacy. From lesson plans to the ongoing resegregation of schools (Rosiek & Kinslow, 2015), from the suspension rates of Black and Brown preschoolers to the pushout of Black and Brown teen boys and girls that fuel school-to-prison pipelines (e.g., Laura, 2014; Morris, 2016), contemporary US education reflects its architect. Myriad additional complexities and concerns are indeed significant, documenting the depth and breadth of anti-Black and anti-Brown bias in US schooling systemically and as formal curriculum, the textbooks and assessments through which students flow.

The point here is not that there aren't other forces in public education in the United States, that public education is inherently a failed project, or that public education should be dismantled. A free and public education for all is essential to any nation or state project that might begin to claim a responsible citizenry, an informed economy, or knowledgeability for its own sake. Such a vision requires a deep reflexivity, one that can address the inherent hatred of its foundation that continues to be normalized today.

Formal curriculum, from the training of teachers to the scoring of students, is an intentionally racist project. Updated IQ tests, standardized assessments, lesson plans, and textbooks may in fact be new and improved. They also function as they should, to separate the haves and the have nots, educational winners and losers (McDermott & Aron, 1978) along clearly demarcated racial lines. In spite of ongoing calls to the contrary, the fix is in, gaps manufactured by false equivalencies and intentional racism—systemic, institutional, and interpersonal, from philosophy to textbook and from textbook to student.

Everyday Curriculum: Oppression and Violence in and out of Schools

In schools, students are taught if they work hard they will be rewarded, an understanding that reflects a formulaic societal rhetoric of meritocracy: hard work equals reward. Questions of gaining knowledge are also implicitly and explicitly tied to goodness in a moral sense—as Ann Gibson Winfield (2007) notes, the jeremiad is alive and well. It is also in schools that students are taught that it is primarily Anglos who do good works—an understanding that is reflected as much in the textbooks students receive as it is in school, district, and state scores on annual standardized assessments, so-called achievement tests.

Education is full of such measurement. Teachers attend not as much to students as to their observable behaviors and attainment of measurable objectives, markers that often help make school more about teachers' expectations and students' ability to parrot teachers' prescribed answers. Most teachers are Anglo, as are most teacher educators, and race and culture are inexorably intertwined. Leaving aside the raced nature of culture for this short essay, expectations about students' behavior and the degree to which they appropriately reach prescribed answers—for incorrect procedures can invalidate correct answers—are also racialized if not racist.

As presented in the previous section, formal curriculum and the structures of schooling are intentionally racist in the construction as well as their contemporary execution. Enacted curriculum, how understandings are negotiated between classroom and school actors (students, teachers, aids, administrators, etc.), is also racist. While such a claim might seem to be either hyperbole or an overreach, children of color are much more likely to have their ways of being (ontologies, how they exist) recast as cognitive deficits (epistemologies, what they know), and/or their everyday understandings are more likely to be undervalued while differences in those daily experiences from their Anglo, middle-class peers are inflated. When combined, this further compounds an appearance for Black and Brown students that differences are in fact deficits, experiences and understandings are not of value, and that the only ways one counts is as a negative (Dumas, 2014, 2016). Put bluntly, from a systemic and institutional perspective, Black and Brown children are much more likely to serve as the failures so that their Anglo peers can be counted as successful than the inverse (e.g., Gershon, 2017a; Kozol, 1998; Lipman, 2003; Varenne & McDermott, 1998; Wozolek, 2019).

The only way to get out of being measured is to pay for that omission, often another hurdle more deeply felt by communities of color, given the conflation of race and social class in the United States. Students at private schools, of the type that cost as much if not more than a year in college, are not required to take annual standardized assessments. Because time in a private school greatly increases one's chances in getting into college, public education often becomes as overpopulated with students of color as private schools become overpopulated with Anglo students when compared to a district's overall racial demographics. As described above, such racialized and racist schooling in the United States is also not news.

When assembled, it becomes expressly clear that children receive a curriculum of lying in school that strongly informs Anglo students' sense of privilege while reinforcing understandings of students of color as less than and deficient. What makes a curriculum of lying so malicious is that it helps to establish race as a natural-seeming deficit, an understanding internalized by students and reinforced by educators, statisticians, politicians, and pundits.

Then there is the curriculum of choking, strangling the ontological and epistemological life out of students of color in school (Wozolek, 2015, 2019) and in daily life for people of color of all ages (Mills, 1998). People of color learn they can't be themselves and be successful in many iterations of schooling, that asking questions will often be considered impertinence, and that to survive one must hold onto multiple versions of self in which one's true self is suppressed (e.g., Cooper, 1892; Du Bois, 1903). I've seen many young students of color corrected for saying "ax" instead of "ask," in spite of the fact that the context and meaning are clear and that African American Vernacular is an officially recognized form of English in the US. But in my 23 years of teaching I have yet to see an Anglo student be similarly corrected for saying "y'all."

If you are a young person of color, outside of school, it's okay for police to kill you, your siblings, your cousins, your mom, your dad, your uncle, your aunt, your grandmother, your grandfather because you are not white. Police are regularly relieved of responsibility for thinking in the moment by grand juries while you or your family are shot or murdered for thinking in the moment, from putting your hands up (Michael Brown) to running away unarmed (Walter Scott), to changing lanes (Sandra Bland) to saying you can't breathe (Eric Garner). You can be shot for toy versions of guns that white folks regularly wear in public to exercise their rights in open carry states like Ohio, whether you're a 12 year old playing in the street (Tamir Rice) or an adult hanging out in Walmart (John Crawford). White kids who dress like you are cool, but Dressing While Black can get you legally murdered (Trayvon Martin). Doing what the police tell you to do can get you shot (Levar Jones), riding in a police car can get you killed (Freddie Grey), and opening your door and Mothering While Black can get you (accidentally) murdered by police (Bettie Jones). Beyond a shadow of a doubt, this is a curriculum of dying. This understanding should be extended to Native and trans peoples, as Native women and trans people of color, for example, are being disappeared and murdered at exponential rates, understandings that permeate all aspects of society including, especially, the place young people spend most of their time: schools.

People are educated not only through their own experiences but by watching the experiences of others (Lave & Wenger, 1991), as well as within and across various communities (Wenger, 1999). When viewed as constellations of events, what may at first seem like disparate curricula become the warp and weft of an interwoven set of understandings connected through a combination of experiences, perspectives, ideas, and ideals. In short, they become a curriculum.

In this case, it is a racist curriculum of lying, choking, and dying. That it is directed at people of color does not mean that it is not learned by everyone and, through its constant repetition and reinforcement, it is what we are teaching our children. It is an implicit and explicit understanding that schooling in the US has always been, and may yet ever be, a Jim Crow space (Gershon, 2017b) designed by eugenicists (Winfield, 2007) that is running, not incidentally biased, but instead tends to run as planned. That the color of your skin is a strong determinant in your life choices and of an everyday curriculum that is a constant reminder that your future health and general well-being, that of your children, your grandchildren, and ancestors to the founding of our nation are inescapably impacted by violence and aggression, not the least of which are yet another state-approved poisoning of predominantly poor to working-class people of color (Governor Ron Snyder and administration/Flint, Michigan) and the ongoing, nation-wide, deeply disproportional incarceration of (young) African American men and Latinos fed in no small part by a continuing school-to-prison pipeline (Fasching-Varner, Martin, Mitchell, & Bennett-Haron, 2014).

Coda: Sounding Off

So, hell yes, Black Lives Matter. They Mississippi Goddam matter.[1] They Strange Fruit, Alabama matter. They Inner City Blues, Make Me Wanna Holler, Freddie's Dead matter. So if A Change Is Gonna Come, it's time to decide, Which Side Are You On?

Note

1. All the songs used here are fully referenced below.

References

Anyon, J. (1980). Social class and the hidden curriculum of work. *Journal of Education, 162*(1), 67–92.

Apple, M. W. (2000). *Official knowledge: Democratic education in a conservative age* (2nd ed.). New York: Routledge.

Au, W. (2008). *Unequal by design: High-stakes testing and the standardization of inequality.* New York: Routledge.

Au, W. (2011). Teaching under the Taylorism: High-stakes testing and the standardization of the 21st century curriculum. *Journal of Curriculum Studies, 43*(1), 24–45.

Bobbitt, J. F. (1909). Practical eugenics. *The Pedagogical Seminary, 16*(3), 385–394.

Bobbitt, F. (1913). *The twelfth yearbook of the National Society for the Study of Education: Part I The supervision of city schools.* Chicago, IL: University of Chicago Press.

Bobbitt, F. (1918). *The curriculum.* Boston, MA: Houghton Mifflin.

Carbajal, M. Curriculum theorists: Franklin Bobbitt. Retrieved from https://www.academia.edu/23673610/CURRICULUM_THEORISTS_FRANKLIN_BOBBITT

Churchill, W. (2004). *Kill the Indian, save the man: The genocidal impact of American Indian residency schools.* San Francisco, CA: City Lights.

Coltrane, J. (1963). Alabama. On *Live at Birdland* [Album]. Santa Monica, CA: Impluse!

Cooper, A. J. (1892). *A voice from the South (by a Black woman from the South).* Xenia, OH: Aldine.

Cooke, S. (1964). "A change is gonna come." On *A change is gonna come* [Album]. New York: RCA Victor.

Delpit, L. (2013). *"Multiplication is for white people": Raising expectations for other people's children.* New York: The New Press.

Dewey, J. (1938). *Experience and education.* Kappa Delta Pi.

Doll, W. E., Jr. (1993). *A postmodern perspective on curriculum.* New York: Teachers College Press.

Du Bois, W. E. B. (1903). *The souls of black folk.* Chicago: McClurg.

Dumas, M. J. (2014) "Losing an arm": Schooling as a site of Black suffering, *Race Ethnicity and Education, 17*(1), 1–29.

Dumas, M. J. (2016). Against the dark: AntiBlackness in education policy and discourse. *Theory into Practice, 55*(1), 11–19.

Fasching-Varner, K. J., Martin, L. L., Mitchell, R. W., & Bennett-Haron, K. P. (Eds.). (2014). Breaking the pipeline: Understanding, examining, and dismantling the school-to-prison pipeline [Special Issue]. *Equity & Excellence in Education, 47*(4).

Freire, P. (1970). *Pedagogy of the oppressed* (Myra Bergman Ramos, Trans.). New York: Herder & Herder.

Gaye, M., & Nyx, J. Jr. (1971). Inner city blues (Makes me wanna holler) [Recorded by Marvin Gaye]. On *What's going on?* [Album]. Detroit: Tamia Records.

Gershon, W. S. (2010). Official knowledge. In C. Kridel (Ed.), *The encyclopedia of curriculum studies* (pp. 618–619). Thousand Oaks, CA: Sage Press.

Gershon, W. S. (2017a). *Curriculum and students in classrooms: Everyday urban education in an era of standardization.* Lanham, MD: Lexington Books.

Gershon, W. S. (2017b). Schooling, neoliberal practices, and critical geographies: Contemporary US schooling as a Jim Crow space. In N. Ares, E. Benida, & R. J. Helfenbein (Eds.), *Deterritorializing/reterritorializing: Critical geographies of educational reform.* Rotterdam, the Netherlands: Sense Publishers.

Green, M. (October 16, 2018). Elizabeth Warren falls for Trump's trap—and promotes insidious ideas about race and DNA. *The New Yorker.* Retrieved fromhttps://www.newyorker.com/news/our-columnists/elizabeth-warren-falls-for-trumps-trap-and-promotes-insidious-ideas-about-race-and-dna

hooks, b. (1988/1994). *Teaching to transgress: Education as the practice of freedom.* New York: Routledge.

Hunter, M. (2004). *Madeline Hunter's mastery teaching: Increasing effectiveness in elementary and secondary schools.* Thousand Oakes, CA: Corwin Press. (Original work published 1982.)

Jackson, P. W. (1968). *Life in classrooms.* New York: Teachers College Press.

Kliebard, H. M. (1970). The Tyler rationale. *The School Review, 78*(2), 259–272.

Kliebard, H. M. (2004). *The struggle for the American curriculum* (3rd ed.). New York: Routledge.

Kozol, J. (1992). *Savage inequalities: Children in America's schools.* New York: Harper Perennial.

Laura, C. T. (2014). *Being bad: My baby brother and the school-to-prison pipeline.* New York: Teachers College Press.

Lave, J., & Wenger, E. (1991) *Situated learning. Legitimate peripheral participation.* Cambridge, UK: University of Cambridge Press.

Lipman, P. (2003). *High stakes education: Inequality, globalization, and urban school reform.* New York: Routledge.

Lipman, P. (2011). *The new political economy of urban education: Neoliberalism, race, and the right to the city.* New York: Routledge.

Mayfield, C. (1972). Freddie's dead (theme from *Super Fly*). On *Super Fly* [Album]. Chicago, IL: Curtdom Records.

McNeil, L. (1986). *Contradictions of control: School structure and school knowledge.* New York: Routledge.

McNeil, L. (2000). *Contradictions of school reform: Educational costs of standardized testing.* New York: Routledge.

McDermott, R., & Aron, J. (1978). Pirandello in the classroom: On the possibility of equal educational opportunity in American culture. In M. Reynolds (Ed.). *Futures of Education.* Reston, VA: Council on Exceptional Children.

Meeropol, A. (1939). Strange fruit [Recorded by Billie Holiday]. On *Strange Fruit* [Album]. New York: Vocalion.

Mehan, H. (1979). "What time is it Denise?": Asking known information questions in classroom discourse. *Theory into Practice, 18,* 285–294.

Mills, C. W. (1998). *Blackness visible: Essays on philosophy and race.* Ithaca, NY: Cornell University Press.

Morris, M. W. (2016). *Pushout: The criminalization of Black girls in schools.* New York: New Press.

Page, R. N. (1991). *Lower-track classrooms: A curricular and cultural perspective.* New York: Teachers College Press

Reece, F. (1941). Which side are you on? [Recorded by the Almanac Singers]. *On Talking union & other union songs* [Album]. New York: Keynote.

Rist, R. C. (1973). *The urban school: A factory of failure.* Cambridge, MA: MIT Press.

Tyler, R. W. (1949). *Basic principles of curriculum and instruction.* Chicago, IL: The University of Chicago Press.

Rosiek, J., & Kinslow, K. (2015). *Resegregation as curriculum: The meaning of the new racial segregation in U.S. Public schools.* New York: Routledge.

Schubert, W. H. (1986). *Curriculum: Perspective, paradigm, and possibility.* New York: Macmillan.

Simone, N. (1964). Mississippi Goddam. On *Nina Simone in concert* [Album]. New York: Philips Records.

Taubman, P. M. (2009). *Teaching by numbers: Deconstructing the discourse of standards and accountability in education.* New York: Routledge.

Tatum, B. D. (1997). *Why are all the Black kids sitting together in the cafeteria? And other conversations about race.* New York: Basic Books.

Varenne, H., & McDermott, R. (1998). *Successful failure: The schools America builds.* Boulder, CO: Westview Press.

Watkins, W. H. (2001). *The White architects of Black education: Ideology and power in America, 1865–1954.* New York: Teachers College Press.

Wenger, E. (1999) *Communities of practice: Learning, meaning and identity.* Cambridge, UK: Cambridge University Press.

Wiggins, G., & McTighe, J. (2005). *Understanding by design* (expanded 2nd ed.). Alexandria, VA: ASCD.

Winfield, A. G. (2007). Eugenics and education in America: *Institutionalized racism and the implications of history, ideology, and memory.* New York: Peter Lang.

Woodson, C. G. (1933). *Mis-education of the Negro.* Lindenhurst, NY: Tribeca Books.

Wozolek, B. (2015). *The presence of absence: The negotiation of space and place for students of color at a predominantly White suburban high school* (PhD diss.). Retrieved from Proquest. 1718128030

Wozolek, B. (2019). War of the half-breeds: Communities of color as a resistance response to raced and racist education in the Midwest. In W. S. Gershon (Ed.), *Sensuous curriculum: Politics and the senses in education* (pp. 67–84). Charlotte, NC: Information Age.

Notes from a City on Fire

The Mattering of Black Lives and the End of Retrenchment

David Omotoso Stovall

I write this note from a city that's *lit*. Young people use the term to describe an event that's lively or is in the process of becoming lively. I'm most familiar in hearing it from them in the phrase "The spot is lit!" Instead of the city being in a space that's lively for enjoyment, the city is *lit* due to the disgust, angst, and perpetual reminder that certain segments of the Black population have been deemed disposable in perpetuity. To their credit, many have not succumbed to their own frustrations, but continue to organize in the tradition of Black freedom fighters from the 17th, 18th, 19th, and 20th centuries in the US. Despite recent media attention dedicated to the concerns of Black people in the US, history reminds us that the current moment is nothing new. Instead, we should understand it as a moment of retrenchment to the Dred Scott decision of 1857, when the Supreme Court decided that Black people had no rights that whites were bound to respect.

I write this from Chicago, Illinois. A city deeply entrenched in corruption, benign and explicit neglect of Black bodies in the form of substandard housing, lack of healthy food options, limited opportunities for quality education and living wage employment. It is also a city steeped in Black resistance. Where the aforementioned issues and concerns are rife across the country in urban centers, the uniqueness of Chicago often lies in its unadulterated commitment to law enforcement, particularly the Chicago Police Department (CPD). At the time of publishing, the city of Chicago spends 40% of its budget on CPD (Aspholm 4, 2020). Before you begin to imagine where those resources could be redirected to, think of what a city looks like in certain communities that are often characterized as being "epicenters" for crime in the city. In many instances, these neighborhoods on the South and West sides of the city operate under the guise of a police state with deep surveillance, false arrests, and perpetual intimidation of residents.

It is also important to note that I am also completing this chapter under the wrath of three global pandemics: the novel coronavirus known as COVID-19, white supremacy, and capitalism. All three have allowed for the rest of the planet to realize what Black folks have been saying all along—*anti-Blackness is real and the normalized state sanctioned death of Black people in the United States is real.* In the current moment, the most publicized instances of malicious Black death at the hands of the police or former police come in the form of George Floyd, Breonna Taylor, and Ahmaud Arbery. Coupled with the disproportionate numbers of Black people to die from COVID-19, the precarious realities of Black life in the US are laid bare. As cities burn in rebellion across the US, it is a perpetual reminder that Black lives have never mattered to the larger power structure. Like many who have decided to rebel against a system that dehumanizes Black people in perpetuity, I am tired and often feel like I am drowning in restlessness and fatigue. Because this is nothing new, for many of us the rebellion is long overdue.

While camera footage of despicable behavior by police may be new to certain segments of the US populace, for many communities of color it is a perpetual reminder of the trauma of our daily lives. For many, it is understood as normal. This moment, like many moments before it, is a time where people have found their conditions to be intolerable and have decided to respond. Given the call of the editor of this volume, the remainder of this account is written in the spirit of solidarity and humility. Simultaneously, it is also the attempt to continue the tradition of pushing critical consciousness in education to envision and build spaces with young people and communities intended to interrupt and reframe commonly shared notions of deficit.

When an earlier iteration was part of a newsletter for Division B (Curriculum Studies) of the American Educational Research Association (AERA), I referred to myself as a "fellow traveler" of curriculum studies, mostly as an "outsider" from educational foundations. At the same time, I have paid close attention to curriculum studies scholars who continue to embrace a radical imaginary and have committed themselves to school/community engagement (e.g., Au 2018; Berry 2018; Matias 2016; Taliaferro-Braszile et al., 2016, to name a few). In making the attempt to continue such traditions, I offer the following meditations on Chicago, its connection to the Movement for Black Lives (Black Lives Matter), the current educational/political moment and the necessity of recognizing these moments of resistance as precious and necessary.

I am a lifelong Chicagoan. For the last 48 years of my life I have developed intimate knowledge of the hypersegregation, isolation, and marginalization of this urban space. The city in which I was born and raised has positioned itself as a "global city" centered in the expansion of the central business district and certain neighborhoods that provide immediate access to beach areas, rail transit, and a plethora of amenities. Tourists are able to enjoy museums, performance venues, and lakefront access with limited visibility of the undercurrent of the city. While some spaces are experiencing unprecedented "development" in the form of high-rise/high-rent apartments, bicycle trails, and hipster restaurants, others find themselves in neighborhoods suffering from abject abandonment. The vast majority of these areas are Black and poor. Race and class are coupled to demonstrate a moment where city officials have made it clear as to who are members of the "valued" population, while others experience what it means to be disposable. Since 2000, the city of Chicago has lost over 260,000 Black residents, accompanied with the closure of over 150 schools since 2004. The vast majority of these schools are in Black neighborhoods where many residents are experiencing some form of housing and/or food insecurity.

In addition to this reality, this happens in a city that is hypersegregated, due to years of housing discrimination in the form of redlining and restrictive covenants. This segregation leads to a series of conflicts as people in certain neighborhoods are displaced. As they are displaced to other communities they are put in proximity to people to whom they have no historical or familial connection. Because the neighborhoods that people are displaced to also lack resources (viable schools, infrastructure in the form of street repair and garbage pickup), tensions run high. Instead of "gang violence" an alternative assessment would include the idea that these conflicts are engineered due to a manufactured dearth of resources. If we couple school closings in this equation with the lack of affordable housing, and law enforcement that is employed to oversee the various conflicts, many of us bear witness to state-sanctioned violence in neighborhoods under the auspices of containment and disinvestment.

Unfortunately, the current recognition of police brutality in the city is one that many in neighborhoods across the South and West sides of the city have come to know as normal. This extends into school space through disinvestment in the form of public school closures and strategies of containment for working-class Black and Brown populations. When schools are removed from communities, it has depleted the area of a central resource. If this is coupled with depopulation, it becomes more difficult for those schools to remain open. Because schools are funded by way of a per-student allotment formula, attendance fuels whether or not the school will remain open.

Additionally, Chicago Public Schools (CPS) has created an application process around the idea of school choice that further depopulates schools. Known as "GoCPS," the application allows for families to rank twenty schools and apply to them (Chicago Public Schools, 2018). While this may be understood as allowing for families to "choose" the best educational options, a different story emerges. The GoCPS application also continues the depopulation of the schools that are consistently at the bottom of the list of 20 schools selected by parents. If a school is perpetually ranked in the bottom five of a family's selection, it will be impossible for the school to remain open. On the South and West sides of the city, this has led to devastating results. High schools with room for 2,000 students barely have 100 students. For all intents and purposes, this has ended the traditional neighborhood comprehensive high school.

Unfinished Business

In the classic mode of gentrification, public housing is destroyed while housing stock in proximity to the central business district (downtown) and transit is prioritized. Given the city's current national spotlight due to gun violence, an alternative take would reveal that we are in a situation where the "chickens have come home to roost." Since the late 1990s, Chicago has destroyed over 80% of its public housing stock. Many of those who remain continue to experience a rash of disinvestment strategies that all but guarantee those having the least getting even less in terms of city services and infrastructure support. In the spring of 2013, 49 schools were closed in one fell swoop. Almost 90% of these schools were over 90% Black and were located on the South and West sides of the city. Amounting to the largest single set of school closures in the history of the US, the city shares similar events with Philadelphia, New York City, and New Orleans in relation to the dispossession of residents with the least resistance to market forces and rationales of competition (commonly known as neoliberalism).

Beyond the process of being set up to fail, this should be considered an act of retrenchment to the Dred Scott decision. As a constant reminder of the afterlife of slavery and bondage (Hartman 1997), Black working-class residents of Chicago are perpetually reminded of their disposability, while the actions of government are rationalized as conscript with market trends and "responsible" lawmaking. If families don't have places to live or places to send their children to school, and are experiencing disproportionate persecution from law enforcement, we have returned to Woodson's (1933) assertion that young people are not only being lynched in classrooms, but also in their respective homes and neighborhoods.

The City as Site for Curriculum

The previous sections are not intended to instill a fit of depression. Instead, the idea is to provide an alternative view of what others consider to be "development." Given the fact that it is merely development for the few, it is also important to understand the city of Chicago as a site of curriculum. The concentric circles of housing, employment, education, food security, and health care allow students to engage their city through an interrogation of their realities. Often referred to as "studying up," a deep interrogation of the form and function of systems of power allow students to dig into the things that affect them while working with others to change the current condition.

Where the Movement for Black lives is wrongly reduced to solely operating as a protest movement/moment, the current situation in Chicago and throughout the globe challenges us to remain consistent in our work in-between public demands for justice. Barbara Ransby reminds us that this "Black-led mass struggle . . . contextualizes the oppression, exploitation, and liberation of Black poor and working-class people within the simple understanding, at least in the US context that "once all Black people are free, all people will be free" (Ransby, 2018, p. 3). As an inclusive movement that is not solely for Black liberation, but is led by Black people, I consider it an explicit reminder for educators to historicize contemporary contexts through a process that allows students to make connections between their world and the demands for justice that predate them. Most important is the ability of educators to make the connection between students and people in their communities that are working to change those conditions. If young people are able to identify, research, plan, implement, and evaluate their work on their own terms, it is reflective of a process that centers their experiences as critical in any push toward educational justice (Duncan-Andrade & Morrell, 2009). The following two sections are examples of local attempts to connect struggles across the city as young people and families continue the legacy of demanding their humanity. Both instances should be understood as sites of curriculum that allow for educators to engage thoughtfully and critically.

A Woodlawn Story

While the aforementioned dynamics continue to manifest themselves in certain communities, in other neighborhoods, the phases of gentrification are incomplete. As a personal example, I currently live in one of those communities in transition. Known as Woodlawn, the community is adjacent to the neighborhood of Hyde Park, home to the University of Chicago (U of C). Once a community of recently arrived European immigrants, the coupling of systemic racism by way of unfair housing practices with the second iteration of the Great Migration prompted massive white flight, leaving Woodlawn void of city services and infrastructure. Documented extensively in Moore and William's (2012) ethnography of the genesis of a large Chicago street organization (gang), the lack of education and employment infrastructure deeply influenced the growth and development of one of the largest African American street organizations in the city, the Black P Stone Rangers. Following the rise and fall of the Black P-Stones, numerous shifts take place in Woodlawn (i.e., deindustrialization, federal recessions, depletion of safety net and long-term living wage employment, etc.) resulting in depopulation and further disinvestment.

Directly in concert with Harvey's (2007) concept of "accumulation by dispossession," the story of Woodlawn grows deeper in complexity. As the area began to depopulate in the late 1980s and early 90s, housing stock was either demolished or abandoned. Soon after, because the eastern sector of the community is proximal to the lakefront, developers targeted vacant land for new housing development. During this time a small plot of land was brokered by a local church and community organization. A small pocket of affordable housing was built, but has been poorly maintained over the years. In addition to its proximity to the lakefront, the eastern portion of Woodlawn has direct access to public rail transit (providing swift travel to and from the downtown central business district). Despite the housing bubble and financial crisis of 2008, abandoned buildings are still being repurposed, transforming them into luxury condominiums and/or expensive single-family homes. Additionally, over the past five years, a public housing development (Grove Parc Place, which was formerly named Woodlawn Gardens) that used to sit at the entrance of the local train station has been razed. The development has been replaced by a set of mixed-income properties, which require low-income residents to "qualify" for acceptance. In the new development, only low-income renters are required to work at least 30 hours per week, cannot have a recent felony conviction, and cannot have a recent history of drug addiction. Where some may view this as "needed improvements" to the area, the narratives of race and class are intimate partners in the sordid story of the dispossession of long-term, working-class and low-income African Americans residents of Woodlawn. To provide viable food options for the new and/or qualified gentry, a new large chain grocery store was erected to serve Woodlawn.

Simultaneously, the University of Chicago has emerged as one of the primary beneficiaries of said accumulation. As much of this new "development" is marketed to faculty, staff, and students, the U of C shuttle bus currently makes stops throughout the southeastern corridor of Woodlawn. Continuing U of C's vision to expand its corridor beyond the southern boundary of 61st street, a squash center has been built on land where a section of Grove Parc Place once stood. As U of C is one of the primary landholders on the main corridor in east Woodlawn (63rd Street), much of the land is held in trust until a suitor of their choosing makes a bid on the vacant lot. Despite the transition, these not-so-subtle developments fuel displacement throughout the neighborhood. The process has slowed since the financial crisis of 2008, but is reaching levels witnessed before the crash.

To ensure continued interest in the community, a significant police presence is felt throughout Woodlawn's eastern corridor. Depending on the time of day, there can one to three parked police cruisers on my block.

Beginning in 2014, the Chicago Police Department began a practice of using the neighborhood as the training ground for first-year officers. This has been a trend across the city in select African American neighborhoods, as city officials feel pressure to address "high-crime" areas. At the current moment in the east Woodlawn, police sergeants hold meetings with the street teams of officers in the middle of the block as a demonstration of police presence for new residents. Police bike patrols ride throughout the neighborhood no less than six at a time. In the summer of 2014, the aforementioned first-year patrol officers could be found walking in groups of threes throughout Woodlawn alleys. In the summer of 2015, beat patrol officers walked the streets of Woodlawn, again in groups of three, to demonstrate to community members that the eastern corridor will be protected. Instead of a sense of safety, a reframing of the situation would consider this show of power as a sign of containment, alerting certain residents that they are now being watched and are no longer wanted in the community.

Deepening the concerns of long-term residents of Woodlawn is the building of the Barack Obama Presidential Center (OPC). While Mr. Obama has touted the center as a space that will support education, job development, and the training of civic leaders, he has also rejected the prospect of a community benefits agreement. In most cases a community benefits agreement (CBA) is developed by a community organization or a coalition of groups to ensure that the new development will not operate as the catalyst for future displacement of long-term residents in a neighborhood. If there is no CBA around a central development hub, the results often come in the form of either displacement for those forced to leave or isolation for those who are able to remain. In the case of the OPC, a coalition of groups who refer to themselves as the Obama community Benefits Agreement Coalition (of which the Black Youth Project 100—part of the Movement for Black Lives coalition, is a founding member) has made a set of concrete asks of Mr. Obama and his collection of developers. These demands include commitments to employment, economic development, education, housing, transportation, and sustainability (Obama Community Benefits Agreement Coalition, 2018).

Designed in the form of a city ordinance, the demands include a request that 5% of revenue generated for the center be used to develop a community trust fund to support neighborhood development initiatives. Another demand calls for the OPC to operate as a library with a full-time librarian and staff that is open every day that Chicago Public Schools are open with full access for neighborhood schools. It also requests that the high school across the street from the proposed center (Hyde Park HS) remain a neighborhood public high school without selective enrollment or other special designations that would prevent Woodlawn youth from attending. In concert with responsibility to the employment of Southside residents, the ordinance requests that "35% of the apprenticeships and 20% of journey workers, across all trades, hired by the contractors must come from the Southside and their demographics must reflect Southside communities" (Obama Community Benefits Agreement Coalition, 2018).

As testament to his work as a community organizer fighting against environmental racism on the Southside of the city, one would think these demands to be in concert with the stated goals of the presidential center. Instead, the Obama CBA Coalition has been met with staunch opposition from OPC staff and Mr. Obama himself. In the past, his rationale for rejecting a CBA centers around the idea that if the presidential center abides by one agreement, who's to say that others won't make the same ask. To some, this may appear to be rational in the sense of free market capitalism and expansion of the private sector (neoliberalism), but to others, Mr. Obama's interpretation of the CBA borders on the ridiculous. With a CBA in place, it would be extremely rare for another coalition to try to usurp the terms and conditions of the original CBA. More importantly, if another group attempted to secure another CBA, the Obama Presidential Center administration could politely refuse, stating that there is a CBA currently in place. The tensions that Mr. Obama speaks of do not exist. Instead, his neoliberal lean is to give credence to the private sector in his rejection of demands from entities that the private sector does not sanction. Nevertheless, tensions remain as some support the building of the presidential center without a CBA (city officials, local Woodlawn ministers, and real estate developers), while others hold steadfast to the necessity of a CBA.

Over the past five years, the eastern half of Woodlawn has experienced a spike in property taxes and a decrease in the population of school-aged youth. The local high school, Hyde Park High School, has space for over 2,000 students, but currently has an enrollment below 800. In a strange series of events, although Hyde Park High School was named in the ordinance originally refused by the Obama Presidential Center administration, the school has just received a $40 million grant for renovations (CBSChicago, 2018). Where the naked eye would view this as a windfall for the school, there is another question that should be entertained: *Given the gentrification that is currently hitting the neighborhood, are these innovations intended for the students that currently attend, or is it part of the larger plan to attract the children of the new gentry to attend the school?* To some, the question may appear paranoid, but if the current population of the school is declining, and there's a brand new brick-and-mortar school four blocks away from Hyde Park High School, there are a number of questions that emerge.

Returning to this instance as a site of curriculum, and given the current patterns of gentrification in the city (schools change when neighborhoods change), it is imperative that these inquiries be entertained. If they are not, then communities are guaranteed more of the same with further marginalization and isolation. Given the current moment, the push to raise public consciousness on the intersection of education, housing, and law enforcement remains high (Ewing, 2015). Simultaneously, it should also be noted that movements do not reflect a perfect world where all who come to the table agree with each other's decisions. Nevertheless, it becomes critical to acknowledge the struggle and the role of young people in reinvigorating a public consciousness on the realities of Black life in Chicago and the US writ large. As the fight for a responsible presidential center continues, I remain thankful for the collective of community organizations that are remaining steadfast in the fight for responsible and sustainable community development. They serve as the perpetual reminder that the fight is not done and they are willing to do the necessary work.

A Contested Case with an Unexpected Result

Predating the current recognition of rampant police violence, there was an event that mobilized Chicagoans to rebel against the disposability of Black people. On October 20, 2014, 17-year-old Laquan McDonald was executed by Chicago police officer Jason Van Dyke. The shooting was captured on the dashboard camera of a Chicago Police Department vehicle. Sixteen shots were fired into his body, despite the fact that he was walking away from the officers on the scene. Laquan was killed one month before the mayoral election of 2014. Understanding that he would be in a highly contested election (which resulted in a runoff), the tape wasn't released until the week of November 23, 2015. Recognizing the cover-up and the despicable practices of the mayor, former police chief Gary McCarthy, and Cook County's state attorney Anita Alvarez, young people and community members took to the streets, preventing shoppers on Michigan Ave (the highest revenue-producing commercial district in the city) to proceed with their "Black Friday" activities. While the protest resulted in McCarthy's ouster, many of the organizers and protesters knew that McCarthy was the sacrificial lamb. Coalition members of the Movement for Black Lives Black Youth Project 100 (BYP100) and Black Lives Matter Chicago (BLM Chicago) were at the forefront of the actions, calling for the resignation of McCarthy, Emanuel, and Alvarez.

Given McCarthy's dismissal in 2016, the events since have culminated in one of the strangest turns in the history of Chicago politics. Although Alvarez declared that she would not resign, she was handily defeated in the March 2016 election. Due to the organizing of members of the Movement for Black Lives coalition, their political education sessions were organized around the idea of understanding the role of the state attorney. From their work it was publicly disseminated that the state attorney's office is riddled with contradictions, one being the fact that the office has the dual responsibilities of prosecution and antirecidivism. In layman's terms, what this amounts to is the fact that the same person who's responsible for locking you up is also responsible for keeping you out of jail. Given the contradictions, the public campaign to get rid of Alvarez has also influenced a newfound interest in city governance.

But the story gets stranger. On the heels of the Van Dyke trial, Mayor Rahm Emanuel announced that he would not run for a third term. While this sent shockwaves throughout the city, it also places some important issues into context. Where I do not know Rahm Emanuel or members of his staff, I can say with some certainty that there were a few things that he was forced to consider in his decision to not run for reelection. Because the Van Dyke trial was one of the most contested in the history of the city of Chicago, Emanuel was clear that if the trial resulted in a not-guilty verdict for Van Dyke, the city could go up in flames. Again, this is not my paranoia, but a reality that rebellion would be imminent in one of the most brutal displays of anti-Black state-sanctioned violence in recent memory. In fact, to corroborate this, the measures taken by the city and other institutions within the city boundaries provide a sign that the city prepared for the worst. Local universities delivered emails to students, staff, and faculty, suggesting early dismissals. Chicago Public Schools ended classes in local schools two hours early. Every active officer in the Chicago Police Department was activated to duties on two shifts (12:00 a.m. to 7:00 p.m. and 7:00 p.m. to 12:00 a.m.). Busloads of police officers were spotted on the South and West sides of the city, running drills in case of an uprising. Many of us in Chicago were prepared for the third burning of the city (the Great Chicago Fire of 1871, and the uprisings in 1968 after Dr. Martin Luther King's assassination being the first and second). It is an understatement to describe the times as intense.

Given the intensity of the moment, there is also an eerie calm. It is not a peaceful moment. Instead, it is preparation for the storm. For myself, things slow down and I go into a deep sense of analysis and contemplation. Instead of ruminations about various scenarios, my mind goes into what needs to be done to prepare oneself for an onslaught of police containment and violence. The police maneuvers of checkpoints, barricades, SWAT team deployments, riot gear with automatic weapons, and razor-wire boundaries do not bring a sense of safety, but instead remind me that at any given moment a community can be transfixed into these realities. Unfortunately I have witnessed some iteration of all of them. The moment does not bring nervousness, but a push to prepare my mind and body to prepare to survive the encounter. Writing this as someone who's almost 50 years old still puts my mind and body through multiple states of trauma.

In this preparation I have to put the Van Dyke trial into context. Jason Van Dyke is a white male police officer. Laquan McDonald is a Black teen who has been in and out of the foster care system and mostly attended alternative schools. His autopsy found the drug PCP in his system. He had a knife in his hand when he was shot. Seven whites, three Latinx persons, one Asian-American, and one Black woman were selected as jurors for the trail (Patterson, 2018)—one Black woman in a city that is 31% Black. Again, the odds are terrible. The two weeks of the trial had the city on edge. I prepared my mind to see what my parents witnessed 50 years earlier: a city on fire.

October 5, 2018 was a strange day. My phone was buzzing with text messages that the jury's decision would be announced at 1:45 p.m. Central Standard Time. All of the preparation announcements were buzzing over mainstream media platforms, email listservs, and social media. Some watched television to hear the announcement live. I was in another state wondering if I would be able to travel back to Chicago due to the uprising. The verdict was in: Jason Van Dyke was convicted of second-degree murder. I couldn't even gasp for breath. My mind was still in mode to prepare for the ensuing uprising. Stunned and shocked are words that are too limited to describe what was happening to me. Never in the history of the city of Chicago has a white police officer been convicted for the murder of a Black person. It was a curious time for this first. I tried to put myself in the place of the jurors and figured that they realized if Jason Van Dyke walked out of that courtroom without a conviction, the city would go up in flames. At the same time, there was a caveat. Despite the second-degree murder conviction, he was not convicted of police misconduct. This is a curious decision, but one that the Fraternal Order of Police will probably use to protect his pension. More importantly, as a site of curriculum, the court ruled that Jason Van Dyke was within his duties and responsibilities as a police officer. It was only the continued shooting that was deemed excessive. Again, you are demonstrating proper discretion if you shoot Black people. Just don't shoot *too much.*

In the end, it is still hard for me to think that justice has been served. The Van Dyke trial was not a public indictment of the system of policing. Instead, his murder conviction is still rationalized as the bad acts of one individual. Critical analysis would inform us that the historical actions of police in the indiscriminate killing of Black and other oppressed peoples have not been brought into question. The Movement for Black Lives reminds us that if we do not ask questions of the system and work to disrupt the things that oppress us, we will continue to be victimized by them. The conviction of Jason Van Dyke saved a city from burning, but what will happen when we are imminently faced with this moment again? I do not trust the Van Dyke decision will be used as precedent for the next case of police misconduct.

Curriculum Fugitivity and the Will to Fight

When Opal Tometi, Patrisse Cullors, and Alicia Garza created the #BlackLivesMatter in response to the unwarranted execution of Trayvon Martin, they delivered a challenge to all who make claim to doing justice-centered work. In their challenge they made us revisit the intersections of race, class, gender expression, age, and ability in our work. They challenged us to think about the ways in which transgender people are wrongly persecuted, maligned, and silenced in the ongoing struggle to claim our humanity while working to change our conditions. For the future of critical analysis in curriculum studies, their challenge presents a critical juncture for those working with communities of color toward justice. In an age of hypertesting and market-based rationales that are used to justify the privatization of school districts through charter management organizations, the work moving forward must be centered in the idea that the claim to Black life is a claim to the humanity of all. As a beacon of solidarity, the current situation in Chicago is but a mirror image to many locales throughout the US and the globe. Such truths need to be reflected in curriculum, educational institutions, and our collective psyches. A failure to do so guarantees us more of the same. Keeanga-Yamahtta Taylor is correct in her analysis that

> The gravity of the crisis confronting Black communities, often stemming from these harmful encounters with the police, legitimizes the need for a more encompassing analysis. It allows people to generalize from police violence to the ways that public funding for police comes at the expense of other public institutions, and creates the space to then ask why. (Taylor, 2016, 168)

Our work has been set. It has been and continues to be led fugitively by Black women and members of other oppressed groups. The moment has become a movement to continue to pay attention to beyond celebrity and hits on social media. Our decision to resist the conditions that contain and marginalize us will come in-between and underneath conventional spaces. Let it be known that we are *still* tired. We are *still* sick of the unrelenting thirst the state exudes for Black death. After the fires subside we will *still* be part of loose and well-defined formations that work to claim our humanity and build a world where we are not perpetually in the crosshairs of the state. It is not linear nor will be connected to an explicit white, Western-European, male, cisgendered, heterosexual, Protestant Christian, able-bodied ethic. It is something different. It *must* to be if we expect to get anywhere closer to the things that make us free.

References

Aspholm, R. (2020). *Views from the streets: The transformation of gangs and violence on Chicago's south side.* New York: Columbia.

Au, W. (2018). *A Marxist education: Learning to change the world.* Chicago, IL: Haymarket.

Berry, T. R. (2018). *States of grace: Counterstories of a Black woman in the academy.* New York: Peter Lang.

CBS Chicago. (2018, September 11). *Hyde Park Academy to get $40 in renovations.* Retrieved from https://chicago.cbslocal.com/2018/09/11/hyde-park-academy-renovations/

Chicago Public Schools. (2018). *About GoCPS.* Retrieved from https://go.cps.edu/

Duncan-Andrade, J. M. R., & Morrell, E. (2009). *The art of critical pedagogy: Possibilities for moving from theory to practice in urban schools.* New York: Peter Lang.

Ewing, E. (2015). "We shall not be moved": A hunger strike, education, and housing in Chicago. *New Yorker.* http://www.newyorker.com/news/news-desk/we-shall-not-be-moved-a-hunger-strike-education-and-housing-in-chicago

Hartman, S. (1997). *Scenes of subjection: Terror, slavery, and self-making in nineteenth century America.* New York: Oxford University Press.

Matias, C. (2016). Feeling white: Whiteness, emotionality, and education. Rotterdam, the Netherlands: Sense.

Moore, N., & Williams, L. *The almighty Black P Stone nation: The rise, fall and resurgence of an American gang.* Chicago, IL: Chicago Review Press.

Obama Community Benefits Agreement Coalition. (2018). *Community benefits agreement (CBA) for the Obama library: Development Principles.* Retrieved fromhttp://www.obamacba.org/principles.html

Patterson, B. E. (2018, September 14). *Chicago Is 31 percent Black, but there's only one Black juror at this Chicago cop's murder trial: What gives?* Retrieved from https://www.motherjones.com/crime-justice/2018/09/chicago-jason-van-dyke-jury-selection-murder-trial-2/

Ransby, B. (2018). *Making all Black lives matter: Reimagining freedom in the 21st century.* Oakland, CA: University of California.

Samudzi, Z., & Anderson, W. *As Black as resistance: Finding the conditions for liberation.* Chico, CA: AK Press.

Taliaferro-Baszile, D., K. T. Edwards, N. A. Guillory, & V. Agusto (2016). Race, gender and curriculum theorizing: Working in womanish ways. New York: Lexington Books.

Taylor, K. Y. (2017). (Ed.). *How we get free: Black Feminism and the Combahee River collective.* Chicago, IL: Haymarket.

Taylor, K. Y. (2016). *From Black Lives Matter to Black liberation.* Chicago, IL: Haymarket.

Watson, D., Hagopian, J., & Au, W. (Eds.). (2018). *Teaching for Black lives.* Milwaukee, WI: Rethinking Schools.

Woodson, C. G. (1933). *The miseducation of the Negro.* Trenton, NJ: Africa World.

Letter to Rev. Dr. Pauli

Reagan P. Mitchell

The Black diaspora is a chocolatized spectrum that functions as a ridiculer. By "ridiculer," I am acknowledging how collectives of organisms and matter act as the satirists and humorists within and between communities. For example, when Zora Neale Hurston (1937/1990) refers to "the rose as breathing out smell" (p. 10), she describes a moment in which Janie's consciousness is expanded via the rose ridiculing her senses, and Hurston is arguing that the act of ridiculing goes beyond Janie's sense of smell. The rose's ridicule is also a proverbial nudging of Janie to get in touch with and be present in the world in which she exists. This chapter similarly thinks about the chocolate spectrum, like the rose, as a space of ridicule, calling to those within and outside of the spectrum to get in touch with the Black diaspora. Additionally, I am referring to the "chocolate spectrum" to signify the multiple ways of being in, between, and across Black communities that is inclusive of the many sexual orientations, gender identities and expressions, abilities, languages, and the like of being Black. My defining the chocolate spectrum in this light is my attempt to further understand the Black diaspora as a nonstatic, dynamic entity. At the core of the Black diaspora is a force of ridicule that works across time to enliven consciousness and/or to posit reminders of possibilities to be erotically funky in time and dreaming. Altogether, Black diasporic ridicule assumes many subjectivities ranging from, though not limited to, pornographic to musical expressions. The funkiness is through the formulations of Black diasporic ridicule constantly in motion denormalizing, dethroning, and discombobulating actors and specters of white supremacy while creating radical spaces of expression (Stallings, 2015).

These images are exemplified through Georgia Anne Muldrow's musical composition "Great Blacks" (2015). This composition is about communing with ancestors whose experiences were lived within and against the Black diaspora. Specifically, Muldrow states, "I'ma be fine, divinely designed. My heart do the beating, but the blood ain't mine" as a recognition that Black lives are always already connected through the blood, experiences, and ontologies of the Black diaspora. As a queer Black scholar and musician whose ways of being, knowing, and doing are entangled with the diaspora, Muldrow's work provokes the question: How far might I lay back or sit on the varieties of Black diasporic foundational beats, between, through, and/or with in order to gain differing realms of consciousness? Although there are several inroads to the act of ancestral communing across spaces and places (e.g., Audre Lorde, Zora Neale Hurston, Sun Ra, or Octavia Butler, to name a few), in this paper I will be thinking specifically with and about the work of the activist legal scholar, and Black feminist Pauli Murray.[1]

To think with Murray, I will be working within the spirit of Michelle Wright's (2015) concept of epiphenomenal time. Similar to the way that physicists like Einstein conceptualized time, Wright uses epiphenomenal time as a way to discuss the "now," through which the past, present, and future are always interpreted" (p. 4). For Wright, the current moment is not "directly borne out of another. . . . it does not preclude any and all causality: only a direct, or linear causality" (p. 4). This is important because, as Wright argues, a linear approach to understanding the Black diaspora can silence and leave out voices, perspectives, and experiences. Instead, Wright's rhizomatic approach, what I will discuss in terms of the *multilogical,* is an attempt to acknowledge the many resonances (Gershon, 2017) that speak to and through my body, Black communities, and Black ways of mattering (Love, 2019). While I have teased apart notions of the ancestral, presentness, and futurity in this text, I am not suggesting that that my engagement with these times is in any way monological or linear. Rather, my engagement is multilogical, existing with an idea and ideal of rhizomatic, epiphenomenal time. My emphasis in describing the ancestral, present, and future as multilogical is intended to acknowledge their omnidirectional presences in discursive rumination. These omnidirectional presences exist in nonlinear trajectories, emphasizing possibilities of simultaneity. Therefore, the Enlightenment narrative of linear time is problematic because it: (a) Only acknowledges select voices; (b) silences possibilities in realizing the presence of simultaneity and polyphony; and (c) freezes the pathways of interaction/intra-action in anthropocentric and overall monolithic mediums (Barard, 1998). In the context of this discussion the body/bodies I am considering are those situated in the Black diaspora that are both human and nonhuman (Barard, 2007). This means both the body of those who are enslaved, and the metaphorical body found within the act of enslavement. Both are significant as both the person and the act are entangled across sociopolitical and cultural histories, places, and times. Furthermore, I wish to consider how we might act as both witnesses (Hartman, 1997; Moten, 2003) and engage in speaking to the voices within this multilogical engagement with the Black diaspora.

It is also important to note that this discussion is partly hinged on a prior response (Mitchell, 2019) I gave to Ligia (Licho) López López's (2018) book *The Making of Indigeneity: Curriculum History and the Limits of Diversity*. Specifically, I am attending to López López's argument that "The future, as a category of thinking, is up to what emerges in the playful act of ridicule" (López López, 2018, p. 104). Here López López is critiquing multicultural curriculums. Her critique attends to the failure of multicultural curriculums due to what is generally shallow, oversimplistic, and neoliberal values. Thus, scholars like Christine Sleeter (1996) and Kristin Buras (2014) remain in chorus with López López's work in that focuses on the decentralization of constituencies and neoliberalism are central culprits in the ethical decimation of multicultural curriculums. For radical Black diasporic US educational movements, this nullification of ethics was expressed in the deemphasis of coalition politics rooted in the understandings to aiding the constituency (Howard, 2011; Pérez, 1997).

Similar to López López's work, in his *Afro-Surreal Manifesto*, D. Scot Miller (2012) states that "Afro-surrealists create sensuous gods to hunt down beautiful collapsed icons" (p. 16). Miller, in resonance with Black diasporic media histories, is engaging and meditating with Black speculative fictions. His singular aforementioned statement, as well as the collective manifesto, is an articulation of the nonstagnancy of the Black diaspora because it acknowledges the magic and mysticism that are central to the diaspora and Black experience. The "beautiful icons" is an acknowledgment of the presence and multitudes of deities constantly at work providing magical possibilities for Black diasporic consciousness building in this present moment. In his comparison of Afro-futurism to Afro-surrealism, while sharing many commonalities, an essential difference is the emphasis of

Afro-futurism's focus on the future. However, Afro-surrealism has its feet in the past, present, and future, with gelatinous hierarchies of ever transposing present relationships—meaning that while time is still applicable, the ever-developing dispute is, simply, over *whose* time. Thus, when attempts are made to impose a rigid Enlightenment time template to the chocolate spectrum/the Black diaspora, Afro-surrealism permeates, envelopes, and destroys that template. Yet, the ethos of Enlightenment time is always in a state of becoming, sustaining linear trajectories situating chocolatized queer, feminist, gender fluid/nonconforming, dis/abled, impoverished folx senses of time as deficient.

My interest in the combination of López López writing "The future, as a category of thinking, is up to what emerges in the playful act of ridicule" (p. 121) and Miller's argument that the "Afro-surrealist create[s] sensuous gods to hunt down beautiful collapsed icons" (p. 16) is in consideration of how the Black diaspora, situated as the chocolate spectrum, acts as a sort of ridiculer.

Before I discuss Pauli Murray, I will situate Black feminist praxis. I continue with Michelle Wright's text *The Physics of Blackness* (2015). From this work, I attend specifically to her discussion on epiphenomenal time to think about how Enlightenment constructions of time are problematic yet essential to understanding how some narratives become privileged, while others are negated. In the case of the discourse I am engaging, time is important to considering institutional epistemic violence. I then return the idea of rigid time and the epistemic violence created for Pauli Murray. In continuing this discussion, I situate Murray as an Afro-surrealist and ridiculer who is aligned with the scholarship of Licho Lopéz Lopéz and D. Scot Miller. Lopéz Lopéz's necessity of ridicule along with Miller's resistance of Afro-surrealism's "quiet servitude" provide a backdrop to consider Murray as both an ancestral entity while simultaneously situating he/r as a figure who was "touched by ancestral entities" (Miller, 2012, p. 11). The penultimate section is an abridged annotated timeline of Murray's life. Afterward, I conclude with a letter to the ancestor, Pauli Murray.

Black Feminist Praxis

> It stirred her tremendously. How? What? Why? This singing she heard that had nothing to do with her ears. The rose of the world was breathing out smell. It followed her through all

> her waking moments and caressed her in her sleep. It connected itself with other vaguely felt matters that had struck her outside observation and buried themselves in her flesh. Now they emerged and quested about her consciousness. (Hurston, 1937/1990, p. 10)

> The existence of a self-defined Black woman's standpoint using Black feminist epistemology call into question the content of what currently passes as truth and simultaneous challenges the process of arriving at the truth. (Hill-Collins, 1990/2009, p. 290)

In the first quote, Zora Neale Hurston (1937/1990), in her novel *Their Eyes Were Watching God*, situates the protagonist, Janie's, consciousness. Hurston brilliantly, inverts and plays on humanoid-dominated control through the rose metaphor. The rose, as Hurston notes, is not a docile vegetation. Through Hurston's touch, it is transformed from a passive, carbon dioxide recipient in service to humans, to an agent providing collective consciousness, denoted through its breathing out. Perhaps the human, Janie in this instance, is in service to the rose. However, the rose is not literal. Rather, the rose provides a tangible context to pose the inquiry composed of "How? What? Why?" It is the "How? What? Why?" that serves a similar function of a map's compass rose to aid in orienting one to the directional specifics. Thus, the rose in this case serves to collapse metaphoric regions between human and vegetation, self and outside world. This bares semblance to intra-actions occurring between spectrums of organisms that complicate entangled agential constructs (Barard, 2007).

Distillation of Hurston's statement through the following Hill-Collins's work presents another avenue where one can dream, inquire, and allow oneself to get *muthaphukin'* weird. In situating Hurston and Hill-Collins alongside each other, while visually vertical, the engagement is quite rhizomatic (Deleuze & Guattari, 1992/2003; Ibrahim, 2014). Here I am shifting away from the tendency of imposing notions of how or when Black feminist praxis start or end. Rather, utilizing Huston and Hill-Collins as mediums of discursive sustenance considers ancestral Black feminist diasporic ruminations. Furthermore, this acknowledgment seeks to pose a broader reminder about the cultural understandings of ancestry. Altogether, for Black communities locally, nationally, and globally, ancestry is not something abstract or untouchable. Rather, ancestry, in Black diasporic contexts, is an engagement with the prophetic (Lorde, 1984; West, 1993;

Mitchell, 2018)—prophetic, in the sense of how ideas, philosophies, and ideologies are spoken into existence through memory and embodiment. The prophetic also extends into the region of doing, whereby mere reflection is not enough. The prophetic in the Black diaspora is about reflexivity, whereby the process of reflection creates a change in one's consciousness that inspires a call to action.

Therefore, both Hurston's and Hill-Collins's statements articulate a Black diasporic/Black feminist praxis in that they frame reflexivity, expressing an expansion of consciousness and progress toward action. For Hurston, this is present in the way that Janie navigates and reimagines her agency through the fluidity of her intimate relationships. In this fictive account Huston simultaneously highlights misogyny and abuse that is all too common in intimate spaces. Additionally, Hurston Afro diasporically situates Janie as a beacon of governance. Janie's governance is indicated in her decolonial resistance of the state to determine the status of how she conducts her intimate relationships. Specifically, the institution of marriage is not the sole reason to remain tied to another. Therefore, Janie understands her marriage as subpar due to the contaminants of misogyny, emotional, and physical abuse, which overrule state control. For the Black diaspora, this harkens back to matriarchal governance, as documented in multiple dynasties in Africa, the Vodun priestess in the Caribbean, the intellectual rigor and vigor in US of individuals such as Anna Julia Cooper, and lastly, who this chapter is dedicated to, Pauli Murray.

In Hill-Collins in *Black Feminist Thought* (1990/2000), acknowledgment of the Black diasporic/Black feminist praxis comes in as genealogical chronicling of how and why Black feminist praxis has been forced to exist collectively as a set of marginal knowledges. At the core of Hill-Collins's scholarship it is a praxis of doing. These processes take a variety of formations. Broadly, this praxis considers how theory begets practice and how the practice begets theory. Altogether, praxis is the discursive relations that present the navigational apparatuses in exploring/unearthing the responsibilities one incurs to the event.

In processing the contextual meanings of praxis, it is Patricia Hill-Collins who poses the inquiry "What is it going to take for Black people to be free?" (Hill-Collins, 2020). Hill-Collins's public recitation of this inquiry highlights a gap in which the praxial engagement is necessary. Thus, her statement simultaneously acknowledges the problem (e.g., Black oppression resulting from white supremacy) while also calling those in witnesses to get dirty in the materiality of doingness (e.g., considering the marginalized communities that must get free in the process of Black liberation). A formulation of the "doingness" is situated in Black feminism. This sentiment is exemplified in Fannie Lou Hamer's statement, "I'm sick and tired of being sick and tired" (Hamer, in Brooks & Houck, 2013, pp. 57–64). While Hill-Collins poses an inquiry regarding Black liberation, Hamer's statement describes the culmination of tensions incurred through emotional, spiritual, and physical trauma she and collective Black communities have endured on US soil. Hamer is simultaneously witnessing while stirring communal consciousness. Hill-Collins and Hamer enact consciousness awakening to incite those touched by the vibrancy of their respective inquiries and declarations as a means to materialize their awakenings toward doing radical Black liberation. Collectively, Hill-Collins's and Hamer's exemplification of the doingness in Black feminism can be heard as a conceptual drone, calling for move to action. All-in-all, abstracted, nongrounded theorization is never enough when considering the plight of Black liberation.

To further root these understandings of Black feminist praxis in present times it is also essential to consider the function of radical coalition politics historically, presently, and futuristically as read in the always is, in the ethos of Wright. Alicia Garza, cofounder of Black Lives Matter and founder of the Black Futures Lab, is essential to consider—with particular attention to the movement building and futurity work she and her conglomerates have done with the Black Futures Lab.[2] This stood out as a watershed moment in which the task assumed was to engage the complexities of need through equity building work for Black communities, the premise being to consider meanings of effective policy creation, promoting, and sustaining equity to better serve Black US communities. The depth and research in the reports produced by the Black Futures Lab was both nuanced and in depth. This project is composed of coalitions with numerous organizations throughout the US to survey approximately 31,000 Black people. However, the power of the project has been in the engagement with radical intersectional politics/resistance in order to tease out the meanings of equity in realms of the state in respect to Black LGBTQIA+ communities. With the realization of metanarratives of Black equity of movements as being trapped in conceptual spaces of cis-heteropatriarchy, the work of Alicia Garza and the collective Black Futures Lab is, in the collective spirit of Lopéz Lopéz's and Miller's work, a utilization of ridicule and resurrection of collapsed Gods (or rather godx) to attend to the nation-state's supported negligence of equity in futurity-building projects for Black communities. However, I would pose the reminder that in regard to Black diasporic movements, this project is a radical reimaginative one (Kelley, 2002)—radically reimaginative in that it is situated in a continuum of praxis grounded in deep coalition politics, which perhaps has been the most profound and influential aspect of Black feminist praxis. Similarly, Garza and the Black Futures Lab parallels to Pauli Murray's navigation of public spheres with coalition politics as the central ethos.

Wright, on Time

> Our constructs of Blackness are largely historical and more specifically based on a notion of spacetime that is commonly fitted into a linear progress narrative while our phenomenological manifestations of Blackness is what I term Epiphenomenal time, if the "now," through which the past, present, and future are always interpreted. (Wright, 2015, p. 4, emphasis in original)

Michelle Wright (2015) reminds us that the Black diasporic narrative suffers from a toxic linearity and rigidity. Wright, in this statement and throughout her text, *The Physics of Blackness* (2015), critiques rigid spacetime narrative constructions. She proposes the epiphenomenal engagement with time as a way for engaging varieties of inquiries as well as getting open to the nonacknowledged gaps in Black Diasporic narratives. The acknowledgment of these gaps in which voices shifted from, as Christina Sharpe (2016) would frame it, the "wake"?

In referencing the collective of Wright's epiphenomenality and Sharpe's wake, I need to take a step back to process the dynamics of event versus tension in regard to historic narrative constructions. A defining of event and tension are necessary. Event is something occurring in a particular and interval of time, whereas, a tensions are the manifestations of the resonance that caused the event to occur. While events occur and pass, the resonance is always in play, assuring that another event variation will happen again. Take for instance, the aforementioned discussion of Black feminist praxis. Cis-heteropatriarchal metanarratives situate Black women's intellectual geographies as nonexistent and/or absent of intellectual rigor and depth. Yet when US history is explored, it becomes clear that at every point there have always been constituencies of Black women and the spectrum of queer folx at the helm raising hell. Whether it is Harriet Tubman, Ida B. Wells, Audre Lorde, Alicia Garza (and so many others) or, in this case, Pauli Murray, there is no question of Black feminisim's role in the introduction of moral, ethical, and political discourses in US consciousness. So, the issue is about the tensions that keep these essential points of US historical discourse continually submerged, some of them being: racism, sexism, homophobia/antitransism, and classism. In our contemporary context, the expression of oppression looks different (in some cases) than when Harriet Tubman, for example, lived. The event would be the physical condition Tubman lived through. However, the tensions are the ideologies of racism, sexism, and classism, which produced the conditions of the event, and persist well after the event has ended. Therefore, it is the culmination of these and other tensions that are presently in play which constrict Black feminist praxis from being acknowledged institutionally and in the collective narrative of US history.

Yet when the event materializes and shifts out of plain sight, this act is situated by some as "passing." However, if the event passes, that is no indication that the tensions have dissipated. This dynamic of the event versus the tension is exemplified in a multitude of ways; however, one example in the context of this discussion is historical narrative, that is, how social foundations in historical narrative tropes shape, route, and create stagnancy in the depiction.

One way to root the discussion of time and Black feminist praxis is in relation to the how physical and conceptual institutions function. Wright (2015) reminds us that narratives, post-Enlightenment, and Western expansion are scaffolded with rigid verticality. I utilize the term *rigid verticality* to describe how the linear pathways of historical narratives are often presented. A problematic result of rigid verticality in narrative depictions is the inability to conceive points of simultaneity. Therefore, if historical events are depicted solely as occurring neatly one behind the other as isolated occurrences, the messiness and blood generated by tensions from an event are suppressed. Considering how intellectual geographies on US soil suffer (or benefit, depending on the hegemony of one's subjectivities) from a linear narrative construction that does not allow a complexity on voices and thought. For example, the legacy of eugenicist ideologies that remain present in standardized testing, the subsequent racist ideas of intellectual ability rooted in questions of race, and, as a result, the development of zero-tolerance policies that disproportionately harm Black youth in American schools (Stovall, 2017; Meiners, 2015; Winfield, 2007). With awareness of these eugenicist legacies, it is essential to consider the infrastructures that operate/embody vertical narrative ethics.

One instance to consider is how higher education values some narratives, incorporating them as a part of the broad institutional memory, while others are relegated to the margins. It is the verticality of institutional memory that parallels the linear structuring of narratives. Inquiry into how rigid vertical narrative structuring functions reveals how hegemony allows a metanarrative to form and then to ring supreme as objective truth when collective broader narratives, perhaps subnarratives in comparison, appear as though they never happened. An example of these instances within and across institutions can be seen when considering the rate at which racial profiling occurs on campuses and in classrooms. Furthermore, if one were to situate these occurrences in tandem with the sprinklings of diversity workshops, situated in many cases as a checkbox as opposed to being a long-term institutional commitment, then the verticality of the "spacetime" according to Wright allows for the metanarrative for institutional aphasia (Stoler, 2011).

Broadly, in institutional contexts, it is the rhizomatic inquiry spacetime considerations that reveal and acknowledge constant becoming, messiness, web creation, and emergent overlaps metanarratives attempt to silence. Thus, to frame institutional progression as either a horizontal or a vertical project, as opposed to rhizomatic, limits the imaginative ranges of events, and tensions reverberate in sustaining oppressive ideologies (Gershon, 2011). Although a full analysis of rhizomatic versus vertical understandings would require much more room than this part of my discourse might allow, it is important to consider how this rhizomatic inquiry might unpack consistent the expungement of Black women/Women of color's experiences from institutional narrative.

In the following section I lean into Afro-surrealism's entrenchment in the mystical in relation to Murray. Ralph Ellison's Afro-surrealist scene of the battle grand royal in *Invisible Man* (1952) aids our understanding of Murray's ethics. While the depiction presented of he/r is of ultimate ethical badassery, I would also add that this was rooted in he/r sense of Black diasporic mysticism given to h/er through familial bonds. To refer of someone as an ancestor acknowledges a transition of physical to spiritual entity; Murray the Afro-surrealist, demonstrates this ancestral indebtedness.

Afro-surrealism, the Imagination, and Murray

> Afro-surrealism rejects the quiet servitude that characterizes existing roles for African Americans, Latinos, women, and queer folk. Only through the mixing, melding, and cross-conversion of these supposed classifications can there be hope for liberation. Afro-Surrealism is intersexed, Afro-Asiatic, Afro-Cuban, mystic, silly, and profound. (Miller, 2012, p. 11)

> The discovery that Ransom and other men I deeply admired because of the dedication to civil rights, men who themselves had suffered racial indignities, could countenance exclusion of women from their professional association aroused an incipient feminism in me long before I knew the meaning of "feminism." (Murray, 2018/1987, p. 238)

Black speculative fictions, in all its genre bleeds, redirectives, materialities, and queerings, bring possibilities of how to dream alternative realities. As presented earlier with Alicia Garza and the Black Futures Lab, the primary power in those fictions is realized through dreaming. An Afro-futuristic sense of dreaming opens up the negated vortexes and portals in time pertaining in regard to equity for the spectrum of marginalized Black communities. Yet, considering the spectrums of Black speculative fictions, Afro-surrealism is engaged in dynamics of Black distribution as well as the ancientness of the shape-shifting. Additionally, it deals with realms of incompleteness in the translatability and untranslatability to rigid time constructs.

An example in which this is witnessed is in Ralph Ellison's *Invisible Man* (1952). Specifically, the scene of the battle grand royal, whereby the nameless protagonist and other Black males are invited to take part in staged fistfight before a white audience. This scene presents the protagonist coming to this gathering to give a speech before rich white patrons, only realize the reality that these whites have to be elected to force the protagonists, and the other Black gentleman, in a spectacle of buffoonery. This scene concludes with the protagonist and the other gentlemen fighting each other for the money flung into the air for the skewed desires of fetish, so prevalent in the white patrons.

What I love about this scene, as well as the broader novel, is how Ellison formulates an entire discourse chronicling the dystopic moral bankruptedness of society, which can be interpreted in a number of ways. The interpretation of these points around Ellison's framings of moral bankruptedness functions as two inquiries for me. First, it begs the question: Could the battle grand royal be a commentary on white male attempts to shield their desires, fandoms, and/or lust for Black bodies through situating Black males in extreme subordination? Second, it asks: Could this scene be Ellison's depiction of the transgressions of white oppression in Black communities, which translates to the materiality of white psyches as composed of a belief that excuses the violent actions toward Black communities without awareness of their incompleteness and underdevelopment in the frame of acknowledgment of overall humanity?

In the aforementioned example, Ellison is the ridiculer through creation of a fictional dismal circumstance elevating the accepted violent products of racism. He elevates the discourse so that the reader can call attention to personal points of unconsciousness in their psyches regarding the ways they are actors in the suppression of communal equity. Ellison as the ridiculer functions as someone who through spectrums of humor is able to cause their audience to go into points of visceral existence.

Thus, riffing on Lopéz Lopéz's assertion of futurity and the playful actions of ridicule, it is Afro-surrealism via chocolate spectral resonances that ridicules the psyche, hopefully toward a reengagement with sensitivity and intimacy, especially those that simultaneously evoke point of pleasure and pain. Additionally, Miller asserts that the Afro-surrealist is a queer and queered entity that is not wrought with "quiet servitude." Altogether, Lopéz Lopéz's and Miller's ideas describe the how the ethos Pauli Murray's ethics existed in he/r life—specifically, Murray as a consummate ridiculer and Afro-surrealist. It is in Murray's commitment of service to ancestral ruminations, as documented in he/r autobiography in addition to the biography, *Proud Shoes: The Story of an American Family* (1956), where s/he chronicles lives that made he/r whole. In this sense, as Miller would emphasize, Murray's love and respect for her familial narrative is an act of "hunt[ing] down beautiful collapsed icons" (Miller, 2012, p. 16)—the icons being the radical Black females resisting "quiet servitude" (Miller, 2012, p. 12). For Murray, these figures (godx, goddesses, gods, etc.) are not dead, but rather entities charged with magic and mysticism rooting the systems of how s/he thinks and h/er overall equity. As Patricia Hill-Collins posed in her inquiry, "What is it going to take for Black people to be free?" and her analysis of the intersectional project as the requirement is for a number of other marginalized communities to gain liberation in the process of Black people becoming free. It is Murray the Queer Chocolotized ridiculer and Afro-surrealist providing analytical nuance to equity projects.

Situating Pauli Murray

> Mrs. Roosevelt, but officially we seem to lack the imagination and the courage to take the hard road but the straight road. Some of us cannot compromise with the "race supremacy" any longer, for to do that would be to give up the last shed of integrity we have left. We must speak out, appealingly, caustically, bitterly, as long as we are able, that Americans may not forget for one moment this race problem is a war issue, and that fundamental approaches must be made to eliminate it, now, not after the war. (Murray, in Bell-Scott, 2015, p. 103)

This section is intended to highlight a few of the many events that root Murray's consciousness. However, I find it necessary to contextualize my letter and dialogue about Murray with a few details about her life. Aspects of Murray's timeline present a long-term engagement with equity projects. The following chronicling and annotation of Murray's life, intellectually/spiritually/academically, that I present is abridged, and I would suggest going to the Duke Human Rights Center Pauli Murray Project at the Franklin Humanities Resource[3] online archive for additional information.

Murray was born in Baltimore, Maryland, in 1910. However, it was not long until s/he was sent to live with her family in Durham, North Carolina, in 1914. S/he was the child of Agnes Fitzgerald and William Murray. Pauli Murray's shift of residence came in response to he/r mother, Agnes's, death that was the result of a cerebral hemorrhage. This circumstance left Murray's father, William, with the task of single-handedly caring for six children, an impossible task for him. As a result, Murray was sent to Durham, North Carolina, to be in the care of h/er aunt, Pauline Fitzgerald Dame. In 1928 Murray entered Hunter University in New York City. S/he eventually completed her Bachelor of Arts degree in 1933, after leaving in 1930 and reenrolling in 1931.

With Franklin Delano Roosevelt's Works Progress Administration (WPA) and New Deal policy, he established the Civilian Conservation Camps (CCC) in 1933, to attend to the growing rates of unemployment in the United States. However, the CCCs only attended to unmarried men.

It was Eleanor Roosevelt and Hilda Worthington Smith who encouraged President Roosevelt to provide a presidential order to establish similar camps for women. In 1933, Murray joined Camp Tera, one of the WPA camps established for women located in Lake Tiorati, New York, where s/he met, begun, and sustained a lifelong friendship with Eleanor Roosevelt. In 1941 Murray applied to Harvard University Law School, however, s/he is turned away because of he/r gender. S/he ended up enrolling in the University of California at Berkeley Boalt Hall School of Law, where s/he graduated in 1945 with a master's degree in law. In 1951, Murray published *States Rights on Race and Color*, an especially essential legal text utilized by Thurgood Marshall's development in *Brown v. Board of Education.*

The following year, Murray was denied a professorship at Cornell University because letters of support came from Eleanor Roosevelt, Thurgood Marshall, and A. Phillip Randolph; 1951 was approximately one year after Senator Joseph McCarthy started his tirade of fear in response to communism in the US. Considering Murray's marked status as a political agitator and being in the queer spectrum, s/he was a particular target for McCarthy's fear discourses. Additionally, it is the outwardness of Murray's resistance and h/er recommenders, who were largely viewed a political rebels, which discouraged Murray's application. In 1961, s/he was appointed to the President's Council on the Status of Woman (PCSW) by President John F. Kennedy.

Approximately three years later, in 1964, the Civil Rights Act is passed; in 1965 s/he coauthors "Jane Crow and the Law: Sex Discrimination and Title VII." This article is particularly important, in that Murray and Eastwood presented a critique of the Civil Rights Act and overall legislation that neglected to deal with gender inequity in discussion of racial disparagement. It is in this article that Murray's intersectional political analysis is witnessed in the call for a more expansive analysis of gender at the root of the discourse in the process of creating freedom. This is very similar in Murray's remarks to Eleanor and Franklin, in the context of war efforts. Specifically, the connection that the abolishment of racist practices on US soil must simultaneously be central to the war efforts in relation to World War II. The year 1965 was also fruitful for Murray, in that s/he became the first Black person to receive a JSD from Yale University, after numerous attempts just to gain admission. In 1966 s/he becomes a founding member of the National Organization on Women, which includes such notable individuals as Betty Friedan. From 1968 to 1973, Murray served as a professor of law at Brandeis University. Murray became the first Black fe/male priest in the Protestant Episcopal Church, a role held until h/er death in 1985 from pancreatic cancer.

Resistance was at the core of Pauli Murray's ethos. In this correspondence with Eleanor Roosevelt, Murray's sharpness of pen is present. S/he sharply reprimands both Eleanor and Franklin Roosevelt for their lack of attention to racial disparagement during World War II in 1942. In the statement's conclusion, Murray states, "this race problem is a war issue, and that fundamental approaches must be made to eliminate it, now, not after the war." This simultaneous and call for racial equity as rooted in multiple freedom projects, like those presented by Hill-Collins, is echoed in Murray and Eastwood's legal brief critiquing the 1964 Civil Rights Act. Murray's realizations of radical intersectional and coalition politics are witnessed (1965). Specifically, in 1942, s/he discussed how the war effort was best served with attention to what is going on in one's house, that is, racist acts deployed toward communities that are predominately composed of Black residents and people of color more generally across the US, whereas in 1964 she situates radical racial equity occurring with considerations of gender equity. For Murray, the realization as the project of equity building was being rooted in several world building projects not exclusively situated in one exclusive marginalized community. I find this to be perhaps one of the essential points Murray's ethos on equity. However, I would also pose the reminder that this approach was not developed in a vacuum. Rather, this approach is rooted in Murray's familial consciousness.

This brief chronicling and historic situating of Murray can be read a number of ways. A few to take notice of include he/r commitment to speaking truth, regardless of who is in the set of power, as indicated in her stanch critique of Eleanor and Franklin Roosevelt's complacency in pushing for racial equity. Additionally, he/r refusal to accept partial policies is presented in he/r critique of the 1964 Civil Rights Act. Altogether, Murray displays a moral, political, and bureaucratic savvy to realize that the project of liberation via policy requires a commitment for which the subordinate groups should be advocated. Thus, the challenge to some presented via he/r political navigation brought with it a requirement that gender disparagement be understood as an issue of racial inequity.

The concluding section of this discussion is a letter to Pauli Murray. It is important to commune with ancestors, and in this letter I ask for advice in addition to sharing how I came to meeting her through text. The letter is composed from a series of ancestral multilogical ethos. As presented earlier, I denote the discourse as multilogical in respect to conceptualization of epiphenomenal time and Afro-surrealism. The collective consideration in both discussions embodies epiphenomenal time and Afro-surrealism's ancestral to futuristic in the present.

It's important that I write, meditate, and/or pray to my ancestors. An ancestor is not a historicized entity, rather an ancestor exists as an entity present in an alternative form. I do not feel the physical presence of my ancestors in a physical form; however, sometimes I sense a spiritual presence that requires me, at times, to readjust and/or lessen the fetish with the physical in order to hear/feel an ancestor's presence (Dillard 2012). Pauli Murray presented he/rself in my life in 2015. S/he is that ancestor who I am currently trying to hear/feel more. My realization of Pauli Murray as an ancestor also is in recognition of the diasporic, queer, and geographic kinship networks we share.

Murray is a mystic. Murray is magic, and it is partly through he/r chocolatized ridicule of my consciousness that I am increasingly uncomfortable with the continued rationalized reformulations of Black lynching, nationally and worldwide. S/he has blessed me and many others with the knowledge to analyze how the nuances of how inequity functions. However, I also realize that the uncomforting is not exclusive to me, nor is it incorrect. Rather, the touch of Murray's mysticism is a series of Black diasporic ancestral ruminations reigning down on my consciousness and that of many others. Murray is a medium in the Black diasporic continuum who in her earthly existence leaned into her calling to develop equity. As a community, in the broadest sense, some have taken on Murray's charge (as well numerous other chocolatized ancestral ridiculers) to fight for equitable circumstances for Black communities. However, this journey always needs more instigators and co-conspirators. May the chocolatized ridiculers continue to create unrest in our consciousness. My unrest toward motivation of doing is sustained through writing/thinking/praying to you, Ancestor Pauli.

Letter to an Ancestor

Hello Ancestor Pauli,

I am writing to you in the advent continued state-supported and -sanctioning of violence toward the bodies in the chocolate queer spectrum that encapsulates all sexual orientations, gender expressions, and economic situatedness. I have felt hopeless at times. However, let me assure you that I really fight, and have fought, an epic battle to let hopelessness know that while it has won a few fights, that hopelessness has long lost the battle due to how the ancestors, elders, and overall community supports and loves us. With the body of work and the overall vulnerability in which you lived your life, I have to ask, how did you compete with feelings of hopelessness when all, you and I alike, desired was adequate infrastructural support, love, and respect of your right and our community to live without fear of harm to yourself and our loved ones?

I align with you in *Blacksouthernqueerhood*. While, your birthplace was Baltimore, Maryland, I learned at three years old that you were sent to live with your family in Durham, North Carolina. I was born and raised in Nashville, Tennessee, so that makes us next-door-state neighbors along the Mason-Dixon Line.

I count myself as one blessed by your being, thinking, and doing (Gershon 2017). However, for approximately 36 years prior, I did not understand how much I benefited from the rich ethical discourses you raised and committed yourself to throughout your life. What was it like to publicly critique the Civil Rights Act of 1964 and remind the male locus that women's rights are civil rights (Murray & Eastwood 1965)? It was Carmon and Knizhnik's (2015) book, *Notorious RBG: The Life and Times of Ruth Bader Ginsburg*, a gift from my partner. I mention this book because it was the first time I learned about you and how influential your and Eastwood's scholarship was to late Supreme Court Justice Ruth Bader Ginsburg's consciousness. If you have not had time to check it out, I will give you a very brief synopsis.

The book's title is a play on the alternate names of Brooklyn-based hip-hop artist, Christopher Wallace aka Biggie Smalls aka the Notorious B.I.G. Collectively, Carmon and Knizhnik's juxtaposition of the word "Notorious" with extension to Supreme Court Justice Ruth Bader Ginsburg calls attention to the degrees of radicalism both individuals operated and/or currently operate in their lives. Radicalism was exemplified simultaneously in Wallace's ascendance to one the world's most influential poetic voices and Ginsburg's existence as the most outspoken living Supreme Court justice in the face of violently antispectrum of chocolate/queerness/women/*etc.* policies.

Pauli, your name emerges in Carmon and Knizhnik's book in regard to Ginsburg's chronicling of the readings she assigned her students prior to her appointment to as a Supreme Court justice, while a law professor at Rutgers University from 1963 to 1972 and Columbia University from 1972 to 1980. One article Ginsburg utilizes is "Jane Crow and the Law: Sex Discrimination and Title VII," critiquing the Civil Rights Act of 1964. While your brilliance is lauded by Justice Ruth Bader Ginsberg, another overlap occurs with Patricia Bell-Scott's book *The Firebrand and the First Lady* (2016). I along with others are collectively reminded through your resistant actions that all roads to social justice legalities in the United States lead directly to you. As I write these words to you, I also think of your revolutionary book *States' Rights on Race and Color* (1951), which served as the legal rebar for late Justice Thurgood Marshall's, pre–Supreme Court appointment counterappeal to overturn "separate but equal" as unconstitutional. However, I am not sure if you have witnessed how this mandate has been continually avoided. Have you and Ancestor Bell (Derrick Bell) had a chance to mash it up about this yet (Bell, 1995)?

While I connect most with you as part of the Blacksouthernqueerhood contingency born in the United States, I apologize if it seems as if in my letter I am limiting your message to that of identity exclusively. It is Drury (2011) who writes, "The problem is that when we put historical figures like Murray to work for us as narrowly representative, we inevitably drop out aspects of her life that are complicating and often inconvenient" (p. 142). Again, my connection with you via queer Black identity is not to simplify you or your message. However, we, historically and presently, as queer bodies in the chocolate spectrum, nationally and worldwide, have been in struggle with violent heteronormativity, racism, and poverty. Historically and presently violent heteronormativity has been given extended mobilization through the modalities of pseudoscience, the religious right, and social Darwinist ideals. As a result, I and many others in the queer chocolate spectrum are fatigued in response to these ideologies, which have been and are translating to violent lynchings rooted in heteronormative violence, depression, impoverishment, self-harm (Wozolek, Varndell, & Speer 2015). As you might have observed, the current political landscape of the US is even more fragmented than when you were with us in physical form. Your presence and wisdom is welcomed now more than ever.

Your nibling in the Black diaspora,
Reagan P. Mitchell

Notes

1. https://blackfutureslab.org/
2. https://paulimurrayproject.org/
3. https://humanrights.fhi.duke.edu/pauli-murray-project/

References

Barard, K. (1998). Agential realism: Feminist interventions in understanding scientific practices. In Mario Biagioli (Ed.), *The Science Studies Reader*. New York: Routledge Press,

Barard, K. (2007). *Meeting the universe halfway: Quantum physics and the entanglement of matter and meaning.* Durham, NC: Duke University Press.

Bell, D. (1995). *Brown v. Board of Education* and the interest convergence dilemma. In Kimberlé Crenshaw, Neil Gotonda, Gary Peller, & Kendall Thomas (Eds.), *Critical Race Theory: The Key Writings That Formed the Movement* (pp. 20–29). New York: The New Press.

Bell-Scott, P. (2016). *The firebrand and the first lady: Portrait of friendship: Pauli Murray, Eleanor Roosevelt, and the struggle for social justice.* New York: Harper Collins.

Brooks, M., & Houck, D. (2011). *The speeches of Fannie Low Hamer: To tell it like it is.* Jackson: University of Mississippi Press.

Buras, K. (2014). *Charter Schools, Race, and Urban Education.* New York: Routledge.

Carmon, I., & Shana K. (2015). *Notorious RGB: The life and times of Ruth Bader Ginsburg.* New York: Vintage.

Deleuze, G., & Guattari, F. (1992/2003). *A thousand plateaus: Capitalism and schizophrenia.* London: Continuum.

Dillard, C. (2012). *Learning to remember the things we've learned to forget.* New York: Peter Lang.

Drury, D. (2013). Boy-girl, imp, priest: Pauli Murray and the limits of identity. *Journal of Feminist Studies in Religion, (29)*1, 142 147.

Ellison, R. (1952). *Invisible man.* New York: Penguin Random House.

Gershon, W. (2017). *Sound curriculum: Sonic studies in educational theory, method, & practice.* New York: Routledge.

Gershon, W. (2011). Introduction: Towards a sensual curriculum. *Journal of Curriculum Theorizing, 27*, 66–81.

Hartman, S. (1997). *Scenes of subjection: Terror, slavery, and self making in the 19th century.* Oxford, UK: Oxford University Press.

Hill-Collins, P. (2020, April). *Critical conversations: Intersectionality and sociology-Patricia Hill-Collins.* Cambridge, UK. Retrieved fromhttps://www.youtube.com/watch?v=Qnr9VK_o-3k

Hill-Collins, P. (1990/2000). *Black feminist thought: Knowledge, consciousness, and the politics of empowerment.* New York: Routledge.

Howard, A. (2011). Bernice Johnson Reagon and the necessity of coalition work. *Journal of Curriculum Theorizing, 27*(1), 1–6.

Hurston, Z. (1937/1990). *Their eyes were watching God.* New York: Harper & Row.

Ibrahim, A. (2014). *The rhizome of Blackness: A critical ethnography of hip-hop culture, language, identity, and the politics of becoming.* New York: Peter Lang.

Kelley, R. (2002). *Freedom dreams: The Black radical imagination.* Boston, MA: Beacon Press.

López López, L. (2018). *The making of indigeneity: Curriculum history and the limits of diversity.* New York: Routledge.

Lorde, A. (1984). *Sister outsider: Essays and speeches by Audre Lorde.* Berkeley, CA: Crossing Press.

Love, B. (2019). *We want to do more than survive: Abolitionist teaching and the pursuit of educational freedom.* Boston, MA: Beacon Press.

Meiners, R. (2015). *For the children? Protection innocence in the carceral state.* Minneapolis, Minneapolis: University of Minnesota Press.

Miller, D. (2012). *Afrosurreal manifesto: Black is the new black.* Chicago, IL: Epicenter.

Mitchell, R. (2019). The chocolate spectrum as ridiculer. *Journal of the American Association for the Advancement of Curriculum Studies, 13*(2), 1–3.

Mitchell, R. (2018). Derrida, Coleman, and improvisation. *Journal of Curriculum Theorizing, 32*(3), 1–12.

Moten, F. (2003). *In the break: The aesthetics of Black radical tradition.* Minneapolis: University of Minnesota Press.

Muldrow, M. (2015). Great Blacks [Recorded by Georgia Anne Muldrow]. On *A thoughtiverse unmarred* [MP3]. Tucson, AZ: Mello Music Group.

Murray, P. (2018/1987). *Song in a weary throat: Memoir of and American pilgrimage.* New York: Liveright.

Murray, P. (1956). *Proud Shoes: The Story of an American Family.* Boston, MA: Beacon Press.

Murray, P. (1951). *States' rights on race and color.* Athens: University of Georgia Press.

Murray, P., & Eastwood, M. (1965) Jane Crow and the law: Sex discrimination and Title VII. *George Washington Review, 34*(2), 232–256.

Pérez, M. (1997). Interview with Bernice Johnson Reagon. *Radical History Review, 68*, 4–24.

Ravitch, D. (2013). *Reign of error: The hoax of the privatization movement and the danger to America's public schools.* New York: Alfred A. Knopf.

Sharpe, C. (2016). *In the wake: On Blackness and being.* Durham, NC: Duke University Press.

Sleeter, C. (1996). *Multicultural education as social activism.* New York: State University of New York Press.

Stallings, L. (2015). *Funk the erotic: Transaesthetics of Black sexual cultures.* Urbana-Champaign: University of Illinois Press.

Stoler, A. (2011). Colonial aphasia: Race and disabled histories in France. *Public Culture, 23*(1), 121–156.

Stovall, D. (2017). *Born out of struggle: Critical race theory, school creation, and the politics of interruption.* New York: State University of New York Press.

West, C. (1993). *Prophetic thought in postmodern times.* Monroe, ME: Common Courage Press.

Winfield, A. (2007). *Eugenics and education in America: Institutionalized racism and the implications of history, ideology, and memory.* New York: Peter Lang.

Wozolek, B., Varndell, R., & Speer, T. (2015). Are we not fatigued? Queer battle fatigue at the intersection of heteronormative culture. *International Journal of Curriculum and Social Justice, 1*(1), 1–35.

Wright, M. (2015). *The physics of Blackness: Beyond the middle passage epistemology.* Minneapolis: University of Minnesota Press.

Democracy in the Break

A Riff[1] in Support of the Movement for Black Lives

Denise Taliaferro Baszile

> The revolutionary character of the Negro's struggle is manifest in the fact that this struggle has done more to democratize life for whites than for Negroes.
>
> —Bayard Rustin, *Protest to Politics*

> Without the idealistic, strenuous, and patriotic efforts of Black Americans, our democracy today would most likely look very different—it might not be a democracy at all.
>
> —Nikole Hannah-Jones, *1619*

May I *shoot* straight? May I bypass the usual academese and shoot straight from the place where all my study meets my experiences lived meets an always engaged practice of critical witnessing meets a cauldron of feelings—angry hot, too sad, and so tired? Honestly, I am rewriting this introduction for the fifth time. When I was writing the first version, Michael Brown was murdered and Ferguson was on fire. The second and third versions were written just after Sandra Bland's killing by traffic stop. The fourth version, written not too long ago, was scribed just after a Dallas police officer took out Botham Jean, who was minding his own business, in his own apartment. And this fifth version is animated by the murders of Ahmad Arbery and Breonna Taylor just weeks ago, both of whom were also minding their own business. Last week, George Floyd was murdered and now the world is on fire. Not to mention that in the midst of this recent and relentless stream of state-sanctioned violence, we should also take note of the violence ravaging the lives of Black trans women, and the thousands upon thousands of Black deaths officially due to COVID-19 and unofficially and most certainly indicative of the conditions commonly referred to these days as the "afterlife of slavery—skewed life chances, limited access to health and education, premature death, incarceration, and impoverishment" (Hartman, 2008).

In response to this ongoing accumulation of Black death, people have been in the streets for weeks now, marching, chanting, blocking freeways, facing off with officers, and in some cases burning, looting, and unfortunately in a few circumstances taking lives. The fury, frustration, fear, and fearlessness are palpable. The demands for justice accompanied by calls for policy change and radical rethinking of public/community safety are gaining a hearing of sorts. While the push is for real transformation, the wonder is as always: *Will this wake-up call be enough?* Has it *ever* been enough? As I read the endless dirge of statements of support that crowd my inbox, listen intently to the conversations happening over the airwaves, and browse the chatter over the net, it is difficult not to be weary, suspicious even. While many folks are finding a renewed sense of hope inspired by the multiracial, multigenerational makeup of protesters, I have been trying to listen for what brings them to the streets. My skepticism alights from the fact that many folks who—if they acknowledge systemic racism at all—see it as a discrete problem in an otherwise sound democracy. These folks are registering the recent murders as a bump in the road to progress, a few bad apples, shameful but correctable with a few bold reforms and little sacrifice beyond the theater of protest. And yet for those of us who live and/or invest daily in the struggle for Black lives and othered lives, we know otherwise. We understand that anti-Black violence is historical, persistent, multifaceted, and repeatedly sanctioned by the nation-state. We know that the injustice is intersystemic. We know that reform though achievable is also retractable, in part and in full. We know that there is much work yet to do. While news commentators and others ask whether this is a moment or a movement, we know that this is but a moment in an evolving movement, in a long line of movements, for the survival and well-being of Black lives in the ditches of *this* American democracy, and its varied versions around the world.

As educators committed to teaching toward a more just society, we should be compelled to ponder how we might meet this moment, this movement for Black lives and its comprehensive demands, which not only require reimagining public safety but reimagining beyond the imagined sanctity of American democracy, as it now stands. If we are being honest, democracy already seems a dwindling idea in the face of state curriculums, driven more and more by free-market imperatives. However, in those places where such an idea is still pondered in the way that all schools *should* still ponder such an idea, what is being taught? Even more specifically, what will we teach about this movement, this moment in this movement when confederate monuments are falling, the coalition appears radically inclusive, and the process as normal is being upended? Do we still tell our students that freedom and equality are quintessential American ideals? Do we still tell them that the most important thing they can do is vote? Do we still teach them that representation, rational deliberation, and decision making are *the* keys to good democracy? Or do we tell them that this image of democracy, as hopeful as it is, has only ever worked for some of us but certainly not all of us? Do we provide them an opportunity to rethink democracy from the perspective of those who have engaged it mostly from the outside trying to get in? Do we dare teach it not apart from the white supremacist-capitalism that guarantees it for some and not others? Do we expose them to the wayward practices of the perpetually excluded and disenfranchised that exceed so-called ideal democratic practice? Do we continue to teach democracy in the ideal or might we teach democracy in the break?

If, in fact, we are only teaching democracy from the perspective of the ideals articulated by the European colonizers turned founding fathers, then we are preventing any possibility of reaching those very ideals—free, of course, from their fetters. Guaranteed. On the other hand, to teach democracy in the break is to lean into the undoing of the ideal curriculum, by entering the teaching moment through the moment that marks Blackness as broken, through "the hold" of the slave ship (Hartman, 2008) and the hold the slave ship continues to have on Black life/death (Harney & Moten, 2013). It is to experience democracy as already broken and still in the process of breaking. It is to relinquish our desire to return things to normal, to refuse the call back to order. It is to enter the process by which we reach past inclusion, recognition, and settlement on negotiated terms and lean into disruption, abolition, and movement on the way to that something we can't yet make out beyond the break. It is to be engaged in contemplating and innovating the wayward practices of democracy broken and breaking open to becoming something else beyond itself. What might we be compelled to rethink and reteach if we engage democracy in the break? In whatever ways we might imagine the course by which we should collectively invest in repairing, reforming, or reimagining democracy or what lies beyond, all efforts will stall if we begin and end that process with democracy in the ideal and abstract, with no consideration of what it looks like, feels like, sounds like in the break, that is from the hold of the slave ship and the hold the slave ship continues to have on Black life/death, and thus democracy, too. In the break, we re-member, we protest, we unite, and we evolve.

Disremembering toward Re-membering

> How we collectively remember is bound up with questions of justice. Or to put the point differently, what we choose to forget often reveals the limits of justice in our collective imaginations.
>
> —Eddie Glaude Jr., *Democracy in Black: How Race Still Enslaves the American Soul*

In *Democracy in Black*, Eddie Glaude Jr. joins a chorus of scholars from Du Bois to King, who argue that white supremacy *holds* democracy hostage. Glaude (2017), in his analysis of the "Great Black Depression" of 2008, offers the sobering reminder that "our democratic principles do not exist in a space apart from our national commitment to white supremacy. They have always been bound tightly together, sharing bone and tissue" (p. 9). What this deathly entanglement renders is, in Glaude's words, "a value gap" which is "the belief that white people are valued more than others" (p. 6). But even more so is the *fact* that the value white people have accrued over four centuries has been absolutely parasitic of Black life/death. To put it poignantly, Black people have been and still are in so many ways, owned, traded, and leveraged as labor, as threat, and as that which the human is not (Wilderson, 2010). Anti-Black racism is as American as apple pie and democracy. Yet this is not to say that the European colonizers turned founding fathers invented anti-Black sentiment, but it is to say that they elevated it to ideological proportions and baked it into the structural foundations of a burgeoning American democracy and built "bone and tissue" on chattel slavery, land grabs, genocide, proto-genocide, white supremacy, and capitalism. What we are left with is this value gap structured by whiteness and a logic of anti-Blackness, ardently maintained, as Glaude (2017) portends, by the course of our racial habits, one being the tendency toward "disremembering." Disremembering is the habit of actively forgetting egregious events of the past, like the *fact* that slavery, genocide, and Indian removal surrounded the writing of all the founding documents; that the possibility of American citizenship is carved from and consolidated by a doctrine of race, contrived in support of white self-interest, economic and psychic; that, for these reasons, the American ideals of freedom and equality are consistently met with the enduring conditions of unfreedom and inequality.

This technology of forgetting, if you will, is not necessarily the natural progression of things distant or aged or even traumatic; rather, it is often an engineered forgetting, deliberately designed to reproduce specific identities—some compliant and complacent, if not content; some deluded and dangerous; some daunted and degraded; as well as others. The stories we tell in the/as the curriculum do not simply, or in some cases, do not at all reflect who we are but more importantly they nevertheless shape who we imagine we can and cannot become (Woodson,1933; Wynter, 1994). This very concern is expressed by W. E. B. Du Bois (1935) in the final chapter of *Black Reconstruction*. In "The Propaganda of History," he interrogates the tendency toward disremembering and its deformative effect on democracy. He offers an impassioned disputation against what had by 1935 become the common historical perspective/record on the Civil War and Reconstruction. Drawing on textbook studies and historical accounts, Du Bois surmises that the overwhelming majority of these propagated several falsehoods, and thus left the "educated," with no idea of the part the "black race has played in America; of the tremendous moral problem of abolition; of the cause and meaning of the Civil War and the relation which Reconstruction had to democratic government and the labor movement today" (1935, p. 713). He goes on to call out the propensity of (white) historians to fashion this history, as a tool of propaganda for amusement and pleasure, for the benefit of national ego, and in the interest of educating the next generation without regard for the truth of things, but rather telling them only what they *wish* them to know. Nearly a century later, in 2020, we can discern the impact of these shortsighted if not outright false accounts of history, as we find that the standard American curriculum still struggles to offer a critical and comprehensive rendering of slavery (Shuster, 2019) as a central cause of the Civil War; rarely mentions Reconstruction; incorporates the role of Black people in American history-making in piecemeal ways and often on terms of misappropriation as objects rather than subjects, in ways that avoid the elephant of elephants in the room—the idea that America could not and cannot and will not exist as something else if not for the labor and laboring of Black people and Blackened peoples.

What this disremembering conjures, above all else, is the depravity of the white political imagination (Olson, 2004), one that cannot fathom beyond the belief that something is inherently and irreparably wrong with Blackness, with Black people, and thus one that cannot comprehend that a more just world in any and all forms lies, at least in part if not in whole, in the abolition work of Black people and our comrades. This matter of depravity is summed up by historian Carolyn Anderson (2017) in her discussion of white rage, which she describes as an invisible almost imperceptible power triggered not by the presence of Black people but more specifically by the advancement of Black people—"blackness with ambition, with drive, with purpose, with aspirations and with demands for full and equal citizenship" (p. 3). It is Blackness in this key, as Anderson elaborates, that has been met every step of the way with white rage, with backlash worked out primarily through legislation and policy.

> The truth is, white rage has undermined democracy, warped the constitution, weakened the nation's ability to compete economically, squandered billions of dollars on baseless incarceration, rendered an entire region sick, poor, and woefully undereducated, and left cities nothing less than decimated. All this havoc has been wreaked simply because African Americans wanted to work, get an education, live in decent communities, raise their families, and vote. Because they were unwilling to take no for an answer. (p. 6)

What a compelling interpretation; it explicates everything from the fall of Reconstruction to the election of Donald Trump, and adds to Glaude's sobering picture of democracy in Black. Getting beyond the ravages of white rage, beyond a democracy of disremembering necessarily calls all justice seekers—of all genres of humans being—to a reckoning, a collective re-membering of the pieces we've been taught to forget (Dillard, 2012).

We should be mindful, however, that re-membering is not really reducible to recalling facts and dates and saviors—you know, sprinkling in barely palatable touches of indigeneity or Blackness or something else framed to fit in. We must engage it, instead, as a process of decolonizing histories and everything else—including our understandings of who we are, of who we have become vis-à-vis a curriculum of disremembering. Re-membering is foundational to democracy in the break, to helping students grapple with, for instance, the forceful take down of the symbols that mark our "narratively condemned status" (Wynter, 1994).

Witnessing the statue of Andrew Jackson poised heroically on the green grounds of the White House, flanked by the sons and daughters of former slaves and those of former slave owners, protesting or protecting with graffiti and rope, should cause us to wonder who this man was; why anyone or everyone might want to tear him down or keep him up; and what is his hold on our imaginations—suffocating or animating? This is *how* we might learn/teach by way of democracy in the break, as already broken, and breaking still.

Protest as Praxis

> A riot is the language of the unheard.
>
> —Martin Luther King Jr., *Where Do We Go from Here? Chaos of Community*

> No justice, no peace.
>
> —Protestors

Historically protesting has been thought of as outside the normal workings of democracy, where protestors are narrated as passionate and irrational, the opposite of the rational, deliberative voter (Gillion, 2020). Surely this has something to do with the fact that it is often the most powerful and accessible tactic/praxis for those who are *repeatedly not heard*, who cannot seriously impact law, policy, or change of any kind without raising some hell—Black people, Indigenous people, undocumented people, poor people, exploited people, *people* as in power to the people. From the right to be free of bondage to the right to vote to the right to *not* be barred from facilities and resources to the right to walk down the street, barbeque in the park, watch birds, or relax in our own homes without being violated, harassed, or attacked—there is no civil or human right for which Black people have not had to fight. There is no scenario of American democracy, where Black people have been included simply because we are, like everyone else, humans beings. From abolitionism to Black Lives Matter (BLM), protest before the vote, for vote, and with the ongoing suppression of the vote has been our modus operandi. While protest is often reduced to rioting, it is perhaps better thought of as a form of wayward praxis indicative of democracy in the break, and thus requires a more nuanced understanding of its forms, purposes, strategies, and impacts.

First, protest can and does take many forms—soapbox speeches, slave stealing, slave harboring, inciting slave insurrection, sit-ins, teach-ins, boycotts, marches, occupations, looting, destruction of property, and other *violence*, as well. Regardless of form, the immediate purpose is to be disruptive, to shatter the silence, to block the way, to refuse to fund, to unsettle, and to upset things as normal. Protest is an effort to capture attention, to demand a *hearing* where no hearing has been afforded through the system, through the normal course of things. As such it always requires breaking the rules, written and/or unwritten, whether the written rule that says don't steal property or don't admit Black people or don't block the entrance or the unwritten rule that reads organized Blackness as a violation of order in and of itself—on the Edmund Pettus Bridge, or the Sacramento State House, or on the Mall in DC, or in the form of a Black militia visiting Stone Mountain.

Some quibble over peaceful protest versus rebellion, but I would argue that a truly *peaceful* protest is not protest at all; something must be disrupted, silenced at the very least. To simply work within the brokenness of the system is to be unable to escape the problem of the system itself. Moreover and arguably working outside the system, unsettling the system is *always* a violent process (Fanon, 2017). Wretched but true, isn't it? To see the truthfulness of this idea would demand, of course, that we expand our understanding of violence and its operations—physical and metaphysical, sanctioned and unsanctioned. Consider, for instance, how some news commentators, politicians, and even some activists themselves have responded to the looting and burning in this most recent round of BLM uprisings. Many have disparaged the violence as something other than real protest by referencing Dr. King's dedication to nonviolence as the exemplary way to protest injustice. While some of these violent acts may indeed have nothing to do with protest, some of them are clearly ways of protesting, and as activist and author Kimberly Jones (2020) has reiterated, rather than using one form to disparage another form, we should be compelled to ask *why?* Of course, *why?* would take us somewhere still too scary for most to go—the root cause, the hold of slave ship and the hold the slave ship still has on us, all of us. Why do people so conveniently disremember that the nonviolent *strategy* of the civil rights movement was met with the fierce and unrelenting violence of *white rage*? Wasn't its purpose to incite the violence that captured the attention of the world, revealing like nothing else could the shamed faces of injustice? For sure, the violence in these recent scenarios has brought 24-hour coverage of the streets from New York to Los Angeles, for nearly three weeks. Though protests continue throughout the summer of 2020, the violence has subsided and the media have largely retreated, save a dutiful mention during each nightly newscast. My point is not to suggest that we teach students how to enact violence as protest, but neither should we *paint* pictures of protest movements as driven any less by violence than nonviolence in its varied forms and performances. Protest is a response to violence, a kind of violence, and a call for an end to violence. No? Don't we justify it when it is for the purpose of maintaining the current relations of power masquerading as rational and fair, but scorn it when used to disturb, disrupt, and unmask the injustice of these very power relations?

Second, though protest as spectacle, as improvised performance works to capture attention, there is much more to it than that. Sometimes protests simply fizzle out, sometimes they grow into movements, and sometimes they are symbolic of the fact that a movement is already in motion. In movement form, protestors are activists, who raise awareness, who educate the public about failures of the state, who rattle the common sense. Mostly, we cannot depend on the state apparatus—mainstream schools and media—to do this work, we have to create or be creative with other tools. In the past the educative work was done with pamphlets, soapbox speeches, door-to-door calls, breakfast programs, and Black owned newspapers; today movement activists leverage the mobile phone and the talk-back power of the net—YouTube, Instagram, Snapchat, TikTok, and Twitter. This technology has allowed people to bear witness and to educate on the issues at hand. They represent the rhetorical undercommons, where people can learn, process, and reflect on details, paradigms, critical histories, positions, probabilities, breakdowns, and more. Consider Nikole

Hannah-Jones's insightful *1619* podcast, Jeffrey Robinson's truth telling in "Truth about the Confederacy," Tanahesi Coates's rearticulation of the long-standing argument for reparations, and most recently Kimberly Jones's passion-filled breakdown of the economic injustice that consumes Black life/death. These are important counteranalyses that rethink, elaborate, clarify, and are accessible in a way they have not been in the past—not in the official curriculum of schooling or even the informal curriculum indicative of mainstream narratives driven by media controlled historically and primarily still by white money and the white imagination.

Finally, as protests charge the rhetorical undercommons, and in so doing, shift the common sense of complacency, the movement grows in size and impact. Barring that group of people who are committed to white ignorance (Mills, 2008) as a refusal to know, we can assume that most people are open to knowing otherwise and at least interested in more justice for more people. It is this group of people—of various backgrounds and circumstances—who are persuadable by the kind of collective unmasking characteristic of protest moments and movements, in this case of Black protest. Black people's commitment to speaking the truth of our realities unfettered by the need to attend to or take care of white people's feelings offers a kind of clarity that brings people to the cause of the movement (as in a variety of movements for more justice for more people). Recently, we've witnessed this kind of rhetorical self-determination in Kimberly Jones's lesson on looting and Gary Chambers Jr.'s lesson on Robert E. Lee for the East Baton Rouge Parish school board.

In his new book *The Loud Minority: Why Protest Matters in American Democracy*, David Gillion (2020) points out that historically scholars have not mined the connection between the process of the protestors—who use disruption to work outside the status quo—and the democratic process. Doing so, however, reveals that protestors can and have swayed the vote and shaped policy by impacting the decision making of nonprotesting voters (Gillion, 2020). We might surmise, then, that this wayward practice of protest is the most viable path pushing toward the kind of revolutionary change that potentially comes with more justice for more people. And I say potentially, because protest—like everything else—can also be leveraged by those who are not invariably interested in more justice for more people, by those who can only see that in order for them to have, everyone else must lose. To this end, the message that grows the movement, I think, is the one that underscores how and why "all struggles against hegemony must embrace blackness for full liberation, because blackness embraces all struggles against hegemony" (Ziyad, 2017).

This is *what* we might learn/teach by way of democracy in the break, already broken, and breaking still.

Toward the Commons-not-yet

> We owe each other everything.
>
> —Stephano Harney and Fred Moten, *The Undercommons*

Just as there has been no radical change toward more justice in the US without the force of protests and the social movements they impel and/or reflect, there have been no impactful protest movements, particularly for issues of racial justice, without cross-racial coalition building. In a system of representative democracy where Black people comprise barely 13%, along with other unacknowledged and underrepresented groups—including Indigenous at 1.3%, Asian at 5.9%, Latinx at 18.5%, among others—our interests are considered only to the extent that they converge with elite white interests (Bell, 2018) or to the extent that we build cross-racial coalitions and enact protest. Historically, the significance of cross-racial coalitions cannot be overstated, as they predate the founding of the country itself, and have brought an end to chattel slavery, an end to de jure segregation, secured (tentatively) the vote, and currently they are powering protests around immigration and environmental injustices and the current wave of BlackLivesMatter protests against state-sanctioned violence and systemic racism. As important as they are, coalitions are also susceptible to divide and conquer strategies, such as stereotyping, Oppression Olympics rhetoric, and narrating issues at cross purposes. To the extent that we are all in a struggle to bring about a more just society, we work to understand the myriad injustices we face as mutually reinforcing inequalities and indignities that call for more than pragmatic and temporary forms of coalition building. We cannot simply locate the point at which our interests as peoples intersect, because intersection implies that we will meet for only this moment and then subsequently continue to move in our separate directions on our separate trajectories. This is ultimately, it seems, no less problematic than interest convergence as a strategy of whiteness; it allows us to elide the ways in which the racist-capitalist relations we live within and against have made us all complicit, in some way, with the project of empire.

When we reckon with the truth of things, we have to contend with the fact that at any point in time in our histories and our present, when our interests as non-white peoples are addressed because of interest convergence, then we are, by virtue of that fact, working against some other group of people, who have been used in the no-win game of empire building. This is the structure and force of empire replicated in the/as the self. In this way, we have to contend with the reality that Black people and Indigenous people, for example, have not only worked together throughout the history of this country against white domination, but we have also been positioned to work against each other, materially and metaphorically, and in ways that reinforce a pedagogy of empire. Although it is vitally important that we acknowledge and understand our distinct histories and how they shape the different ways we may experience injustice, revolutionary change calls for something more. We have to imagine not simply what we can do together at our points of intersection, but we must confront the much more difficult task of trying to figure how to end rather than rearrange the racist-capitalist structures that govern and discipline our relationships. Is it possible that holding ourselves accountable to this greater task could be the context from which the commons-not-yet emerges? This is *why* we might learn/teach by way of democracy in the break, already broken, and breaking still.

In Pursuit of the Revolutionary-not-yet

> Politics as usual—debate and argument, even voting are no longer sufficient. Our system of representative democracy, created by a great revolution, must now itself be the target of revolutionary change.
>
> —Grace Lee Boggs, *The Next American Revolution*

Since the 2016 election of Donald Trump, a rash of books and conversations have emerged with the "*startling*" news that American democracy is in peril, *again.* In *Democracy in America? What Has Gone Wrong and What Can We Do About It*, for instance, Benjamin Page and Martin Gilens argue that the US's system of representative government is faltering because law and policy are controlled more and more by corporations and elite politicians and less and less by the average American citizens, who according to their analysis have almost zero impact in the legislative process. Ultimately, they suggest that while other countries have been moving toward more equality, the US has actually exacerbated inequality and the answer is a broad social movement to reform democracy (like the Poor People's Campaign?). Although this text makes some important points—like most texts of this ilk—it has almost nothing to say about the way *racism* is inflected in this crisis of democracy. The idea, then, that democracy is only now in peril ignores the historical and current cries for justice and revolutionary change by those who suffer disproportionately at the behest of America's white supremacist capitalism rolled into liberal democracy. From the Poor People's Campaign to the Black Panther's Party's Ten Point Program to the political platform of the Movement for Black Lives, Black freedom dreamers have historically centered race/class (gender is being saved for another paper capable of carrying this heavy lift) dynamics in their protests against inequality and their demands for a more just democracy. To offer an analysis of inequality as democracy's demise without attending to the racial character of the inequality and the persistent attempts to correct it is to underscore the problem of race that has historically and persistently plagued democracy—the society's tendency to ignore its relevance and impact unless by the force of protest. And even then, critical reforms often confront backlash and divestment overtime. If we consider, for instance, the progressive legislation brought on by Black protest movement building, such as the dissolution of separate but equal with the *Brown v. Board of Education* decision or the Voting Rights Act of 1965, we must also account for the ways both measures, among others, have been more or less aggressively dismantled in recent decades through a court, that again and again, dismisses remedies to racial injustice that do not fundamentally serve and protect white privilege, property, and power. Such regressions and cycles of backlash make it patently clear that liberal democratic reform is insufficient; the system, as it is, is incapable of correcting itself. To this end the clarion call of the Movement for Black Lives, one of the more recent platforms for justice, is not for the same-old kinds of reform, but for revolutionary change.

The work of dismantling and reimagining civil society/the world in pursuit of the revolutionary-not-yet is captured in A Vision for Black Lives: Policy Demands for Black Power, Freedom, & Justice, a collaboration of more than 50 Black organizations from across the country under the umbrella of a Movement for Black Lives (M4BL). Broadly speaking, the collective calls for an end to the incarceration and killing of Black people; investments in the education, health, and safety of Black people through divestment from exploitative forces including prisons, fossil fuels, police, surveillance, and exploitative corporations; economic justice for all and a reconstruction of the economy to ensure Black communities have collective ownership, and not merely access; a world where those most impacted in our communities control the laws, institutions, and policies meant to serve us; and a remaking of the current US political system in order to create a real democracy where Black people and all marginalized people can effectively exercise full political power (A Vision, 2015). Overall, the demands articulated in the document are radical, no doubt. They are in step with if not a critical impetus for the growing call to defund the police, which is a response not only to the recent death of George Floyd and others, but a reckoning with a long history of violence carried out by systems of policing, surveillance, legal adjudication, and incarceration designed to discipline Black bodies to protect and serve white/elite/corporate interests under the guise of democracy for all. A Vision moves beyond liberal democratic reforms that channel more money into policing in ways that fail to fundamentally change their relationship to and practices in Black and Brown communities, that is, training, body cams, and the like. Instead it calls for a transformative vision of civil society by addressing the root causes of mutually reinforcing systems of inequality that degrade, devalue, and deaden Black well-being in particular, and the well-being of all communities of color, all people in general. Ultimately, the architects of and advocates for A Vision call not so much for revolution in the old Marxist sense of overthrowing the government, but for abolition, which entails a steady committed and protracted struggle, whose demands for a new kind of society entails fundamental changes not only to our institutions but also necessarily in ourselves and our relationships to one another. Revolutions are ultimately evolutions on the way to better futures, one's that emerge in the heart of the struggle. This is *where* we might learn/teach by way of democracy in the break, already broken, and breaking still.

And the Struggle Continues . . .

It is now three weeks gone since I started on the fifth version and the number of bodies climb—Rashard Brooks, Elijah McClain, and the still ridiculous numbers of Black and Brown people consumed in part by COVID-19 and poor health and little care, and in great measure by the reckless messaging and reopening of the economy at just about the same time that we begin hearing reports of the disproportionate racial impact. Hmm . . . Not to mention, the most recent "breaking news" of increased shootings in Black and Brown communities where jobs have been lost and family and friends have been dying and plans are always being made to suppress the vote. An attempt, no doubt, to call the public back from the brink of defunding the police, but also a failure to see that the so-called Black on Black violence politicians like to taut as the convenient reason to shore up law and order is but another symptom of a democracy in the break, already broken, and breaking still. As the struggle continues, and as we continue toiling in a *field* (of education) that has absolutely lassoed the pursuit of justice to democratic ideals, when might we learn/teach by way of democracy in the break, already broken, and breaking still?

Note

1. A riff is a short repeated phrase in popular music and jazz. I use it here to cause us to ponder how Black freedom struggles have repeatedly sought to hold American democracy to its higher ideals. Blackness is improvisation and refrain—democracy in the break, already broken, and breaking still.

References

A vision for Black lives: Policy demands for Black power, freedom, & justice. https://cjc.net/wp-content/uploads/2017/04/A-Vision-For-Black-Lives-Policy-Demands-For-Black-Power-Freedom-and-Justice.pdf

Anderson, C. (2017). *White rage: The unspoken truth of our racial divide.* New York: Bloomsbury.

Bayard, R. (1965). "From protest to politics: The future of the civil rights movement. https://www.blackpast.org/african-american-history/1965-bayard-rustin-protest-politics-future-civil-rights-movement-0/

Bell, D. (2018). *Faces at the bottom of the well: The permanence of racism.* New York: Basic Books.

Boggs, G. L., & Kurashige, S. (2012). *The next American revolution: Sustainable activism for the twenty-first century.* Berkeley: University of California Press.

Chambers Jr., G. (2020). Activist teaches school board about their racism and confederate history/Now this. https://www.youtube.com/watch?v=QNLI2jZRJa8

Coates, T. (2019). Opening statement on reparations at House hearing. https://www.youtube.com/watch?v=kcCnQ3iRkys

Dillard, C. B. (2012). *Learning to (re)member the things we've learned to forget: Endarkened feminisms, spirituality, & the sacred nature of (re)search & teaching*. New York: Peter Lang.

Fanon, F., Philcox, R., Sartre, J., & Bhabha, H. K. (2017). *The wretched of the earth*. Cape Town, NY: Kwela Books.

Gillion, D. Q. (2020). *The loud minority: Why protests matter in American democracy*. Princeton, NJ: Princeton University Press.

Glaude, E. S., Jr. (2017). *Democracy in Black: How race still enslaves the American soul*. New York: Broadway Books.

Hannah-Jones, N. (2020). *1619*. nytimes.com/1619podcast

Harney, S., & Moten, F. (2013). *The undercommons fugitive planning & Black study*. Wivenhoe, NY: Minor Compositions.

Hartman, S. V. (2008). *Lose your mother: A journey along the Atlantic slave route*. New York: Farrar, Straus and Giroux.

Jones, K. (2020). How can we win. https://www.youtube.com/watch?v=llci8MVh8J4

Lovejoy, P. E. (2013). *The transatlantic slave trade and slavery: New directions in teaching and learning*. Trenton, NJ: Africa World Press.

Mills, C. (2007). White ignorance. In S. Sullivan & N. Tuana (Eds.), *Race and epistemologies of ignorance* (pp. 10–15). Albany: State University of New York Press.

Olson, J. (2004). *The abolition of white democracy*. Minneapolis: University of Minnesota Press.

Page, B. I. (2020). *Democracy in America? What has gone wrong and what we can do about it*. Chicago, IL: University of Chicago Press.

Robinson, J. (2017). Truth about the confederacy. https://www.youtube.com/watch?v=QOPGpE-sXh0&list=PLwfdTKcPlB5mnWMRzTGcv_SGuAqLQ6pvg&index=2&t=71s

Samudzi, Z., Anderson, W. C., & Kaba, M. (2018). *As Black as resistance: Finding the conditions for liberation*. Chico, CA: AK Press.

Shuster, K. (2019). *Teaching the hard history of American slavery*. Retrieved from https://www.splcenter.org/teaching-hard-history-american-slavery

Tuana, N., & Sullivan, S. (2008). *Race and epistemologies of ignorance*. Charlesbourg, QC: Braille Jymico.

Wilderson, F. B. (2010). *Red, white & Black cinema and the structure of U.S. antagonisms*. Durham, NC: Duke University Press.

Woodson, C. G. (2019). *The mis-education of the Negro*. Lavergne, TN: Chump Change.

Wynter, S. (1994). No humans involved: An open letter to my colleagues. *Forum N.H.I.: Knowledge for the 21st century: Knowledge on trial, 1*(1), 42–72.

Afterword

Lester K. Spence

Wozolek and the various scholars she's deftly brought together understand how important the Movement for Black Lives (M4BL) and curriculum studies are to one another. The Ngozi Williams article presents us with a thoughtful first-person examination of the effects of curricula on the Black queer student. The David Omotoso Stovall article helps us understand Chicago's central role (home to the Black Youth Project 100, one of the most important M4BL organizations) in the neoliberalization of education (Lipman, 2011). The Yolanda Sealey-Ruiz, Marcelle Haddix, and Cluny Lavache article imagines a critical pedagogy that places Black and Brown students in the center of the education project rather than on the periphery. Roland W. Mitchell uses the tragic example of Hurricane Katrina to examine how he navigates the troubled waters of the academy as a Black administrator—New Orleans, too, is a key site of educational neoliberalization (Johnson, 2011). Reagan P. Mitchell, taking a decidedly Afro-surrealist approach, suggests we develop a Black feminist praxis to expand our notions of time and space in order to counter all-too-linear conceptions that bound and bind fecund Black possibilities. The Sherick A. Hughes article carefully considers the role math and data should play in knowledge development and in M4BL inculcated attitudinal shifts, providing what could be called a countercurriculum to contest the disinformation provided by white racist accounts of BLM.

The Walter S. Gershon article presents a historiography of curriculum studies as it relates to teaching Black and Brown students a historiography both vicious and true—the curriculum these scholars seek to contest is *violent* (sometimes nakedly so) and dissembling. The Kirsten T. Edwards article uses the insights of critical race theory (CRT) and intersectionality to critique the recent spate of college attempts to diversify through a combination of diversity inclusion and equity programs and affirmative action hiring. Here the concept of marronage comes into play, specifically in Black spaces at historically white institutions (HWI) (Roberts, 2015). Finally, Denise Taliaferro Baszile brings it all into the contemporary moment, using COVID-19, the deaths of George Floyd, Breonna Taylor, Ahmaud Arbery, and others to resurrect/create an American democracy that befits all of its citizens. It's unlikely that at the beginning of this project Boni Wozolek thought this volume would not only make an intervention into the subfield of curriculum studies, one that could potentially open the subfield up to new lines of inquiry but could potentially help to create the new postpandemic world that has yet to come into being. However, I believe this can help to do so—can help kickstart that longer project that will likely take up the rest of our lives.

My work over the last decade or so has primarily been about the neoliberal turn—how we've gone from a society with a relatively robust social safety net and sound labor protections to a society without these, and the effect that shift had on Black politics in the United States (2011, 2012, 2015, 2020). I would suggest that one way to read the pieces contained in this volume, as well as curriculum studies in general, is as responding to the same crisis I responded to when I began to critically study Black politics. Inasmuch as curricula are not objective means of teaching students but are themselves generated as a partial response to the political, economic, and cultural demands of the moment, I understand curricula as intensely political texts that can either restrain or expand democratic capacity. And given that those whose demands are often most connected to crisis tend to be disproportionately Black, Brown, Indigenous, and queer, it makes sense that one of the chief questions Wozolek and her co-conspirators seek to ask is how might we turn to curriculum studies to consider why these students are most often at the wrong end of every educational statistic we collect? And then similarly, how might we shift curriculum studies to not only consider and study those lives with the care they deserve but turn curriculum studies to the more radical project of giving those students (and their comrades) the tools they (we) need to actually create a world in which their lives not only matter but their lives determine the fate of everyone else on the planet? Trying to understand this particular period,

I've worked to develop what I call an Afro-realist attempt to understand our current moment. Below I articulate this approach, juxtapose it against its pessimist counterpart, and then connect it to the works in the volume.

Afro-realism

Over the past several years one mode of inquiry has increasingly shaped how we view Black life, particularly within the United States—Afro-pessimism shaped largely though by no means solely by the work of Jared Sexton and Frank Wilderson III (Sexton 2008, 2010; Wilderson, 2020; Wilderson III, 2003).

While term has its roots in African politics—it was originally developed to castigate those who saw Africa's future as being mired in debt, corruption, and internecine strife (Hyden, 1996)—it now has come to refer to a particularly productive conception of Black life that places anti-Blackness at the center of the modern state, economy, and civil society. The concept revolves around a few fundamental claims. The first claim is that slavery is not something that ended, in large part because slavery is not something that *can* end. The idea of social death promoted by sociologist Orlando Patterson becomes critically important here—what distinguishes the chattel slave and slavery in the US from other forms of slavery is that the slave dies a certain type of death that cannot be reversed. Social death reduces the status of the slave to a thing, and that status cannot be somehow reversed or ended. I'm going to come back to this last, but this is worth parsing out.

For Patterson (1982), the idea of "manumission" (that is, the act of freeing a slave) created what Patterson called an "inalienability problem." Inalienability is one of the most fundamental of liberal concepts—in the Declaration of Independence, life, liberty, and the pursuit of happiness are deemed to be among rights that cannot be "alienated," cannot be bought, cannot be sold. With the master-slave relationship, a different sort of problem exists. In the case of the master-slave relationship, the relationship is one of power and domination. The slave exists for the master, the slave exists to serve the will of the master. The slave doesn't own anything and is, instead, owned by the master. How can the slave, then, "purchase" freedom? The slave cannot somehow earn money and then use this money to purchase her freedom, because she'd basically be using the master's own resources to purchase said freedom from the master—whatever money the slave earns is already in effect the master's money. Further, no third party can do it either, because that third party is either using funds provided by the slave, which gets us back to the original problem; or the third party is using funds provided by either the third party his-/her-/theirself or some other party—which does not generate freedom as much as transfers the slave from the original master to a new one. As a result of this dynamic, Afro-pessimists argue, the slave can never be free. Blacks, given this, are still slaves.

The second claim is that modernity itself is based on slavery and on the status of Blacks defined by slavery. Afro-pessimists are not the only ones to interrogate the role of race in modernity—Richard Iton (2008) and others (e.g., Gilroy, 1993; Hanchard, 1999; Mbembe & Dubois 2017; Weheliye, 2005) are also involved in this pursuit. However while the bulk of scholarship here either examines how Black populations across the diaspora selectively use ideas, institutions, and norms developed within the modern West for their own ends, or posits that the conception of modernity itself is in some ways undeniably Black (we can't write about "modern music," for example, without writing about music produced by and to an extent for Black populations), the work of Afro-pessimists suggests instead that Black populations are and have always been the population by which modernity is defined. Although it is clear that settler colonialism provided European states with the land they then used slave labor to successfully mine, Afro-pessimists argue slavery is more important than either of these in creating the conditions for the modern moment.

Finally, Afro-pessimists suggest that desire—more specifically the desire that comes from subjecting Black bodies to a unique form of violence—is more important than material *interests*. They focus on the libidinal economy to the virtual exclusion of the political economy. We know that much of slavery was accompanied by a certain type of gendered viciousness with men, women, and children often victimized by a violence that was random and capricious. Afro-pessimism suggests there is a type of desire at work here that stands above and beyond the use of chattel slaves as the equivalent of fixed capital. And then as chattel slavery is expressly replaced, the libidinal economy is still at work, as shown perhaps in the various acts of violence committed by police against Black bodies.

Politically, these ideas have a range of consequences, of which I'll note five. By suggesting that the fundamental identity of Black populations is their racial identity (more specifically their *Blackness*) and that this identity is to an extent diametrically opposed to other bases for identity (class, for example), it politically supports doubling down on intraracial coalition building over interracial coalition building, positing other forms of coalition building as antithetical to Black interests. Inasmuch as these intraracial coalitions are going to be organized around interests defined by subsections of intraracial groups, these subsections are likely to be defined by and overdetermined by class. By suggesting that development and change are only possible by ending modernity and its political project is deeply antiinstitutional, promoting tearing a range of institutions down and starting anew rather than reconstructing existing ones. By suggesting that the libidinal economy is more important than the political economy, it sidelines considerations of class both in examining Black politics itself and also racial politics. Finally, and relatedly, though the Afro-pessimist position does have political consequences and is often articulated as if it were a radical political intervention, it has little room for politics.

Against this approach I articulate an Afro-realist response, based on a few different ideas. First, Black populations are *not* still slaves. Relatedly, Black populations have agency and have exerted that agency time and time again in American life. When Patterson wrote of slave societies and the complicated question of freedom, he was primarily dealing with the question of *manumission*—the individual act of a master freeing a slave. And in order to prove manumission functioned in generating social death, he examines a variety of slave societies, including the US South. What he does *not* do is address the sticky question of revolution—the instance in which slaves in effect worked to free themselves. Neither *abolition nor flight represents forms of manumission.* The instances he deals with in *Slavery and Social Death* are all instances in which individual Blacks were either "freed" by their masters, purchased their freedom *from* their masters, or had a third party do it for them. Black slaves in the United States during the Civil War and in Haiti during the Haitian revolution did not have their freedom given to them, they took it. In the case of Haiti they did so through a 13-year-long revolutionary struggle. In the United States they did so through the General Strike (Du Bois, 1962; Henderson, 2019; James, 1989). While it is still appropriate to acknowledge that the role of blacks vis-à-vis other racial groups is unique given the history slavery played in developing the transatlantic world, it is not appropriate to suggest that Blacks still have the same relationship with the state, civil society, and the market that they did in slavery. It is more appropriate instead to suggest that while Blackness is "a capacious category of surplus value extraction essential to an array of political-economic functions, including accumulation, disaccumulation, debt, planned obsolescence, and absorption of the burdens of economic crises . . . [and] the quintessential condition of disposability, expendability, and devalorization" (Burden-Stelly, 2020), Black populations have exerted agency and that the state, civil society, and the market have responded to Black action.

I bring up the three in tandem because this approach takes political economy seriously. The market, the state, civil society, and the relationship between the three play a significant role in how we live in the world. Elites in Williamsburg, Virginia changed Black life as well as the nature of the state and the market when they modified the legal status of Blacks in a series of laws passed between approximately 1640 and 1705, rendering them slave laborers (Colonial Williamsburg). When Blacks participated in the General Strike, ending the Civil War, they created the conditions under which a different abolitionist democracy was not only imagined, but briefly brought into being—both the end of Reconstruction and later the creation of the planter-dominated Jim Crow regime should be read as a counterrevolutionary response to this moment (Du Bois 1962). As the Fordist system developed, American cities (particularly ones north of the Mason-Dixon Line) became more and more important, increasing opportunities for Black laborers who worked in this moment to create the seeds of a Black counterpublic (which itself arguably worked to generate a countercurriculum), which they used to counter racist ideas about Black capacity and increase Black political solidarity (Black Public Sphere Collective, 1995; Georgakas & Surkin, 1975; Green, 2007; Smith, 1999). The form of subjugation, exclusion, and discrimination Blacks faced during each of these moments differed profoundly from one another. Taking these dynamics seriously when studying race and Black political life requires that we understand the ideas, interests, institutions, and identities influence one another over time, with interests coming to the fore in some instances (being used to then determine ideas, institutions, and identities), ideas coming to the fore in others (shaping what our interests are, or helping determine the form of new institutions), and identities or institutions coming to the fore in yet others. We can and should understand the Movement for Black Lives as a set of interrelated institutions in part constructed in order to push forward an interest contained in a very specific idea—that Black lives matter. Note though that the idea "Black lives matter" can be operationalized in a number of different ways, in part based on the interests of those doing the operationalizing.

Applying this insight to curriculum studies more broadly, and the works in this volume specifically, it strikes me that in effect one can think about curricula as a set of bundled ideas—ideas about how to teach, ideas about what to teach (about what *not* to teach), ideas about the purpose of teaching, ideas about where, when, and how learning occurs—that in turn shape how different populations think about themselves (about their *identities*), about how different populations think about what they want out of learning (about their *interests*), and then about how schools and other places of learning are structured in order to deliver the curricula (about how *institutions* are structured). When Williams writes of her youthful desire to have "good hair," she implicitly connects this to two sets of institutions—the predominantly white upper-income school district she attended as a child and the broader mass media. In both instances we can imagine both an implicit and an explicit curriculum at work, shaping her sense of what it means to be a Guyanese American, and also what it meant to be Black. When she writes that she cut her hair two weeks after seeing *Black Panther*, she's basically writing of a countercurriculum that gave her a different set of ideas of how to express and affirm her identity. When Stovall writes of Chicago, one of the two central geographic sites of neoliberalization mentioned in the volume (the other, again, being New Orleans, addressed by Roland Mitchell), and he writes of how the power exerted by various elite institutions in the city is hidden by educational institutions, he's making a set of claims about how the neoliberal turn is produced and reproduced by certain policies (closing down public schools, adopting high stakes testing, opening dozens of charter schools), the use of the carceral state, and a tacit decision *not* to teach these dynamics in schools. But he also writes, as do Sealey-Ruiz, Haddix, and Lavache; Roland and Reagan Mitchell; Edwards; and Taliaferro Baszile, about the capacity of Blacks, in the absence of curricula designed to affirm Black life, to create the spaces and the institutions necessary to do so.

In fact, along these lines we can think of Black Lives Matter itself as a bundle of ideas, normative (Black lives *should* matter) and descriptive (Black lives *do* matter), designed to shape identities (to create the conditions for a conception of Blackness so capacious it affirms the lives of Black populations previously deemed anathema to respectable Black life), designed to both critique elements of institutions (municipal spending on police, for example) and offer institutional modifications to them (#defundpolice), and designed to reshape what a range of individuals and institutions believed to be in their best interests (causing institutions to revisit their support for the symbols of the Confederacy, for example). We can think of Black Lives Matter then, as a curriculum, one designed to not simply *teach* about American life (to, as Hughes does, provide a set of critical truths) but designed to generate a critical praxis for modifying it.

But thinking about Black Lives Matter and the works in this volume in this manner requires thinking about it, and about curricula in general, as shifting over time in response to other shifts, and it also requires thinking about curricula in general as *generating* other shifts. As Reagan Mitchell notes, this does not mean that we should think about the changes generated in linear terms. However, it does mean that at the very least we should understand that change (*development*) occurs. That the historical and contemporary dynamics Gershon traces are not set in stone. Further, however, it also involves understanding that curricula do not only change and develop over time (and as an aside, when I write about "development" I do not mean to suggest that "development" is only a positive thing, that in contrast to the notion that curricula are bundles of static anti-Black ideas, curricula are consistently developing and becoming better as they relate to Black life, as it is possible to "go backward"), but within the same time period they also shift depending on the state and local context. One of the challenges in writing about this current moment, particularly given the ferocity of the neoliberal turn, is the challenge of acknowledging the realities of Black rural and suburban life. The changes we note in cities like Chicago and New Orleans are happening in cities nationwide. But just as there is a stark difference between a city that spends $1.8 billion on police (Chicago) and a city that spends $200 million (New Orleans), there are differences between cities like Chicago and New Orleans and suburbs, on the one hand, and rural regions like the Mississippi Delta, on the other. Both the forces arrayed against Black life (in the latter case the big-agriculture looms large) and the epistemologies that work to generate countercurricula differ in critical ways. A number of scholars, push back against the notion that modern Black life in the United States is a Northern and Western phenomenon by suggesting that "the south has something to say" (Hobson, 2017; Laymon, 2013). I would suggest too that the rural also has something to say (Woods, 1998).

Taking an Afro-realist approach requires acknowledging intra- as well as interracial politics. Race does matter. However, within racial groups some exert far more power than others and this power differential has effects. Now the works in this volume recognize Black heterogeneity. A

New Orleans community member made clear to Roland Mitchell that being a Black university administrator wasn't quite the same as being Black in the communities devastated by the federal, state, and local response to infrastructure development (Hurricane Katrina didn't devastate New Orleans, neoliberalism did). The Stovall and Edwards articles (as well as others) acknowledge class distinctions within Black communities. However, even as we write and study, often for the purpose of articulating Black interests, we have to take more care to understand the conditions under which Black interests and Black identities are internally generated.

As I note above, the Hughes article details a number of critical truths, truths designed not just to inform minds but to shift politics. Here's another truth—while racial income gaps exist and have always existed, over the past several decades inequality *within* Black communities is actually greater than inequality *between* Black communities and non-Black ones. Said another way, the gap between the Black 1% and the Black 99% is actually *greater* than the gap between Black and white families (Spence, 2015). Politically speaking, what does this mean? Taliaferro Baszile is absolutely right to note that the increased focus on wealth and politics within political science largely ignores racial politics. But what this volume suggests is that wealthy individuals are not only more likely to have their interests met than individuals not so wealthy, but that a part of the reason this occurs is because they work through powerful institutions both to make sure their interests win out explicitly over other interests, and to make sure that their interests are the only ones that are often even considered. Further, it suggests that separate and distinct from wealthy individuals, corporations exert an enduring political influence over legislation and over legislators.

How does this finding translate into Black politics?

It is both a matter of common sense and Black academic sense that something we'd call "a Black agenda" exists. The writers in this volume all take for granted that race matters and creates the conditions in which we need some coordinated set of policy responses to deal with race and the contemporary manifestations of racism. There is a reason why Blacks are disproportionately the victims of police violence, there are a set of educational outcomes that are better for Black populations, a set of policies that are better for Black populations, and then a set of policies that are poorer for them. But the growing literature on wealth and politics tells us that powerful interests work through institutions to make ideas about their interests reflect common sense, often using arguments about (racial) identity to do so (Einstein et al., 2019; Kelly & Witko, 2012; Macedo & Karpowitz, 2006; Piketty & Saez, 2003; Trounstine, 2015). We know that intraracial inequality is *larger* than interracial inequality. So why wouldn't a similar dynamic occur *within* Black communities? The neoliberal turn writ large occurs through racial politics—through the attempt to associate left and liberal government with (nondeserving) Black, Brown, and Indigenous populations. But the neoliberal turn *also* occurs *within* Black spaces. Class plays a powerful role within Black political life, shaping how the political and social agenda for Black populations is defined at any given time (Arena, 2003; Barlow, 2010; Blume Oeur, 2018; Cohen, 2012; Dawson & Francis, 2016; Johnson, 2011; Owens et al., 2020; Reed., 1999). Although one argument implied in some of the work in this volume is that this dynamic reflects some combination of internalized racism and/or interest-convergence with whites, an Afro-realist account recognizes the complexities of Black interests. Within a school context in Baltimore or Detroit, for example, Black principals, Black teachers, Black administrators, Black parents, and Black students all have subtly different interests, and these interests can shape what they believe Black people should do at any given point in time.

A related way to read the Black Lives Matter movement, on the one hand, and the broader calls for curricula shifts, on the other, is to read them both as attempts to forge a unified Black interest that goes beyond class distinctions. One powerful reason why Black public policy attitudes are consistently more progressive than white ones is because a combination of racism and Black counterpublic work neutralizes intraracial class dynamics to an extent. However, with this said, it's worth considering the fact that Blacks in general have expressed far more willingness to mobilize around police brutality than they've shown a willingness to mobilize around the labor policies that would make the lives of working-class men and women like George Floyd and Breonna Taylor more bearable. I noted above that how one translates the idea "Black Lives Matter" into policy is at least in part based on one's interests, where one is situated class-wise. While many Blacks do translate "Black Lives Matter" into policies that at the very least seek to subject police to democratic mechanisms of accountability, some Blacks translate the phrase into radically reducing the size and the scope of police, while other Black populations translate the phrase into more technocratic reforms. Along related lines, while the recent George Floyd protests saw Black mayors support the creation of Black Lives Matter murals in Atlanta, Baltimore, and Washington, DC, among other places, none of these mayors also supported "defunding the police," and in fact mayors in Atlanta and Washington, DC, have supported *increasing* police funding. What this means for curriculum studies is that we have to be attentive to the role these class dynamics play within Black politics broadly considered, and even within the populations *within* Black communities that we are increasingly concerned about. Within every identifiable subset of Black communities, this is true—Blacks with more resources have both more access to networks of care and more power to set the agenda for these communities than lower-income Blacks in these communities.

One of the arguments fundamental to the Afro-pessimist position is that the relationship between Blacks and non-Blacks are *antagonistic*, distinguishing antagonism from conflict for one important intellectual and political reason. Conceptualizing a given battle between two forces as "conflictual" rather than as "structurally antagonistic" implies that the conflict can be resolved through reason or some process of generating consensus. Conceptualizing a struggle as structurally antagonistic, on the other hand, implies this struggle is *not* one that can be solved by reason or consensus. Structurally antagonistic relations will also end up politically with an unresolved residual that cannot be solved through the rationalist, individualist means offered up by liberal democracy (Mouffe, 2013).

The Afro-realist approach acknowledges the broad idea that there are political differences that cannot be solved by rationalist, individualist means. There are political differences that are in effect *baked in* to the given structure and cannot be resolved by technical fixes. And inasmuch as different racial populations have different relationships with the state, market, and civil society, these different locations can lead to problematic politics. Here Claire Jean Kim's (1999) theory of "racial triangulation" looms large. However, the Afro-realist position suggests that the unresolved antagonism can be resolved politically, not by "changing hearts and minds" or by bringing in "experts" to devise solutions that meet a little bit of everyone's needs. But it can be resolved—in unexceptional circumstances it can be resolved through an intentional type of institutionalization, and in exceptional circumstances through the wholesale creation of new institutions which have the capacity to themselves create new identities and new interests.

I began this work with a brief discussion of slavery. I want to come back to slavery to make two important comments related directly to the idea above.

First, we know that the transatlantic slave trade was an important building block of the modern moment, but it was not the only building block. Without lands taken forcibly from Indigenous populations, without forcing women to biologically and social reproduce the interlocking set of institutions and populations articulated as the West, the modern moment as we think of it does not exist. The Afro-realist approach acknowledges that slavery, while a constitutive element of modern society, was not the only constitutive element. While we can and should study the specific way anti-Black racism transforms ideas, interests, and institutions, we also have to study the way anti-Indigeneity works alongside of and separate from anti-Blackness. I suggested above that we be sensitive to geographic dynamics in the study of how curricula in rural spaces function vis-à-vis Black populations. Inasmuch as anti-Indigeneity is arguably spatially concentrated as well, focusing on rural spaces also gives us an opportunity to examine anti-Indigeneity in some depth.

Second, to drive home again the critical idea of Black political agency, one way to think about the concept of agency is to think about it as a force that has the capacity to change the nature and quality of Black life. Developing a politics around the idea that "Black Lives Matter" can indeed create conditions that increase the likelihood that Black life matters, and in fact if we think about Black culture itself as providing a bundle of ideas that can constitute the core components of a countercurriculum we can suggest that those conditions are more possible if Black life matters (culture, broadly defined) is articulated in a certain way. And the relationship between Black life matters and Black Lives Matter is reciprocal—Black Lives Matter hasn't focused on police simply because of the reality of police violence, but also because there's a long history of Black cultural production (particularly rap music and hip-hop inflected cinema) expressly critiquing police behavior, providing an easy way for Black populations to understand both why people like George Floyd seemingly keep on getting killed by police *and* a political response to it. Similarly once Black Lives Matter is understood as a political movement, it in turn shapes the work of cultural producers, both in their artistic work (Kendrick Lamar's *To Pimp a Butterfly*, Beyoncé's *Lemonade*, Ryan Coogler's *Fruitvale Station*) and in their political behavior—in the recent wildcat strike conducted by NBA and WNBA players that then spread into Major League Baseball, Major League Soccer, and into at least one tennis tournament (as a result of Naomi Osaka's decision to withdraw from the Western and Southern Open tournament officials instead postpone it).

However, alongside thinking of agency as a force that has the capacity to change the nature and quality of Black life, I suggest we think much broader, that in this instance Black agency not only has the capacity to change Black life, but the capacity to change *life*. Before Black slaves made the decision to conduct a General Strike, both the victor of the Civil War and the terms of that victory were in doubt—the war did not become a war to end slavery until slaves made it so. The protests conducted around the world in response to George Floyd's death were in some ways responses to American policing, which is deeply anti-Black. However, they were also using Floyd's death to arguably drive home similar international dynamics. Even if we move to less explicitly radical politics, to consider the rise of popular culture with racially sophisticated politics, we can find ways that Black popular culture, that a Black countercurriculum shapes cultural production.

HBO has recently become home to some of the most sophisticated efforts to reimagine American popular culture—in 2019 *Watchmen* reimagined Alan Moore's graphic novel (which itself served as both a commentary on the Cold War and also a commentary on the power of the comic book to speak to sophisticated adult themes) and in 2020 *Lovecraft Country* takes Matt Ruff's novel of the same name and puts it to film. Among other things, *Watchmen* introduced many viewers to the 1921 Tulsa Race Riot, one of the most horrific events in American history, one known to many African Americans but largely until this moment unknown to whites. When asked why he depicted it, and why it played such a powerful role in his reimagining, Damon Lindelof pointed to the work of Ta-Nehisi Coates. Until he'd read Coates's work, Lindelof never knew about the event. Reading Coates changed how he viewed America and then how he viewed the work. Similarly, H. P. Lovecraft was racist even for the early-twentieth-century period in which he wrote, but was so groundbreaking that his racism often went unremarked (a prominent speculative fiction award bore his name until the science fiction author N. K. Jemisin fought to have it changed). Matt Ruff was one of a few sci-fi writers to explicitly tackle the elephant in the Lovecraftian room—as racist as Lovecraft was, as racist as the period Lovecraft wrote in was, no one had ever written a Lovecraftian novel from the standpoint of Black people living in that period. What gave him the idea that such a thing was possible? In the acknowledgments, Ruff (2016) thanks Cornell University Professor James Turner. James Turner helped to found Cornell University's Africana Studies Center—one of the first in the nation. When we write of the importance of a new curriculum, we should focus on its impact not just for Black, Brown, Indigenous, and queer students—I'd make the argument that they don't really need it as such. Rather, the new curriculum is for the purpose of creating a new world. Afro-realism is neither pessimistic, believing the world has to be broken in order for Black people to live, nor is it optimistic in that it believes that Black life abundantly generates paths, even if those paths are solely fugitive. Finally, it is not incremental, solely taking the world as it is and arguing that change occurs and should occur slowly in bits and pieces. Taking an Afro-realist position means taking the position that another world is possible—and that it is our fundamental responsibility to bring that world into being.

References

Arena, John. 2003. Race and hegemony: The neoliberal transformation of the Black urban regime and working-class resistance. *American Behavioral Scientist*, *47*(3):352–380.

Barlow, Andrew L. 2010. The contemporary crisis of neo-liberalism and Black power today. *Black Scholar*, *40*(2):24–33.

Black Public Sphere Collective. 1995. *The Black public sphere*. Chicago, IL: University of Chicago Press.

Blume Oeur, Freeden. 2018. *Black Boys apart: Racial uplift and respectability in all-male public schools*. Minneapolis: University of Minnesota Press.

Burden-Stelly, Charisse. 2020. Modern U.S. racial capitalism: Some theoretical insights. *Monthy Review*, *72*(3).

Cohen, Cathy J. 2012. Obama, neoliberalism, and the 2012 election: Why we want more than same-sex marriage. *Souls*, *14*(1–2):19–27.

Colonial Williamsburg. 2018. *Slavery and the law in Virginia*. History.org. http://www.history.org/history/teaching/slavelaw.cfm.

Dawson, Michael C., & Francis, Megan Ming. 2016. "Black politics and the neoliberal racial order." *Public Culture*, *28*(1), 23–62.

Du Bois, W. E. B. 1962. *Black reconstruction in America: An essay toward a history of the part which Black folk played in the attempt to reconstruct democracy in America, 1860–1880*. New York: Russell & Russell.

Einstein, Katherine Levine, Palmer, Maxwell, & Glick, David M. 2019. "Who participates in local government? Evidence from meeting minutes." *Perspectives on Politics*, *17*(1), 28–46.

Georgakas, Dan, & Surkin, Marvin. 1975. *Detroit, I do mind dying: A study in urban revolution*. New York: St. Martin's Press.

Gilroy, Paul. 1993. *The Black Atlantic: Modernity and double consciousness*. Cambridge, MA: Harvard University Press.

Green, Adam. 2007. *Selling the race: Culture, community, and Black Chicago, 1940–1955*. Chicago, IL: University of Chicago Press.

Hanchard, Michael. 1999. Afro-modernity: Temporality, politics, and the African diaspora. *Public Culture, 11*(1), 245.

Henderson, Errol Anthony. 2019. *The revolution will not be theorized: Cultural revolution in the Black power era*. Albany: State University of New York Press.

Hobson, Maurice J. 2017. *The legend of Black mecca: Politics and class in the making of modern Atlanta*. Chapel Hill: University of North Carolina Press.

Hyden, Goran. 1996. African studies in the mid-1990s: Between Afro-pessimism and Amero-skepticism. *African Studies Review*, *39*(2), 1–17.

Iton, Richard. 2008. *In search of the Black fantastic: Politics and popular culture in the post-civil rights era*. Oxford, UK and New York: Oxford University Press.

James, C. L. R. 1989. *The Black Jacobins: Toussaint l'ouverture and the San Domingo revolution*. 2nd ed. New York: Vintage Books.

Johnson, Cedric. 2011. The neoliberal deluge: Hurricane Katrina, late capitalism, and the remaking of New Orleans. Minneapolis: University of Minnesota Press.

Kelly, Nathan J., & Witko, Christopher. 2012. Federalism and American inequality. *Journal of Politics*, *74*(2), 414–426.

Kim, Claire Jean. 1999. The racial triangulation of Asian Americans. *Politics & Society*, *27*(1), 105–138.

Laymon, Kiese. 2013. *How to slowly kill yourself and others in America: Essays*. Chicago, IL: Bolden.

Lipman, Pauline. 2011. *The new political economy of urban education: Neoliberalism, race, and the right to the city*. New York: Routledge.

Macedo, Stepen, & Karpowitz, Christopher F. 2006. The local roots of American inequality. *PS: Political Science and Politics*, *39*(1), 59–64.

Mbembe, Achille, & Dubois, Laurent. 2017. *Critique of Black reason*. Durham, NC: Duke University Press.

Mouffe, Chantal. 2013. *Agonistics: Thinking the world politically*. London: Verso.

Owens, Michael Leo, Rodriguez, Akira Drake, & Robert A. Brown. 2020. Let's get ready to crumble: Black municipal leadership and public housing transformation in the United States." *Urban Affairs Review*, *57*(2), 31.

Patterson, Orlando. 1982. *Slavery and social death: A comparative study*. Cambridge, MA: Harvard University Press.

Piketty, Thomas, & Saez, Emmanuel. 2003. Income inequality in the United States, 1913–1998 (Updated). *Quarterly Journal of* Economics, *118*(1), 1–39.

Reed, Adolph L., Jr. 1999. *Stirrings in the jug: Black politics in the post-segregation era*. Minneapolis: University of Minnesota Press.

Roberts, Neil. 2015. *Freedom as marronage*. Chicago, IL: University of Chicago Press.

Ruff, Matt. 2016. *Lovecraft Country: A Novel.* 1st ed. New York: HarperCollins.

Sexton, Jared. 2008. *Amalgamation schemes: Antiblackness and the critique of multiracialism.* Minneapolis: University of Minnesota Press.

Sexton, Jared. 2010. People-of-color-blindness: Notes on the afterlife of slavery. *Social Text, 28*(2 (103)), 31–56.

Smith, Suzanne E. 1999. *Dancing in the street: Motown and the cultural politics of Detroit.* Cambridge, MA: Harvard University Press.

Spence, Lester K. 2011. *Stare in the darkness: The Limits of hip-hop and Black politics.* Minneapolis: University of Minnesota Press.

Spence, Lester K. 2012. The neoliberal turn in Black politics. *Souls, 14*(3–4), 139–159.

Spence, Lester K. 2015. *Knocking the hustle: Against the neoliberal turn in Black politics.* New York City: Punctum.

Spence, Lester K. 2020. Live and let die: Rethinking secondary marginalization in the 21st century. *Souls, 21*(2–3), 192–206.

Trounstine, Jessica. 2015. Segregation and inequality in public goods. *American-Journal of Political Science, 60*(3), 709–725.

Weheliye, Alexander G. 2005. *Phonographies: Grooves in sonic Afro-modernity.* Durham, NC: Duke University Press.

Wilderson, Frank B. 2020. *Afropessimism.* 1st ed. New York: Liveright Publishing.

Wilderson, Frank, III. 2003. Gramsci's Black Marx: Whither the slave in civil society? *Social Identities, 9*(2): 225–240.

Woods, Clyde Adrian. 1998. *Development arrested: The blues and plantation power in the Mississippi Delta.* London and New York: Verso.

Contributors

Kirsten T. Edwards is a faculty in the Department of Educational Policy Studies, as well as affiliate faculty for African and African Diaspora Studies, and the Center for Women's and Gender Studies at Florida International University in Miami, Florida. She currently serves as a mentor professor in the Office of the Vice Provost to Advance Women, Equity & Diversity. Her research merges philosophy, college curriculum, and pedagogy. More specifically, Dr. Edwards is interested in the ways that the globalization of higher education perpetuates racial asymmetries and anti-Blackness.

Walter S. Gershon, PhD, is associate professor of Critical Foundations of Education at Rowan University. Dr. Gershon's scholarly interests focus on questions of justice, access, and dignity regarding how people make sense; the sociocultural processes that inform their everyday sense-making; and the qualitative methods used to study those processes. Situated at the intersection of critical studies of education, social science, and qualitative research methods, Walter's work often utilizes emerging theoretical and methodological understandings to explore everyday experiences for marginalized children and youth. In addition to journal articles and book chapters, Walter is the editor of three books and two scholarly monographs, *Sound Curriculum: Sonic Studies in Educational Theory, Method and Practice* (Routledge, 2017; AERA Division B, Outstanding Book Award, 2018), and *Curriculum and Students in Classrooms: Everyday Urban Education in an Era of Standardization* (Lexington Books, 2017; Society of Professors of Education, Outstanding Book Award, 2019).

Marcelle Haddix is Distinguished Dean's Professor of Literacy, Race, and Justice at Syracuse University, where she is an inaugural codirector of the Lender Center for Social Justice. She holds a courtesy appointment as professor in nutrition and food studies and is affiliated faculty in African American Studies, Composition and Rhetorical Studies, and Women's and Gender Studies. In the Syracuse community, she facilitates the *Writing Our Lives* project for urban youth writers, the Breedlove Readers Book Club for middle and high school Black girls, and the Soulful Saturday Sistas Black women's literary club and free library project. Dr. Haddix was selected as the 2021 winner of the Divergent Award for Excellence in Literacy Advocacy, given by the Initiative for 21st Century Literacies Research. A 500-hour certified registered yoga instructor, Dr. Haddix is cofounder of the Sankofa Reproductive Health and Healing Center and a founding member of the Café Sankofa Cooperative.

D'nae Harrison is an award-winning interdisciplinary artist from Philadelphia, Pennsylvania. In 2014, she obtained her Bachelor of Fine Arts degree from Pennsylvania State University. In 2016, D'nae received the Philadelphia 76ers: Mentoring Art Contest First Place Award, conferred by Allen Iverson. In 2017, the City of Philadelphia commissioned D'nae to create a 52-by-52-in. oil painting, which remains downtown on permanent display. During the same year, her work featured with Six Summit Gallery in New York Fashion Week '17 (Fall). In 2018, her work showcased at the former Robert Miller Gallery in Chelsea, Manhattan, during the *Eminent Domain* exhibition. In 2020, her notable *Shaded Oppression* painting received MOZAIK Philanthropy's 2020 Future Art Award and honorarium. During the same year, Harrison's *Save the Date* mural located in iconic LOVE Park, featured on various news outlets such as WHYY, NBC10, CBS3, Yahoo! News, Hyperallergic, Culture Type, and the *Philadelphia Tribune* in efforts to raise voting awareness during Mural Art Philadelphia's project To the Polls 2020. In 2021, the Philadelphia International Airport commissioned D'nae to create the *Shaded Rocker* rocking chair, which remains throughout the terminals at the airport and are on permanent display.

Sherick A. Hughes, MA, MPA, PhD, the Holton Distinguished Professor of Education at the University of North Carolina at Chapel Hill, engages scholarship on: (a) the social context of education and policy, (b) critical race studies and equity, (c) anti-Black racial bias and debiasing strategies, and (d) qualitative and mixed methodology. His scholarship has informed universities, school districts, nonprofit agencies, media (e.g., Patriot Act with Hasan Minhaj on Netflix), and arguments before the North Carolina state Supreme Court. Hughes received a 2016 Distinguished Scholar Award from the esteemed American Educational Research Association (AERA), and a 2020 award from the American Society of Professors of Education for the book titled, *Autoethnography.*

Cluny Lavache is currently the coprincipal at Bedford Academy High School, which is one of the top-rated high schools in New York City. Her research revolves around the academic achievement of African American students in urban settings, and the impact of success on African American students through student and teacher racial congruency. Her interests also include how teacher education programs can challenge preservice teachers to understand their role and the impact they have on teaching students who are culturally, linguistically, and economically diverse. Dr. Lavache is a member of Delta Sigma Theta Sorority (Brooklyn Alumnae Chapter, a member of American Education Research Association (AERA), and a member of Association for Supervision and Curriculum Development (ASCD). Dr. Lavache has been School Leaders Fellow for Math for America; Corwin Fellow in Financial Literacy Summer Institute Federal Reserves at Teachers College, Columbia University; and Mentor/Facilitator at New York City Men Teach (NYCMT). Most recently Dr. Lavache is working on establishing her own consulting firm, Lavache Systems.

Reagan P. Mitchell, PhD, is an assistant professor in the Division of Liberal Arts at the University of North Carolina School of the Arts. He was born in Nashville, Tennessee, and received his Bachelor of Music from Middle Tennessee State University, his Master of Music from the University of Northern Colorado, his Educational Specialist degree from Louisiana State University, and his Doctor of Philosophy from Louisiana State University. The merger of Reagan's formal training and performance as a musician and pedagogical training as a curriculum theorist has an intrinsically inter- and transdisciplinary feel. Through his expanded course of study, he has laid the foundation for a program of research on the cultural and historical influences of race, space, gentrification, auditory architecture, and communal wisdom on education. Reagan's scholarship brings together curriculum theory, Black diaspora studies, ethnic studies, critical race theory, critical geography, and sound studies.

Roland W. Mitchell is the E. B. "Ted" Robert Endowed Professor and dean of the College of Human Sciences and Education at Louisiana State

University. His research theorizes the impact of historical and communal knowledge on postsecondary education. Roland has authored seven books and numerous scholarly works. His coedited book with Sara Carrigan Wooten, *Crisis of Campus Sexual Violence*, was awarded an Outstanding Academic Titles award and was highlighted on the Top 25 Favorites list of the *Choice* editors. He is coeditor of the Rowman & Littlefield book series Race and Education in the 21st Century. Based on his scholarly record and related activity, Roland was selected as a Southeastern Conference (SEC) Academic Development Fellow. He has a deep passion for impactful community service, as evidenced through his membership on the advisory boards of the Louisiana Department of Children and Family Services and the Louisiana Governor's Taskforce on Community Policing and Reform.

Yolanda Sealey-Ruiz is an award-winning associate professor at Teachers College, Columbia University. Her research focuses on racial literacy in teacher education, Black girl literacies, and Black and Latinx male high school students. A sought-after speaker on issues of race, culturally responsive pedagogy, and diversity, Sealey-Ruiz works with K–12 and higher education school communities to increase their racial literacy knowledge and move toward more equitable school experiences for their Black and Latinx students. Sealey-Ruiz appeared in Spike Lee's *2 Fists Up: We Gon' Be Alright*, a documentary about the Black Lives Matter movement and the campus protests at University of Mississippi (Mizzou). Her coauthored book (with Detra Price-Dennis) advancing Racial Literacies in Teacher Education: Toward Activism for Equity in Digital Spaces will be published in April 2021. Her first full-length collection of poetry *Love from the Vortex & Other Poems* (Kaleidoscope Vibrations) was published in March 2020, and her sophomore book of poetry, *The Peace Chronicles* was released in July 2021.

Lester K. Spence, PhD, is a professor of political science and Africana studies at Johns Hopkins University. He specializes in the study of Black, racial, and urban politics in the wake of the neoliberal turn. Dr. Spence is the author of *Stare in the Darkness: Hip-hop and the Limits of Black Politics* (winner of the 2012 W. E. B. Du Bois Distinguished Book Award) and *Knocking the Hustle: Against the Neoliberal Turn in Black Politics* (winner of both the *Baltimore City Paper* and *Baltimore Magazine*'s 2016 Best Nonfiction Book Awards). In addition to his book projects, Dr. Spence's numerous articles can be found in spaces like the *American Journal of Political Science, Political Research Quarterly, Souls: A Critical Journal of Black Studies, Contemporary Political Theory*, and the *Du Bois Review: Social Science Research on Race.* Dr. Spence's forthcoming work includes three book-length projects: an examination of the contemporary politics of HIV/AIDS in Black communities (under contract with Columbia University Press), an attempt to trace the contours of what he calls Afro-realism, and an investigation of the *thick blue line* of urban policing.

David Omotoso Stovall, PhD, is a professor in the Department of Black Studies and the Department of Criminology, Law and Justice at the University of Illinois at Chicago. His scholarship investigates three areas: critical race theory, the relationship between housing and education, and the intersection of race, place, and school. In the attempt to bring theory to action, he works with community organizations and schools to address issues of equity, justice, and abolishing the school/prison nexus. His work led him to become a member of the design team for the Greater Lawndale/Little Village School for Social Justice (SOJO), which opened in the fall of 2005. Furthering his work with communities, students, and teachers, his work manifests itself in his involvement with the People's Education Movement, a collection of classroom teachers, community members, students and university professors in Chicago, Los Angeles, and the San Francisco Bay Area, who engage in collaborative community projects centered in creating relevant curriculum.

Denise Taliaferro Baszile is associate dean of Diversity and Student Experience and professor of Curriculum & Cultural Studies in the Department of Educational Leadership at Miami University. Dr. Taliaferro Baszile's work focuses on understanding curriculum as racial/gendered text with an emphasis on disrupting traditional modes of knowledge production, validation, and representation. Her scholarship draws on curriculum theory, critical race theory, and Black feminist theory and seeks a fuller understanding rather than a simply a legitimate understanding of the dynamic relationship between race, gender, and curriculum. She has published in the *Journal of Curriculum Theorizing, Curriculum Inquiry, Currere Exchange, Race, Ethnicity and Education, Curriculum and Pedagogy, Educational Studies, Knowledge Cultures*, and *Urban Education.* She has two coedited texts: *Race, Gender, and Curriculum Theorizing: Womanish Ways* and *Black Women Theorizing Curriculum Studies in Color and Curves.*

Ngozi Williams, a Cleveland State University student in a STEM program, writes from the perspective of a Guyanese-American woman deeply entrenched in primarily white spaces in Cleveland, Ohio. Her writing explores the effects of white American social norms on young Black American people, and how privilege may insulate one from the intersection of complex marginalization. Through her work, she seeks to examine the responsibility we all bear for elevating the social and cultural Others within our society.

Boni Wozolek, PhD, is an assistant professor at Pennsylvania State University, Abington College. Her work considers questions of social justice, qualitative research methods, and teaching practices that focus on the examination of race, gender, and sexual orientation in schools. Most recently, Dr. Wozolek was a 2021 Critics Choice Award recipient for her book, *Assemblages of Violence in Education: Everyday Trajectories of Oppression*. She is also a 2021 recipient of the Early Career Award from the Critical Issues in Curriculum and Cultural Studies special interest group of the American Educational Studies Association (AERA), and the 2020 recipient of Taylor & Francis' *Educational Studies* Award, "Best Paper of the Year" for her article, "Hidden Curriculum of Violence: Affect, Power, and Policing the Body." Dr. Wozolek's past publications can be found in journals such as *Cultural Studies ↔ Critical Methodologies*, the *Journal of Gender Studies*, *Educational Studies*, the *Journal of LGBT Youth*, and the *Urban Review*. Forthcoming projects include a special issue with the *International Journal of Qualitative Studies in Education* (*QSE*).

Index

www.ingramcontent.com/pod-product-compliance
Lightning Source LLC
LaVergne TN
LVHW050152080826
844660LV00002B/175

* 9 7 8 1 4 3 8 4 8 9 1 7 9 *